1.00

June 2005
Linda,
   Enjoy the Show!
Continue to live with
Passion!
        Cheers—
   Margaret E. Broderick

PASSION
V.
ARROGANCE

MARGARET E. J. BRODERICK

PASSION POWER PRESS

Passion Power Press, Inc.
Indianapolis, Indiana

Publisher's Cataloging-in-Publication

Broderick, Margaret.
Passion v. arrogance : a Dana and Goliath story of
wine, women and wrong! / Margaret Broderick. -- 1st ed.
    p. cm.
    Includes index.
    ISBN 0-9762597-6-1

1. Wine and wine making--Indiana--History. 2. Banks
and banking--Corrupt practices--Indiana--Case studies.
3. Women-owned business enterprises--Indiana.
4. Discrimination in banking--Indiana--Case studies.
5. Sex discrimination against women--Indiana--Case studies.
 I. Title.

TP557.B76 2005   641.2'2'09772
                  QBI04-800136

Printed in the United States of America

ISBN print ed. 0-9762597-6-1

Library of Congress Cataloging-in-Publication Data

DEDICATIONS

To all the girls I loved before…wait, wrong book. Instead, let me thank my rock, my posse, the friends who listened to my bitching and rejoicing with the same passion with which I express it.

I am the way I am because of the interaction I have allowed in my life…good, bad or indifferent. When you learn to sort that out, it is indeed very powerful. Indifference was gone long ago…bad has almost disappeared… which leaves only good. That is a very peaceful place to be. I wish it for all of you. This dedication seems an inferior way to thank those who put up with me….

To the kind people that frequented Gaia Wines: You celebrated our dream and that warmth still touches us. Thank you for believing in all we did. It made everything worth it.

Money Folks, Good Friends & Family: Glenda, Tracy, Brian, Tim, Rusty, Amy, Greg and Abby—You all kept the dream alive, your belief and love for Angee and I made us stronger. It constantly convinced us anything is possible. With considerably more ease, may all of your own dreams come wonderfully into reality.

Baby Sister, AB, and Dr. Eye: I wish you had been part of it to the very end. I miss each of you every day. **Jules:** No one has changed and grown more than you. That you wish to be more like me is tragic but flattering. **Pam & Sang:** Thanks for the merlot mop up, the late night functions, the Hollywood movies, road trips in search of wine, fire pit rallies. It kept us going. **Mortimax:** You once ruled the cosmic, karma world. Sorry I sucked you in to all this. Remember to always be able to yell, "So, fire me." You left the struggle too early, but that was a good thing. **Peggy:** Who would have thought you would have come back into my life with such influence and caring. The real ones never, ever, are far from our hearts.

My boyfriend, Dave L: You are a smart, supportive farmer. A man I happily call my friend and confidant. My challenges pale in comparison. You have touched my heart.

My husband, David T: Your words "Don't do that to yourself" ring in my ears if I head down a destructive path. I never tire of your thoughts and confidence. I am so appreciative of the 19 years of lunches and the intellectual conversations that go with them.

Joni: You got more of my calls, full of anger, frustration and sadness, than anybody. Without fail, you managed to be focused, caring and supportive. You remain a passion in my arrogant heart.

Notorious DLG: You face your own challenges with grace and strength. You have dealt with me with the same. For that, I am a better person.

My Soul Mate, Angee: You are, quite simply, the best person I have ever known. Never did you fail to believe in me or us and that has made all the difference. I am proud to be your wife and partner in life. See you at the pier. You are my rock. Are you serious about this? Because, I am! Grow old along with me, the best is truly yet to be!

Technically speaking, I have managed to surround myself with extremely supportive cohorts in this latest shot at fame and fortune. **Bob Juran**, my editor, for calling one more time, and easing me through the process. **Rich Schell**, agri-prenuer attorney who found each chapter a story in itself, was calm and understanding as I ranted. **Karen Ross**, while eagerly awaiting my poetry, understood contemporary, sexy and powerful in the design of the cover.

Table of Contents

PREFACE

METHODOLOGY

The story you are (hopefully) about to read goes beyond definition. Beyond just incredible. Often, grasping to understand the situation, I was sure my head would implode.

As I lived and researched the events of this story, I regularly took notes and, when needed, recorded conversations for reference and clarification. Those recordings were transcribed for easy reference. When meeting notes were taken, a written account of the proceedings occurred shortly after the actual event to preserve the integrity of memory. A time, meeting length, participation and date record was made of meetings.

Obviously, court proceedings were recorded then transcribed and are referenced throughout. E-mails and voice mail messages, when made available and not diminished by the opposition, have been retained.

Meetings often included more than the two parties involved, most with attorneys present, particularly as we moved forward and began to understand the seriousness of the actions taking place.

I personally conducted interviews and research including the expertise of business professionals in the areas of finance, banking, winery operations, and law. Consultations occurred with the legal profession and this manuscript was vetted (reviewed) in its entirety by legal counsel trained and experienced in literary work, including defamation. The entire manuscript was reviewed by persons who lived the experience with me, to ensure the accurate recounting of details and timelines. Names were omitted and non-vital identifying traits were changed to protect both the innocent and the guilty.

Great effort was made to make a clear separation between my opinion and factual events. If in doubt, contact me. I have no problem sharing my opinions.

The intent was not to unnecessarily damage anyone involved in this story. Instead, this story was designed to be an education in passion versus arrogance, right versus wrong and even, at times, women versus men.

It is my belief that the best of all of us are embodied in traits of passion and desire to do what is right. No matter how dire the situation, no matter how dim the prospect of success, no matter how difficult the adversaries, no matter how great the risk of the final outcome, those traits will sustain us.

CHAPTER ONE

The Start of a Dream

*"The future belongs to those that believe
in the power of their dreams."*
Eleanor Roosevelt

"You must do the things you think you cannot do."
Eleanor Roosevelt

"Art is about making something out of nothing and selling it."
Frank Zappa

The story was simple: simply the American Dream. Over lunch, Angee mentioned that making wine and owning a winery would be something great to get into and something from which we could retire. We would do it in Key West, Florida, after her many years as a social worker and mental-health managed-care manager.

Her bright philosophy has always been "When life gives you lemons, make lemonade." She had purchased a home on the east side of town, and, to her surprise, found grapevines. Not a vineyard, mind you, but half a dozen, native American Concord vines. When life gave her grapes, she made wine. After a few failures, she had some great successes and began entering the results in international wine competitions and winning. Family and friends alike requested the wine for personal consumption and gift giving.

Rather than plan for retirement, I countered with "Why wait?" The lackluster economy of the early 1990s was offering me no reasonable employment opportunities. Starting a winery would make a great thesis project for my master's degree in business administration, which I had decided to pursue in the free time presented to me.

After researching the options, I found out that Indiana had state-sponsored programs to help the development of the wine and grape industry. Of course, it made sense for us to stay here and become stable and successful, before moving it all to another state. We would have the state programs to help, Angee would work her current full time job until it got off the ground, and I promised to do everything else.

We should have been more specific. Angee should have defined her "Get off the ground, then retire" timeline; I should have defined what "everything else" meant.

Six weeks after that conversation, I had completed the business plan and we were off to locate possible funding sources...mainly banks.

After visiting six banks and gaining three pending yeses, we considered the effort successful. But it was the best "yes" that would win. Who understood best? This was the Midwest, not wine country, and, although the first commercial winery started in Indiana, there were no strong feelings about the industry or its perceived pinnacle toward success. It would take cash. Even as a growing, profitable venture, a winery would continue to require cash forever.

The bitchy mistress in this business was inventory. Raw goods, the grapes, were harvested once annually. Although there were ways to buy juice after harvest, every fall huge amounts of cash had to be available if you were to introduce new products or restock the best sellers. Equally important was making sure there was increased supply available to meet the demand that had developed, as well as the expanding markets we would pursue.

Just as the season came for a winemaker to marvel at her creations, and as testing and tasting all looked promising for huge sales, there it was: another huge cash outlay. All the quality in the world was no good if you didn't have bottles for the wine. Not just bottles, but corks; not just corks, but capsules; and eventually, if you wanted it sold and out the door for cash, labels. Early spring each year would bring all of those needs to the forefront.

A winery hopes for a successful fall and winter with lots of cash in the door. In fact, most winery and retail operations see 60 percent of their revenue during that time. We were both a retail entity and a winery. Too often, small wineries were resigned to playing catch-up from a slow first quarter.

We knew from the start that choosing a banking partner who had a glimmer of knowledge about the process, and could competently explain it to others, would be important. I also knew that, in reality, there is no sales function in banking. The loan officer, at best, can merely be your advocate. These individuals have to take all the trends, information and passion (which they don't understand at all) and relate it effectively to underwriters.

Underwriters are people you never see and are never able to ask or answer questions to directly. I imagine them in high towers or basement cellars, depending on the economy. I imagine them looking at numbers and charts and more numbers and expensive computer analysis machines and programs that eventually only recite yes or no. It is not a human contact sport by any means.

What a business needs is not a loan officer but a competent human communicator. What you are hoping for is a communicator among the number-crunching drones. If they smile occasionally and get excited about your products or service, it's a plus.

Actually, you should calm them down at that point, because an excited loan officer is a strange animal. Bankers, I believe, don't know how to handle those feelings. It is truly more emotion and passion than their systems can handle.

We were off to find one of these creatures. Two banks had individuals who seemed reasonable, but one underwriting department wanted to structure the loan for $30,000 less than what we had proposed. I am sure some little machine said that would be better.

I continued conversations with underwriters via the two loan officers daily: asking questions, making sure the parameters were best for us. As we walked into the chosen bank to sign loan contracts, I was on my cell phone to the other bank. As we circled around the block looking for a parking space, and until we were in the building, I was negotiating their commitment to the full amount.

While we walked into the big downtown building, I reconfirmed the amount and the terms, and said I would call tomorrow. I thanked the loan officer for all her hard-fought communication between underwriting and entrepreneur. I hung up the phone. Angee and I went upstairs to sign for the funds for our dream.

The stack of documents was thick. It was exciting and scary, and I watched Angee turn pale as she put everything she had on the line for a new business, one that she believed we could turn into a dream beyond all imagination.

It was an opportunity to create something new, different, and beautiful. We were sure it would allow us freedom and independence, change and closeness. Along the way, we hoped it would provide a desirable lifestyle and a little money to enjoy it.

Our original site plan was to be a part of the new municipally developed mall in downtown Indianapolis. The wrath of this real estate development brought a set of challenges that probably didn't have to happen. But we wanted to be a contemporary, urban winery, with no trace of the farming and vineyard views that people were expecting.

In Indiana, as well as most of the country, wineries began as an offshoot of a farming operation. In many cases, creating a value-added agricultural entity offered state tax benefits and incentives. Neither Angee nor I came from farm families or had the strong desire to be farmers. We surmised that growing grapes would be a job better left to the experts. There is a saying about farming: Buy it, inherit it or forget it. Between the early hours and hard manual labor, we opted to forget it and get fruit from the professional folks who knew what they were doing.

Despite the asset of farmland, there was very little chance we would secure funds to start farming, and the risk of grape growing in Indiana, with its often harsh and regularly unpredictable winters, put the chances for success out of even our flexible comfort zone by quite a few miles.

Without the farming land requirement, we began to look extensively in the downtown area, starting with the mall and surrounding areas. While there were good options around, owners and brokers-lessor were getting big heads about the chance to cash in on the excitement of a new retail development. As a result, we found most sites with unrealistic price tags, or terms that left our little winery without much chance of long-term success.

The experience of acquiring a lease from a big mall developer was a lesson in itself. Lack of flexibility, percentage of sales on top of healthy square-foot costs, and finishing out the space architecturally made us seriously rethink the heart of downtown.

The winery had to be accessible to a tourist traffic, and convenient to the day traveler. While out with friends one day, we stopped in a furniture store in the artistic area of Massachusetts Avenue. It was a new and upcoming region of the city devoted to theatres, independent restaurants, and locally owned retail shops.

I inquired about the availability of space in the three-story building with one store owner and asked about the temperament of the building owner.

We got a positive reaction, and I went around the building to get a phone number off the leasing office window. That week I had an appointment to see the basement. We immediately referred to it as the "cellar," knowing it was much sexier. The space was clean and spacious, with exposed brick walls and high unfinished industrial ceilings. Both Angee and I at once saw the possibilities of how perfect the odd space could be for our dream.

The other dream was how workable the landlord/owner and his team (his wife and her sister) were in leasing to us and sharing in our dream. For them, it had been vacant space since the gay nightclub had folded three years earlier. The idea of a destination site with good demographics made sense. They were very easy to work with, and that, coupled with their own enthusiasm for our project, made it a quick deal. We signed a five-year lease on February 14, 1996.

While renovation of the space began, I held interviews with public relations firms and vendors from the small landing that existed upstairs. Angee and I spent every night and weekend researching and buying equipment and merchandise, taking care in each purchase with the limited loan funds secured by the Small Business Administration and our own life savings.

Grape juice was being fermented at offsite wineries, pending our alcohol permit issuance. When we were licensed properly, we would pick up the fermented juice. Angee would finish, refine and sweeten our first six offerings. Producing offsite gave us a ramp-up of product introduction that turned out to be vital, opening and having wine available immediately rather than starting the process upon licensing.

For some reason, the big decisions were always the easiest for me to make. At that time, every decision was big. At the same time, we carefully analyzed our actions to limit mistakes.

One such example was the public-relations firm that we chose. They took the exact language I had given them for press releases and media interviews, and reprinted it on their letterhead. Then we received a bill for $3,000. I was outraged, and quickly decided it could be done once, by me, and for a lot less.

The landlord had subcontracted out the painting, at my request, to speed things up. While the job was being completed properly, I was suspicious when one of the workers asked for the check to be made out to him. Since I wasn't writing the check, I forwarded him to the landlord, who issued a check in his name.

The next day we got a visit from his boss, with an invoice, asking to be paid. We shared with him what his supervisor had requested. As I suspected, the employee had cashed the check, paid the workers, but left with the extra cash and the next three contracts of that company. Despite a call to the bank, it had been a legal transaction, and the painting-company owner learned a lesson about follow-up on job site management.

Angee researched possible names that would reflect the honor and history of winemaking, women, and the creative process involved. She shied away from using her last name as being too much of a cliché. It was a process much like the naming of anything. Once the right one pops up, it's hard to move on.

The name "Gaia" had hit the mark early on. The Greek word for "goddess" provided us with many opportunities. First, and clearly the best was its exotic, romantic feel.

From a marketing standpoint the name was an incredible asset. Despite the fact that there were a variety of mispronunciations, that very difficulty began many of the relationships for our company.

People asked how to say it, how to spell it, and why we had chosen Gaia. So much of wine involves unnecessary intimidation; questions about the name provided people a starting point for asking about wine. If we did a good job of making them comfortable, that pattern would continue and we would have the opportunity to educate the public.

What was intellectually behind the name was the strong connection between the factors tying the industry into the name. The Greek culture was the first to commercialize winemaking, actually making it viable commerce. Gaia is the name for the Greek goddess of earth, from whom all the products come. Finally, it was a goddess name and served to honor the female aspect of our venture.

A fourth and little known fact was that many people believe Gaia to be the origin of the word "gay." Gaea or Gaya spellings lent support to that. Although it was nowhere in our winery literature, Angee and I together felt it was the final indication that this should be the name.

There was one strong opponent to the idea. An early advisor to the winery, someone with considerable history in the industry, made much of the fact that we would, or could, get sued for using the name. We were unaware that there was a winery in Italy with the family name Gaja. Angelo Gaja is an internationally known winemaker. Our advisor was sure that this man, with what he knew of his temperament, would see fit to come to America, even to Indiana, and on hearing of our business name would create a great legal hassle on our little operation.

I did some very preliminary research to defend our choice. The name was not spelled the same, it did not mean the same thing, and, as I would find out later, a title is the one thing that cannot obtain a copyright. Additionally, Gaja products were not widely known in Indiana and were not readily available in our original market.

Gaja did make a well-known cabernet that retailed for about $75 a bottle. I was quite sure that no one would confuse anything about the two entities.

Even early on, we were so committed to this being right that we forged ahead. If Angelo had the time, the attention he brought to Gaia Wines in Indiana could have only given us another ready-made opportunity to introduce our products to an ideal market.

As we finalized money issues, an original commitment to an equity position had to be changed. It was done with good reason, but was an unfortunate starting issue. Without the exact amount to make bank-required ratios, we risked the total financing. Before opening, we would have to find an additional $5,000. Not a large amount, given the project, but it might as well have been five million if we didn't have it. And we didn't.

What we did have was three very supportive "angels."

Getting money from relatives is a difficult challenge that often has to be played out. The theory is that if you can't convince friends and family, who have obviously known you for longer than the bank has, then why should a bank feel compelled to partake in financing your dream?

So, with some discomfort, we had discussions with Angee's mother, her sister and brother-in-law, and a co-worker of hers. With equally remarkable success, we secured the last $5,000.

We attended trade shows in Chicago, Indianapolis, Atlanta and San Francisco, in search of the right mix of wine-related merchandise to complement the winery experience.

Hundreds of vendors offered thousands of choices. Having been to all the Indiana wineries and sixty others nationwide, we were aware of the product mix. We wanted to offer something different. Our theme was distinctly "no gingham ducks," as I referred to it. Nothing would be country, all high-end, lots of glass, lots of contemporary products, full of color and style. It completed our vision of a downtown city winery that made the experience accessible to people at all levels of wine enjoyment and education.

Occasionally, even with my understanding of the entrepreneur-ial spirit, I made awful purchases. There was something sad about the aisle of vendors hawking (or in some cases, not hawking) the latest product that would be perfect for our store. I am not sure if it was a good sales job or a pretty face, but I soon found our small winery with $500 worth of biscotti, because someone told me it was what was big in the coastal wineries. But it was not a good Midwestern fit.

Months, later I would throw out $495 worth of biscotti. I didn't even have the heart to donate it to charity, it was so bad.

It took only two weeks after opening for me to realize something seemed absent. The ambience we had dreamed of was missing. The place was full of dead air. The night I figured it out I immediately went to purchase a stereo system that our first employee quickly set up.

Despite some early miscalculations, few were more wrong and made for a better story than the huge misjudgment I had made about size and weight. As we neared our opening, we ordered half a semi-truck of bottles, all neatly and tightly stacked on pallets. It was then we realized that the mystique of the cellar presented a logistical problem. Everything that would eventually come up had to be brought down, and wine was not light. Neither were bottles. I simply did not have a rational idea of half a truckload, or a pallet of bottles. Depending on the style of bottles, that meant 80 to 110 cases, 12 bottles in each case. Even when they were empty, the repetition up and down stairs was a massive undertaking.

There were no loading docks and no freight elevator because of the historic nature of the building. For years to come we would hear from new employees, usually in the first week, or the first time they had to carry a full case upstairs. The comment was always the same: a some-what out-of-shape, breathless newbie would drag back down the stairs and utter what he or she thought was the most original solution to our problem: "You know what you should do? Get an elevator."

For a while I would laugh and recount the incident that occurred with our first bottle delivery. Approximately 10 pallets were to arrive early one Friday, and we were set to bottle the wine that weekend. First, as you might see, there was no margin for error. Our next issue was the difficulty in pulling a semi truck behind the small alley in the back of the building. Drivers always made it seem like it was the biggest problem they would ever encounter.

Once the truck was in place, its back door swung open to reveal a long, half-empty truck. At the very end were our new bottles. It was an exciting sight. Then it all changed.

I had arranged for Angee, myself and our one new employee to be there to unload. Apparently the humor in this was lost on me, as I told the patient driver. With no pallet lifter, no dock, no truck lift, we would hand-remove every box, breaking down the pallets and carrying each box one at a time down two flights of stairs where they had to be restacked.

There was always the feeling that we—all right, I—was the butt of many trucking faux pas stories at the truckers' annual banquet. The driver shook his head and agreed he had time to get some dinner. His arrival was already hours late and he had to be gone by the next morning for another pickup. This was 3 p.m. on Friday. By 9 p.m. that night, we were convinced that the process was going to take more time the next day.

Beyond that, we were incredibly sore and tired. Not just "Boy, this was a long day" tired. Not just "Wow, great physical activity" sore. After 9 p.m., we disbanded for the night. I had to figure something out. As we drove to the last restaurant that was open for dinner, I can clearly recall that the only place that didn't hurt on me was my lips. Moving from the table to the salad bar was a battle. I knew the next day would provide no relief.

Over dinner, as Angee and I ached with every move of food to our mouths, I realized we would need a flexible, strong workforce fast and first thing the next morning.

Even thought it was after midnight before we got home, I was up early the next day. The solution was either brilliant or idiotic, but it was the only option we saw. At 7:30 a.m. I drove directly to the homeless shelter less than six blocks away.

Painfully, I slid out of the car and dragged myself across the sidewalk to the front office to inquire about anybody being available for work. The office staff pointed me to the double doors of a room where about one hundred guys milled around even at this early hour. I stepped in and asked if anyone wanted to work. More than half started toward me. Without a lot of discussion, I pointed randomly to the youngest and strongest-appearing of the men.

Eight guys piled into my SUV. Less than two hours later, 10 pallets were unloaded and restacked. It was the best use of effective manpower I had ever coordinated. Without a second thought, the homeless-shelter workforce became our just-in-time labor staff for the next eight years. Although the men who helped changed over that time, the work was always flexible and timely. They were grateful for the work and the cash in hand. I was lucky that they kept coming back and the story of the loading work at the local winery was not a scary tale retold at the shelter.

As happy as we were about how appropriate this new wine cellar was, we always had a plan for the future. We always knew what had to happen next, and there was much delight in the design of the next building which we would call home to Gaia Wines.

A napkin drawing hung on my office bulletin board. The building was round, giving homage to the Earth. Actually, to many it looked just like a big breast. We would incorporate a deck overlooking the city to retain the contemporary flair of a city winery. What could be more romantic than sipping wine atop a winery balcony overlooking the lights of the city? It would provide a venue for weddings and an unobstructed view of the July Fourth celebration, and host countless cookouts.

In our mind, the structure would also become a factor in the skyline of the city and a tribute to wine and to women entrepreneurs. Copper, glass, and water paths would allow it to become an accessible retreat. Even as we finished up for the opening weekend, I could see the future of what we were creating. The next step was always part of the reel that rolled in my head.

With most details addressed, on Indy 500 auto race weekend in Indianapolis, May 25, 1996, we opened our dream, Gaia Wines Contemporary Winery. The first owned by women exclusively. The first owned by lesbians.

During the first sale, I realized I should have paid more attention to the register computer system training, as I fumbled with the keys and the system with half-entered inventory. But there was cash in the drawer that first day, and that was an amazing feeling of success and accomplishment.

We had signed our present life away as we began the journey to our new life and all that it would be.

CHAPTER TWO

MEETING MY SOUL MATE

*"The most we can hope for
is not that someone does not stand in our way,
but instead helps us clear the path that will become our way."*
MEJB

"Bacchus opens the gates of the heart."
Horace
(65-8 B.C.)

I can't for the life of me remember who the "hot lesbian performer" was who brought me to the coffee café with another date. But I can recall clearly spending time with Angee, sitting across from me, at the small table for four.

She was with someone else I had known from two-step country dancing. Her date was an older, nondescript woman with little personality. It's safe for me to make a judgment, because I was with the same.

The evening was actually the end of a country dance party, and we had, by chance, ended up at the coffee house, although I was not a coffee drinker. It was the place to see and be seen. Yet instead of making the rounds, I was engaged by Angee. She was funny, quick and smart, and completely at ease with herself. It seemed as if she would be a fun friend.

When we all finally decided to end the evening, it was disappointing to have to leave Angee, if only, I thought, because the conversation had been so intellectual and fun all at once. This was Saturday, and we would see each other on Monday at the local dive's regular country dancing night.

On Monday I would find out about Angee's partner's plans. She was going to break up with Angee. Certainly switching partners had become comically common within our tight group. What I most objected to was that the partner was sharing that information with other people before she told Angee. I felt some of the pain Angee would feel at not being treated right to the very end.

I could only give a sympathetic look the next time I saw Angee at the dance club. I didn't think about anything romantic, but figured her new free time would give us on opportunity to hang out.

In mid-January I tracked down a number for Angee at work. She gave me her home number and suggested I call her there later. When I called, I figured a discount movie and some pizza would give us a little chance to spend some time together without a lot of pressure. I left a message, and Angee was quick to call me back.

"How about we see a movie and grab a bite to eat," I casually suggested. Her response was a new one. (Feel free to use it yourself, if needed). "I can't, I am papier-mâchéing my mannequin." It was too good to be a real excuse.

"What?"

"Well, I am covered in paste and paper, fixing the arm of my mannequin."

She was weird. I didn't know what to focus on first, the fact that she had a mannequin or that she was repairing her arm. She seemed in a hurry. "Maybe another time."

"Right, Okay, you know, it's no big thing, just a movie and some pizza…" I figured she felt pressured or it was too soon or she thought I was gross.

"No, really, I got to finish this before it dries."

"I'll see you next week." And I ended the conversation so she could get back to her inanimate paper surgery.

I was cordial the next time we saw each other at the club. There were plenty of people to dance with, and switching around, regardless of whom you came with, was commonplace. Although I had never danced with Angee, she approached and asked.

As I led her around the small dance floor, we laughed and talked, but I was detached. Finally she said something.

"Are you ever going to ask me out again?"

"Come on, papering a doll's arm…?" Clearly, I was still bitter.

"I had all the supplies, and once you start you got to finish it." Perhaps I didn't understand the intricacy of hobby work. We swung around a few more time before I relented and we made plans for that Saturday.

It was snowy, and not the night to be on the road with my small sports car. I made it to Angee's home safely, and we headed to dinner at one of my favorite locally owned restaurants. Little did I know that the menu listed Angee's favorite entree, duck. We laughed, and the conversation was easy and thoughtful. I paid for dinner and we headed off to a comedy club.

At the end of laughing, we sat in the car out front and it became obvious we didn't want to leave each other. I reached for a local event paper that was in the back seat and we decided quickly on a jazz club farther north of the city.

Instantly, once inside, I felt protective of Angee. I have no idea why. While it is my nature to be polite and respectful, I had a feeling that I had to surround her, be aware of the surroundings, to protect her.

Maybe it was the odd mix of people at this predominantly straight club. Maybe it was something she had shared with me at dinner that I immediately assimilated into my consciousness.

In between band sets, we tried in vain to actually hear a complete song. We had chosen Boston's "More than a feeling" on the juke box. It was good both being kids of the `70s and `80s.

I had a strong reaction when a woman at the club began to take an interest in Angee, asking her to dance and spending time talking to her. What was most unusual was that it was not the kind of club for two women to be dancing together. It certainly leaned more to redneck than I felt comfortable with. But I was very comfortable with Angee, and that felt new and grand after a rather tough run of some other dates.

As we headed to the car, it was apparent that the weather conditions had worsened. My Porsche was covered in snow and ice. The driver's-side lock was frozen. We used Angee's gas card to scrape off enough ice to see through the front window, and I crawled over the passenger's seat to get in. She was unfazed and helpful. It was the first battle that challenged us together. We had success.

My house was much closer than Angee's, so I offered to head there and have her spend the night. She was not interested. Or perhaps more accurately, she wanted to be in her home. The Porsche never progressed so slowly for so long. I was sure that anyone traveling the highway that night would find us in a ditch the next morning.

Arriving safely in front of her house, we said our goodnights and Angee hugged me with a series of back pats. Not a good sign of how the longest date in my life should have ended. There was no invite in, if only to sleep on the couch. There was little comfort in being sure that she would feel bad if I didn't make it home. I headed across town by myself.

After the cold goodbye, I was somewhat shocked by the enthusiastic greeting from Angee the next Monday of country dancing. Again we made plans for the following Sunday. No sense eating up a Friday or Saturday on a second date, I thought to myself. Later in the week, I received a huge bowl arrangement of white flowers and, poking out of the middle, on a plastic stick, was the Boston CD with our song.

For Sunday dinner I made more of an effort than I would have originally thought. I lit the house throughout with candles and had a blazing fire in the family-room fireplace. Filet mignon and a fondue dessert made up dinner. I set up a full round of CDs in the player: Kenny G, Celine Dion. As I was ironing my jeans, the bell rang.

Being right on time was a new thing for my dates, but I was pleased. Angee would often refer to the setting as my "dyke trap." Everything was perfect.

After another wonderful evening of conversation, laughter and sharing of thoughts and ideas, Angee got up to leave. I followed her to the door and politely helped her on with her coat. But I didn't want the evening to end. We hadn't kissed, and I needed more time.

"Don't go." It came out as a statement rather than a question. In one uninterrupted movement, Angee dropped her purse, and the coat fell off her body onto the floor. Neither of us bothered to pick it up as we headed back to the couch.

Getting comfortable, I stretched out on half the couch, careful not to take up too much space. Angee sat upright at the other end. We continued talking, and she pulled my feet onto her lap to begin rubbing them. Game over. There wasn't a better, sweeter move that could have been made, given the massage whore that I am.

We talked about the music playing, none of which she was familiar with. That I could change. She was sweet, easy, and so very comfortable with herself.

One hour later she would tease, "What's a girl got to do to get a kiss around here?" Forty-five minutes later we would kiss. It was the kind of kiss that made you wonder why you hadn't been kissing your whole life. That was January.

In July, on my favorite holiday, the Fourth, a crowd gathered at Angee's home. It was significant because she had been so cautious about visitors after years of dealing with crazy clients and abusive family members.

Our friend Julie stood by with a song by Trisha Yearwood I had carefully chosen. "Down on My Knees" began playing while all our guests were in the front yard on this perfect sunny day. Angee was in the backyard to start the grill.

I glanced at my watch again to confirm the timing. Earlier in the week, a dancing friend had inquired what I would do if Angee said no. It had never occurred to me.

I called Angee to come to the front yard. Confused, or maybe irritated, she joined everyone in the front yard. I looked to the sky and pointed upward as the plane made its first pass with my marriage message.

I fell to my knees, (well, actually, gently bent to my knees), and as the song played on I opened the box with two matching channel-set diamond rings.

All Angee could do was hold on tight and repeat yes, yes, yes. That night, as we watched fireworks from the top of a downtown parking lot, I briefly wondered whether we would be here if she had said no.

We had easily shared a lot over a brief time. Angee was working intensely in private therapy and in a group setting, to deal with a violent, abusive childhood. I had felt comfortable sharing my recent business failure. Almost immediately into our relationship, I found myself telling her that I would soon be looking for an apartment, having sold my house to give another $1,200 to the IRS on a debt that had been paid in full yet was so badly misallocated that an even greater amount remained.

We often joked about relocating to Key West, Florida, creating a simpler, carefree life for us, if only for a while. All she ever asked was if her dog, Charlie, could come along.

That kind of trust and love is what would become the basis for everything we would do together. As long as we were together, nothing life dealt would detour us. There would be no challenge that was not faced as a team. I believe that is the very definition of love.

I never had to look for an apartment. Angee's offer to move into her home was gentle and sincere. We began a new life together, and would come to know that the power of two was formidable.

This ease and energy of our partnership made me progressively invincible. Even as I struggled with the failure of my business as a reflection of the failure of me, I never received any doubt from Angee. There may have been times when, in her nurturing way, she would question me to clarify a thought process or decision. However, it was never critical, never demeaning, and often she believed in me more than I was able to believe and trust myself.

Any disagreements we had were incredibly few. I remember redecorating our new home together as she headed off to work. She was sick and really needed to stay home and recover. While I respected her dedication, it was often at the risk of her own well-being and health, be it mental, emotional or physical. I think it was the first of only a few times I ever raised my voice during our discussion.

Angee is fearlessly trusting, even when common sense should tell you no. On vacation in the Keys, we had walked out of a restaurant by the ocean to walk along the shore while we waited for my sister, who was vacationing with us.

A plain white van pulled up with three men. It was the kind of vehicle you might see rented for terrorist activity. They slowed to a stop, blocking any view from the restaurant. The passengers-side window was down and they asked how to get to the beach. It seemed an odd request, given that they were facing the water.

As Angee moved in to understand them better, the side panel door slid open, revealing the third man. More than that, it gave ample space to grab someone.

Perhaps I had seen too many movies, yet my reaction was immediate. He leaned forward and I grabbed Angee's arm, even as she was still trying to give some direction. I pulled her back out of reach from the van and we moved to be in view to others at the back of the van.

It was a split second that now seems forever, but with cleared space, I ended the conversation and continued to hold tightly to Angee as the man in the back lunged slightly forward out of the van. We stepped around the van and into the street, convinced that getting hit was a viable option over being pulled into a nondescript van with three men.

Angered at her naiveté, I tried to understand what Angee was thinking. She was only trying to help, and any normal internal signals that should have alerted her to danger were missing. This factor, despite her terrible childhood, seemed odd.

While I, who had gratefully never experienced the fear or danger that she had, was acutely aware that the situation was not right.

My mistrust of everything became her protection. I felt it was my best and greatest responsibility—to make sure that nothing ever hurt her again. My job as protector was one I was very good at and, silently, relished.

Angee and I share everything. She is every part of my life. There is no one I trust more. The feeling that it is and always will be the two of us is a great comfort. It also gives me great strength, knowing that together there was, and still is, nothing we can't do, and no struggle we won't support each other through.

We don't fight, instead preferring to enjoy the time we get to spend together. I am forever glad that we don't waste time like that. We have meetings and we talk and make lists. When things need to get done, we divide and conquer. When the world seems too rough, we relax in each other's arms with music, candlelight and a glass of wine or a Bailey's and Grand Marnier combo on ice, which we nicknamed "nectar of the goddess."

All of our work is together and toward common goals, and it makes

all the difference in the world. There is compromise, and understanding. More than knowing our strengths, we know each other's
weaknesses, and they are never exploited to be hurtful, or demeaning.

I remember my dream as a young girl, of how romantic it would
be to walk through a gallery, enjoying the art, the music, being
consumed in the senses surrounding me and the hand of a love in
mine. That hand is Angee's. I am very lucky.

CHAPTER THREE

A Fellini Film
Casting and Lessons

"Work is the refuge of people who have nothing better to do."
Oscar Wilde

For one all too brief moment in time, Gaia Wines employed an Asian dwarf, a pagan polygamy head witch, a black woman married to a gangster pimp, a bisexual mom, and a gay clergy person. Those were the good ones.

Angee had known Dawn from a former life in the nearby Indiana University setting. Dawn had come to Indiana from Washington, D.C., working with a research professor whom she admired greatly.

Unknown to us, she had become aware of and began to track the path of Gaia Wines. It was a small leap she made when she arrived at our doorstep to inquire about employment realizing she was ready to do something different with her career.

I have made some significant hiring mistakes, and for some time would continue to make them. Maybe it was the retail nature of the job, or the transient nature of the college-age folks who approached us. But all too often, a new employee lasted less than 30 days. We came to appreciate anything beyond 90 days as a dream.

Initially I was against hiring Dawn. I didn't particularly like her, nor do I remember trusting her. That lack of trust was less a comment on Dawn and more about my growing distrust of anyone. Angee, however, was confident that Dawn would be a good addition.

Dawn started out part-time and quickly became irreplaceable. Despite her rough edge and sharp tongue, she had a growing legion of customers who found her to be caustic while being both knowledgeable and inviting. It was a weird combination.

Despite my hesitations, I found myself depending on Dawn more as Gaia Wines grew. Her flexibility was an asset. She was able and willing to embrace all that was becoming Gaia in its many forms. She was married at the time, and yet her personal life never seemed to interfere with her dedication to our business, or her love and dedication to Angee and me. So often, she was a comforting port in the constant storm that small business can be.

Although it was unofficial, before long Dawn was the first full-time employee. Her ability to learn quickly and maintain both a personal opinion—which she rarely hesitated to share with us—and an understanding for the vision we had made her priceless. Some of my proudest moments came in hearing her succinctly repeat, with unflinching accuracy, our vision and plans.

Three years into our working relationship, I was driving her crazy, or at least adding to the trip. She moved to another small business and a less competent boss. I don't think I ever shared my pain or sense of loss when she told us that she needed to leave to avoid killing me.

It was then that her appreciation for my crazy, obsessive dreaming and management style took root. When it would come time, it was easy for her to return.

Casting: When a certain gentleman walked into the winery to interview, I was impressed by the fact that he was wearing a suit. It was impressive even if it was because he had come from his other job. He seemed sharp and personable, as if he could handle himself.

It could have come from years of being a double minority. He adapted quickly and made friends with everyone as a matter of course and of defense. He worked hard and enjoyed the camaraderie of the Gaia Wines family.

Lesson: That feeling of family became a common theme with the employees that made it past the one-year employment mark. Each was a talented and dedicated individual who added personality and more character and credibility to our operation.

I realized something else. People were drawn to the family that we seemed to inadvertently create. They were proud of their association with our business. We rapidly became friends and family.

Developed from experience, I don't trust anybody. But I distrusted these folks the least.

The mix we were beginning to attract was as varied as the people you pass on any big city street. The blend of people looking for the excitement and romance of the winery was distinctive. That is probably a good way to describe the Indiana native that joined Gaia Wines.

Casting: She was a big, fun girl from a small town in the Midwest. She worked full time at a community center and was looking for extra cash. She had crazy soap-opera-drama friends, and a huge smile and laugh. At the same time, she was strong with opinion and rarely failed to share it. She quickly became a part of the core family.

During an offsite trip in southern Indiana, she showed her commitment to the cause. In part, trying to save money and because rooms for wine festival were in short supply, Angee and our staff, male and female, had to share rooms. We thought it would be only a slight problem, because the old hotel, the best in the area, did offer pull-out beds.

Apparently a regular check of the pull-out bedding option was not a high priority of this place. Sadly, this dedicated employee found she was sleeping, at least trying to sleep, in the shape of a "v". The bed would not pull out completely, nor did it flatten out. So with her hind side hitting the ground, she slept with her feet up in the air, slightly above her head, which was also raised.

While we all joked about it, she made it through like a trouper. She was able to joke as well. I never really heard her complain. We treated her to a massage as soon as we made it back home.

Lesson: It's amazingly funny what people will do when they believe in the dream. You should recognize and reward them publicly and sincerely.

Casting: The gentlest man one would ever want to meet came in one day to add another retail job to his already busy schedule. His years in the retail arena made him well suited for the winery. He was a manager for a large national upscale retailer, and it was hard to envision why he would want to spend what little free time he had at another retail location.

But he loved what he did at Gaia Wines and often wished, as we did, that it afforded him an opportunity full-time. He was very neat and kept the winery in topnotch shape. As I passed him during a private function, while most of the staff was feeling stressed, I smiled and asked him how he was doing. "This is easy and fun," he replied.

Lesson: I never saw him lose even one bit of himself to the pressures that we sometimes faced, and that made Gaia Wines a better place for its guests. The attitude of well adjusted, happy people will spill over to your customers. Keep talented people focused on their talents.

With higher than average turnover, we found ourselves most times plowing through employees. What appeared at times to be a good fit usually took only a pay period or so to show that it was not someone who would be with us long-term.

Despite accepting this turnover as the nature of any business with elements of retail, restaurant and customer service, we were determined to raise the bar. Not accepting employees who could not comply with basic duties turned into the quickest way to weed out some folks.

Essential to the issuing of paychecks was having an accurate time card. There was little time to assume what actual hours had been worked, given the seven day schedule. Days could easily start at 6:30 a.m., and we often entertained private events until past midnight.

Casting: We also expected employees to handle their own affairs, which is why it was so unexpected when an employee's mother called to begin harassing us. He had not completed his time card or his required paperwork, and as a result he was not issued a check. Even though he had directions about what needed to be done, apparently his first reaction was to call his mother. After a few days of calls to Dawn demanding payment and to talk with me, I took her call.

"Pay my son" was the basic demand. Rather than get into a verbal battle, I remained surprisingly calm. That only served to make her more irate, as she began threatening legal action, seemingly proud that she had a family lawyer.

I caused her more angst when I asked for the name of her attorney and said I would contact him or her directly to discuss the issues. She froze, with no name to give me. "Don't bullshit a bull shitter" is my mantra.

When this failed to get me riled, she went back to her demands. Again, I calmly broke her rant by asking how old her son was, knowing full well he had to be 21 to be working with alcohol. When she told me his age, I stated our policy about not being able to share information with anyone other than the employee if he was of legal age.

Lesson: I never figured out why he had been so hesitant to comply, but he did come in later that day to complete the missing information and receive his last check. It is vital that you establish your organization's working systems and observe them despite outside pressures or special requests. Clearly outline the process and lines of communication. Make sure they are understood and followed.

Casting: One of the first private functions we hosted was in the relatively small, front tasting room, well before we expanded into less crowded space. As a result, tables pushed dangerously close to merchandise and surrounded lots of glass gift items.

We served dinner for the private birthday party, and navigating around glass and food product proved to be a challenge. A pretty tasting room associate, an energetic part-time actress, did a well thought-of job engaging customers and handled with wit the hassle that sometimes came with the retail environment.

Mid-party, a jar of spaghetti sauce hit the floor by a table in the middle of the first room. She dutifully headed over to clean it up. She was responsive and apologetic, making quick work of cleaning up, even though it had not been her fault. Next to the mess was a table of three women and one male guest.

The party wrapped up with both guests and host pleased with the outcome. As we stood around rehashing the pluses and minuses, I saw a regularly confident new associate become very uncomfortable. I pressed to see what was wrong.

Although she initially hesitated, I was shocked when she finally shared with us what had happened during the cleanup. While she was down on her knees slopping up the sauce, the male at the table began making comments and sounds as if she were down on her knees for his pleasure. I was furious.

Even at a woman-owned business, this male felt it appropriate to harass a female while at a table of female guests.

It was bad enough that no one at his own table thought to reprimand him and make apologies to our employee. Angee and I were also concerned that our employee had not felt comfortable saying something to us, that somehow we would condone the behavior because they were paying customers.

"Listen, we do not accept that behavior and would have dealt with it, if you had come to us during the event," I told her. Sadly, in typical female-server mode, she felt it best just to take it.

"This is a female-owned business, and treating women improperly will never be acceptable," Angee said. The normally jovial woman felt terrible and was close to tears: She was even hesitating to respond to our reaction, feeling that somehow she would be abused again.

"We will always support our employees; they should be treated right. One of the benefits of owning your own business is that you can pick and choose what business you do. We don't need anybody's money that bad," I said.

Our energetic actress seemed shocked. "What could you have done?" she pleaded.

"I would have asked the man to apologize and leave, and told his host. If need be, the entire party would have been shut down."

Lesson: At once, it became our policy. Our associate let out a deep breath and seemed more comfortable. That event set the tone, and our reaction became policy with respect to how our employees were to be treated. If you feel in your heart that something is wrong, commit to correcting it immediately. Over-analysis and delay undermines the response/policy being equal to the action/event. Commit to people first, if that is your most precious resource.

Casting: People come in all shapes and sizes and with very different lifestyles. That's not a tough concept to grasp. But without fail, Gaia Wines seemed to grasp the most different! At over 6 feet and pushing mid-300 pounds, another employee was a brash, imposing man, at least physically. But he had a humor about himself that was an asset in making people comfortable, one he had probably developed shortly after he hit that height.

As we prepared for the staff holiday party, invitations were sent out to employees and offered each one the opportunity to bring a guest. We made it vague, since we realized that not everyone had a wife or husband. Nothing is worse than going to a party without someone by your side. So we went out of our way to make people feel comfortable.

It was on this occasion that the 6-footer chose to push the limits-if we had any-of the guest policy. Somewhat awkwardly, he asked about bringing significant *others*. I had been forewarned by another employee as to his situation, but I let him continue, for the sake of practice, to own the right to share his situation.

Would it be okay for him to bring *two* partners? "Two guests?" I tried to clarify, "That would hardly be fair to others." He continued to explain. I listened calmly.

He had two wives, non-traditional family, to be sure. Even more so, given conservative Indiana. He lived with another couple, and while this second woman had a male partner, she was also considered within the family as partnered with him. He was surprised that I did not hesitate to tell him she was welcome. He even looked confused. "You don't have a problem with that?" he said.

"As a lesbian, I know, if you can keep two women happy, then you are to be feared and revered. "More power to you," was my answer.

Lesson: Leave room for individual interpretations of the rules and regulations you have set, if needed. The value of respecting someone's situation will provide him or her with appreciation and dedication.

Casting: At the risk of sounding backwardly prejudiced, I have found that gay men are excellent cleaners. No one had ever kept the winery as clean as when we had a young gay man working for us part time. As one of our early employees, he was kind, funny and available.

His part-time status worked out well, because he was on disability. He took great care in navigating the winery landscape and loved the interaction with people. We all believed it kept him healthy.

It was odd when we started getting customers telling us that they had stopped by during open hours to find us closed. The first few times we brushed it off. Surely they had been there after eight and thought it was only 7:30 p.m.

It took about four occasions for us to actually track the days of "early closing." They were all days that he was on the schedule.

We tightened the schedule, stayed around a few nights, and followed it up with impromptu visits after we had left. Then the next inconsistency surfaced.

It came to our attention during the labeling of wine; we would come to a case of wine down a few rows on the pallets to find one or two bottles missing from a case. We were still running with a volunteer bottling staff, and the first few times chalked it up to sloppy casing during bottling with a new crew.

But when we adjusted production and monitored case filling more closely, we found out again that bottles were being removed after the fact. Someone was stealing, not from the floor, full of product, but making the incredibly inconvenient effort to dig down three or four stacks of heavy wine cases to steal an unlabeled bottle or two. That he varied the product choice made it harder to track. It was quite an effort.

The final incident came when he was supposed to show up with a friend on Saturday to help bottle. Both he and the friend were late and that cut into the already small bottling crew.

Being Saturday, we already had concerns about using people's free time. Being late was not like him. Leaving early yes, but being late, no.

His friend showed up first and explained the tragic night they had had. After being stopped by police, on suspicion of drunk driving, he had switched to the driver's seat to protect his unlicensed friend. As a result, he had spent the night in jail. When he finally walked in to the winery, he knew the end result.

"I'm fired, right?" he said calmly, like it was part of his plan.

We listened to his story to make sure the facts were correct. Then just as calmly as he had asked Angee, responded that it would be impossible for him to maintain his alcohol license allowing him to sell wine. As a result, he could no longer be employed by Gaia Wines.

Later, we discovered that he had regularly locked up the store shortly after we left in the evening and would then head across the street to a gay bar to drink with his buddies.

Lesson: When he left, the mystery cases containing 11 bottles instead of 12 also stopped. But the winery was never cleaned as well again. Often, a business owner must choose between the asset of talents and the liability of actions. Chart each step you wish to take in your process, set timelines for behavior to change or adjust, and be decisive in your decision when the time comes to make it.

Our part-time chief financial officer had been convinced from the beginning that Gaia Wines should move head-first into the wholesale business. He was sure that an effort at the wine shop and restaurant level would provide a more stable cash flow as we grew. I was less enthused at the thought of selling our product for less and of maintaining relationships with distributors who truly wanted little to do with locally produced wines.

But I warmed to the idea of a three-pronged business model: retail, wholesale, and private functions. A business model allowing diversified service and product mix and diversified revenue streams made sense.

Casting: At a lunch meeting that followed my awakening, I mentioned the idea to a state official who was to assist us in more profitable growth. He excitedly mentioned that his daughter had worked for a distributor and said I should chat with her.

I liked his daughter immediately. I mention this because that is a rare occurrence for me. Her loud high-heeled shoes could be heard miles away as she made her way down the winery staircase during each visit.

It was not the only thing loud about her. Her big thick red-black hair framed a small chiseled face. She was full of nervous energy and talked without pulling any punches, with strong, honest power. She was a force to be reckoned with.

She had worked in the restaurant business and for a small local distributor and had gained some insight into the business segment we were venturing into. We talked for over an hour and she asked who "had our back" from a legal standpoint. Could she help, as a gesture of friendship, review corporate papers and our plan?

As a public defender, she truly believed she was doing "God's work," protecting criminals from our legal system. The work had impacted her with a no-nonsense, straightforward, strong-woman aura that made her obsessive-compulsive manner unapproachable by most people—particularly, I imagined, to the opposite sex.

I felt with her assistance, as she had said, we could be an unstoppable force. We had embraced her as part of the team. She joined us at that year's Ernst & Young Entrepreneur of the Year award dinner as an early thank-you for her efforts, before any work had been done.

Noticeably, there was disappointment when she failed to come through on some promises she had made to check over things, which we credited to, or blamed on, her commitments to the court system. When she back-pedaled on being able to help us out, I felt it was just another case of perpetrating deception by an outside professional. It would be eighteen months before we would talk again.

Lesson: Never close the door on a resource or an opportunity. If you must temporarily close the door, at least do not flip the deadbolt.

CHAPTER FOUR

IN SEARCH OF INTESTINAL FORTITUDE

"He who knows, does not speak. He who speaks, does not know."
Lao-tzu
(604-531)

"Training is everything."
Pudd'nhead Wilson

"Talking is one thing," he remarked to himself.
"Doing is another." Snail to Tigger.
The Te of Piglet
Benjamin Hoff

As an industry, other wineries were pretty much in agreement when I announced that we had a sales position available. What in the world would a sales person do? This was unsettling yet I realized most business owners are not business people. But of all the functions I had assumed in the growing company, I knew it wasn't until we had a successful, productive, competent sales person (or team) that we would be able to see the level and surge of growth and profitability that we were inching toward at this point.

Not one winery in Indiana had a full time sales person. Yet we all expected growth to happen magically. Most assume just by being, there should be regular increased sales, and better profitability.

Casting: Our own efforts started with our first employee. This guy had helped on build-out of the space and was excited about the opportunity for his first private function, a social club that enjoyed good food and wine. He had learned that a criterion for membership was that these folks must have a net worth of $1 million and up. He got set for a profitable night.

What I could not tell him at the time was that there is a reason people have a net worth of $1 million plus. It's not because they spend hundreds of dollars at Indiana wineries. Anyway, he dressed appropriately in a tuxedo shirt and bow tie and attended to their every need. A private chef was brought in for our first private function.

Lesson: At the end of the function, the total commissionable revenue was $42.08. One guest bought one poster and one bottle of wine. It was heartbreaking for all of us. But our first sales person, who tried hard to hide his disappointment, had learned a lesson in the sales world. People do things for *their* reasons, not yours. Let people learn from their experience, not just yours.

Sadly, individuals who attempt to portray themselves as sales people are very often the victims of mutual mystification. While it sounds simple enough, ask someone close to you if they know what this term means and then if they can explain it.

It is so simple a concept that the beauty is breathtaking. It happens all the time, between friends, lovers, and strangers. Mutual mystification is the perception effecting reality, of what you are trying to communicate being unduly influenced and sometimes terribly clouded by your own set of experiences.

It could very well be the root of all evil as we know it. But when managed properly, one's ability to be effective is dramatically increased.

Someone says to you, "I want an elegant affair," "I want a good bottle of wine," "I want you," and surely, we would, under normal instances, react the way everyone else would…elegant in my mind, a good bottle of wine is what I like and I want you too. But, for what?

Casting: I graduated to college interns as a part-time solution to our sales challenges. Over the course of two years, we employed five local interns plus an international intern-which almost led to international incident.

Two were good, one was okay and three got fired. These are not great odds if you are trying to take advantage of an increase in sales and business that is growing double digits by word of mouth anyway. Growing a company beyond that which is organic requires better odds and much better skills.

A sale is not easy, nor is it pretty, if you don't know what you are doing. It requires skills, which, as a society, we are never formally taught. Like money management and banking, we don't have sales classes in grades K-8. We don't learn to go toe-to-toe, feeling equal with our customer and feeling that we can be the ones to say no to the sales process as well. It is the companies' and manager's fault, one hundred percent.

I could paper a wall with the résumés from "mortgage loan sales people." If you cannot ask for the business, take the money and make the decision about the piece of business, you are not a sales person. But companies regularly tell pharmaceutical representatives, mortgage loan processors and customer service people that they are sales people. Then they wonder why they fail. What's more ironic, the folks who hired them wonder why they are not producing.

Beer Guy

One intern placement came as two guys I hired for our millennium product and related celebrations. Not being a beer drinker, I was unaware of the devastating effects of a night of college beer drinking. Most every morning these two gentlemen spent the first part of their morning processing the night before.

One intern was put on the phone for sparkling wine sales. Never has a phone been dialed so slowly. When I approached him, teaching him a process and some techniques, he was responsive but inconsistent. One day, frustrated with my "badgering" management style (expecting accountability), the young man actually turned to me and said, "I just have to show up to get my college credit."

He found out that he could "just show up" someplace else all over again next semester. He received no credit for his time with us. In his exit interview, he told me he had learned more in the six weeks he spent with us than in four years of college. I was flattered and horrified all at once. I wanted to send my bill to the college, since they already had his money.

Beer Guy II

The other intern brought in at the same time showed some ability. He loved the game because it made him sexy. It stroked his ego, and while, eventually, you want to leave ego out of it, it was a good place to start. He was tall, blond and good-looking. Once he became familiar with the concept that I was neither impressed nor interested, we were able to begin to assemble his abilities. He actually wanted to be better.

He attended the sales process meetings we had contracted for, and in three weeks was up and running. That's a pretty good training curve. He was implementing processes that were providing him with increasingly consistent results. He became more of a presence for our business by attending after hours functions, and serving as an industry representative at events that would allow him greater access to more companies, and thereby, decision makers.

Then we had a problem. Think about it: handsome man, winery industry, alcohol-laden events, and the opposite sex.

He walked in the morning after an event, happy with the results and how the rest of his evening had gone. As he moved on with his day, the calls started coming, messages from last night's lady. She'd left an earring. He claimed he was unfamiliar with this ploy. I explained.

Three days later, he had not returned her call and the calls were still coming. Then there was the next event. Pretty soon two or three calls were coming at any one time, and although he was selling, it was counterproductive to the image a female-owned winery wanted to present. It became time for our heart-to-heart talk.

In reality, we talked of another organ. My progressive behavior modification was quick in coming and simple in message: Keep your dick in your pants.

I explained that when he left our place of business he continued to be the image that hundreds of people see, and, as small as this community was, the reputation was going to damage not only the company but also him, personally, at some point.

Surprisingly, as quickly as he had learned to sell with consistency, he learned that his appeal could, and should, be controlled. He completed his semester and we considered his time at Gaia an overall success.

Lesson: Often the most valuable asset is your and your company's reputation. Guard it from damage at all costs.

A sale, unlike most professional skills, is rarely taught well. It is that fear of the unknown that keeps so many people from being really good at it. Much like entrepreneurship, it is not for the faint of heart. It requires—rather, demands—no less than the same toe-to-toe, unwavering lack of fear.

Rejection cannot be an issue that paralyzes you. On any given day, you will experience that rejection more times than you can imagine. The best timesaver for sales people has to be to get to that "no" as quickly as possible.

Sometimes that means the sales person is saying no first. Being the rejecter is a skill you have to learn as well. To be able to tell someone, nicely and calmly, that their expectations and your product/service is not a fit is an empowering process. Once more, it is not for the weak.

My ongoing joke was that I made the worst sales person decisions in the world but I was always quick to get rid of them. Yet I never fired anyone outright. It was simple to make the case that, for whatever reason, their job performance was not in line with our expectations. Their choice was to bring it in line or we would find someone that was a better fit.

As a small business owner, I was also acutely aware of the use of our resources. They were not unlimited, and it was something we made painfully clear during the interview process.

Assessing Every Fit

We interviewed a very tall woman, whom I had met at a business venture at her boss' company. She had found out about our opportunity and went to elaborate lengths to create an introduction package that would catch our attention. She was talking to Dawn one day when I walked in and she made a point to make contact with me, although she had no appointment. She offered up a big bag full of candy, with each piece carrying a part of her cover letter.

Our first clue as to her ability to be successful should have been that none of the candy was really very good, it was predominantly off brands. After six weeks of multiple interviews, testing and reality questioning, this candidate was ready to leave her office in a new building with a $15 million company, secretary, cell phone, retirement, 401K and $80,000-plus salary for a commission-only position.

Every interview was at the winery, which meant she had to drive through the area-and to our location-on more than one occasion. I was purposefully blunt about the corporate change she was about to make. I made our little company sound as bad as possible. I wanted no rose-colored view in terms of how difficult it would be without what she was used to-plenty of resources. She would share an office and answer the phones.

At one point, we had made the interview process so glaringly tough that she actually asked if we wanted her to take the position and what she would have to do to get the job.

Three days into her new employment with Gaia Wines, she showed up late and didn't sit down. It was a frequent, immediate sign with which I had become familiar.

"I don't think this is going to work out," she stated. Since I was somewhat prepared, I asked her to take a seat and said we would go over her thoughts after three days. She had set a couple of sales appointments with friends and had been at the winery's birthday party with her husband.

"What is it that you think is lacking?" I asked.

"Well, I have no cell phone and no office and there is just a lot going on," she responded. I asked her to tell me more. It went nowhere. Nothing had been different from what she had been told and encountered during the interview process. Getting irritated, I cut to the chase.

"Look, you are not going to stay, and I am not going to ask you to, so would you do me the courtesy of not feeding me bullshit. Offer an honest and professional response to your decision."

"I am not comfortable with the neighborhood."

"The same area you have been coming to for two months during interviews; you are now uncomfortable with the area? Can you share with me, what does that mean?"

"Look, I'm not going to be made to feel uncomfortable here." She looked close to tears. Interesting. This once bold, candy-assed sales-person was uncomfortable with a question. She left immediately.

Dawn walked in 15 minutes later and looked around. She had the best sixth sense about the longevity of sales people.

"Oh, what the hell happened? Did you make her cry?" she asked.

"Almost, but I stopped short, hardly really worth it," I replied.

Lesson: As Dawn and I processed the latest victim of our contin-uing "sales hell," we came to the conclusion that perhaps the neigh-borhood of Gaia and its liberal sexual diversity was too much for the conservative woman from Republican Corporate Middle America. If someone is not offering the best efforts during the honeymoon period, don't assume it will get better as time goes on. It will be almost impos-sible to determine the real motivation for people's actions, and you should waste precious little time trying to make a square fit into your triangle. It will never work.

To a Greater Call

I loved the next sales guy in a way I have never loved a man. He was a perfect godlike vision. He was handsome, with bright, striking eyes and a perfect model face and body. His clothes were always unmis-takably pressed and crisp and it put me to mind of an old girlfriend from college. In short, he could have fathered my children....um, child.

He was polite, respectful and enthusiastic about the opportunity. He had also worked in his family's small business, respected his father and the efforts he had made in growing his own company. He liked wine, Dawn and me. We were on our way. He tested well and had really good answers. Then we got to the questions about lying.

There was never a reason to lie, he said. Okay, I countered, but given the presumed fact that everybody lies, what would cause him to lie? He assured us there was no occasion that would cause him to misrepresent a situation, or lie.

Angee and I met him for the final interview at a lunch spot with a guarantee of two things: I would get to eat, and we would see the social graces of the prospect.

He stood up out of respect when Angee reached the table. We all ordered light, but it was impossible to notice that he had severely broken out all around his lips. I wrote it off as some odd infection.

Lunch went well, and we told him on the spot that we would like him to join the company.

Nothing seemed to be of issue: not compensation, not the smallness of the company, not Angee and I as partners.

Four days in, and I was as much encouraged about this guy's ability as about anybody's. He made calls, set appointments and sought and took advice easily.

Having been out traveling for a few days, I was excited to get a face-to-face with our new sales talent and get an update on progress from a hard-numbers perspective. When he arrived, we immediately got to the update. His work was in order, he knew what was going to close, and had percentages on his activity. He had business that was *closing* four days in; I say that not because it couldn't happen but because he had actually been able to do what I always knew was possible. It was the way it was suppose to be.

"I got a call this morning as I was getting out of the shower," he started, "and it didn't have a caller ID, so I knew what it was. Some years ago," he continued, "I was approached out of the blue by the FBI. They had been trailing me and doing research. They knew things about me that only someone who was keeping a close eye could have known."

My boy was cracking around those perfectly pressed seams. He continued.

"My agent called this morning."

"Your handler," I countered, "just like ALIAS, the television series."

"I had already turned them down once two years ago. Yes, it is like ALIAS. I had decided if I had another chance I would take it. I leave in 24 hours. I don't know where I am going. You can't tell anybody."

Right! "What happens next?" I was intrigued.

"I meet her for lunch; I don't know if I'll be back."

What could I say; the father of my future children was off to save our entire world from pending destruction. I was discouraged that it took priority over my desire to grow the company. I went home to tell Angee in person. Dawn called about 11:45 to tell me he had left.

Lesson: When I returned about an hour later there was a sweet, handwritten note in my mailbox and the reports from his four days. The man of my sales dreams was off to a greater calling. I felt safer.

His lips had healed and he learned that not telling is kind of a lie, really. I never heard from him again. There are most definitely events that are out of your control. Sometimes things are out of everybody's control. Mourn and move forward.

Misplaced Passion

The wrong or misaligned commitment with the right skills can be just as frustrating as none at all. We hired a lady who was trainable. I wondered how she ever got out in the morning with as much makeup and maintenance as she seemed committed to. She also possessed a strong commitment to teaching aerobics.

Every day without fail she was out the door to teach, whether or not she had come close to her professional goals. Being pretty and teaching were her priorities, despite the fact she had tested well and was able to articulate a plan. She lacked the ability to choose to follow through on this commitment, to be successful at sales.

Lesson: Successful people are usually not successful at everything they attempt. These are the same type of people who get to the end of a work week and don't know or understand why they have been unsuccessful, or how the week got away from them. They have failed to track their progress or lack thereof. Equally frustrating, they were unaware what steps should or could have been taken and lacked an understanding what needed to happen next.

At the end of one week, it was easy to determine how the time had been spent. And like business ownership, you have to be clear on what you *can* do and what you *will* do. They are two very different tasks. I could tell people what to do to be successful. Yet it often came with some disappointment on their part that I refused to do it for them.

"Let me see you do it" was often a request. My response was simple. I know how do to it and have done it…you will learn nothing from watching me…you must go through the process yourself. Make mistakes, screw up, get lost, say the wrong thing, use the wrong voice and make the process your own. Find your own voice to success.

It was very much like aerobics, where watching the teacher is not going to help you get healthy or lose weight. You will simply be able to admire their style and fitness but hold none if it for your own. An unwillingness to put on the tights means you'll never really sweat.

Support from Home

We began to understand that people don't make their decisions on their own. Whether they don't want to take responsibility or they are fishing for a second opinion, they consult people. So we began to be conscious of those influences.

I got in touch with one potential fit who was working with a recruiter. That was our first sign about his decision-making ability. He wanted someone else to convince him of an opportunity. He was a nice guy, friendly and engaging.

After going through our process and working out details in the compensation program, we took him and his wife for an appetizer and drinks to celebrate. She knew little or nothing about what he had been doing and what our company was all about. But she was determined to understand what his compensation program would include and what kind of advancement was available. I thought it might be good for him to start the job first, but I indulged her questions.

We asked about them, as a couple, how they met. Instead, we found out that he had told the recruiter that he was going to respond to our sales position ad on his own, but was quickly convinced by the recruiter that he should work through their search firm.

Lesson: If someone is easily influenced by others, your impact will be short-lived. The guy really didn't even want to be in the sales business. While he was kind and personable, he was too trusting and could not close a deal.

Before the 30 day window had lapsed on his recruiter contract, he quit. Gently and politely, he left with only a hint of the importance of the timing. He genuinely wanted us to avoid any fees associated with his placement.

International Incident

When I received an e-mail from Land-O-Lakes, I had no idea what they did other than cheese (or is it butter?). Regardless, this big company wanted to talk about placing an intern with our company. We found it very flattering and were just beginning to see both the need and the advantage to having better, more qualified outside sales talent.

Surely we couldn't do it all. Actually, we were finding out we could, but it wasn't the way to go to the next level and still be able to function as something resembling human. However logical it may have sounded, I forwarded them on to a larger operation, something with farms and lots of work, well established. Still, they kept coming back.

What I found they wanted was an expert marketing experience for this intern, whose family owned land, grapes and a winery in a small Eastern European country.

I knew nothing about the country, the customs, or the habits. Could he speak English? I didn't have time to learn a new language, never a strong point with me. We talked back and forth about the options of hosting a newcomer. He would need a place to live, and what we paid wouldn't allow anything livable, even by Midwestern standards. I was assured he had some sort of allowance that would supplement the salary.

Before we knew it, I was at the airport with a "Wine Intern from Eastern Europe" sign, tracking down our new employee. We drove straight to a hotel close by that would be both clean and safe. Finding him housing would come. I was nervous and so was he.

He went through the standard training, albeit a little slowly to allow for his broken English language. He at first appeared polite, respectful and capable. His parents ran a family winery. He was kind and appropriate in bringing us some samples that we saved for a special occasion. That was the first week.

Another employee was kind enough to take him to see some housing options when I couldn't make the appointment. With housing set, it was time to begin to work him fast and furious to make the most of his time with us. But even with housing settled, we had a problem.

Day after day, he wore the same outfit. Now, I am no Imelda Marcos of outfits, but clearly the day-to-day wearing of the same clothes left him no time to wash. I gently asked Angee to speak with him.

In her non-threatening way, she explained that every day there had to be showers, deodorant, and fresh clothes. He changed immediately.

Slowly, he went to more events in public. There was a prestige in introducing our international intern; it was a nice feather in our cap. Soon I was not accompanying him, but rather letting him be part of the off-site team. Even with showers, we had a problem. The guy drank like a fish; he quickly became a spoiled brat.

Lesson: Under pressure and with the potential for large-scale disgrace, people will lie to everyone about everything. Apparently his family had some wealth in the old country, and once settled in to the new country, he felt taken advantage of by females. I am sure I had discussed with the host company the issue of working for women, but his response regarding his level of comfort had clearly been faked.

We talked about the drinking and laid out the requirements as we had for all employees: not at events, not on our time, or on our dime while representing the company at public events. Then things turned quickly; everything became an issue. I talked with his host company about his performance. He was not going to stay any longer than the Americans we had briefly employed.

He complained that the events he went to were not of the caliber he expected. This was despite having been present at an event hosted by our governor.

What we later found out was that he needed to improve his English to run the Western tour program of his family's business. His sister was learning French, and he had, somewhat reluctantly, been given English.

His host company finally found him an assignment elsewhere, and although it was not the tradition, he would be moved. What we found out later was that, in fact, he had disgraced his family and country by being moved. Apparently there was so much disgrace that his government had the nerve to question our company's ethics. We were the small Midwestern winery that could have sparked an international incident.

Then we received a 10 pound brick of cheese from Land-O-Lakes thanking us for our patience and handling of the incident. Cheese was the payoff for world peace. That seemed a small price to pay!

Despite the hassles of no ongoing, consistent sales function, we continued to reach our own goals by taking responsibilities for the mistakes we had made. We continuously refined our process and learned from our failings. I remained ultimately responsible for what happened, whether that was good, bad or indifferent.

I continued to seek expertise where I felt, we or I was lacking. Every weakness had to be addressed, eliminated or restructured to become strength. With each effort, we plowed forward. Each new step was a learning experience, and we passionately embraced what we had learned. I kept a focused eye on the bottom line and a commitment to the people who were already here. We did staff training regularly and hosted quarterly retreats to other wineries, ensuring our staff was the most resourceful.

We structured an organization where the best talent forced others to raise up to the excitement and passion of what we were accomplishing. Equally, they assisted in accessing the best fits to move the company forward.

Valiantly, I denied the acceptance of the 80/20 rule, that 20 percent of the workers do 80 percent of the work. It struck me a as disincentive to the entire organization.

While experts told us that any organization is made up of 20/60/20, I refused to leave the organization at that formula. At every level, I consistently revised our workforce mix. The thought that 20 percent excel, 60 percent are mediocre and 20 percent are sub par, and eventually damaging, is inherent in all organizations. That fact made us all strive to remove any dead weight. With much effort, we asked ourselves "Is this person and their talents in the top 10 percent, and will he or she effectively move us closer to our carefully defined goals?"

If employees did not rise to the challenges that a small woman-owned-and-operated organization offered, then their time with us, no matter how valuable to their learning process, had to be short.

We accepted that reality would be a part of our ongoing, redefined process. The strength we all gained, personally and professionally, from being clear in that commitment, made the external challenges we faced as Gaia Wines unwavering. In fact, our success was based only on our efforts and the forces with which we chose to surround ourselves. It made the way we handled the future full of possibilities...no matter what incompetence might be presented.

Chapter Five

Party like It's 1999*
...Oh, It is 1999!

*With Apologies to AFKAP
(The artist formerly know as Prince)

*To be a success in business,
be daring, be first, be different.*
Marchant

Party like it is 1999; Prince's song was finally here! It was the year we were all supposed to enjoy like no other. We were to be full of joy and celebration, rejoicing that we were experiencing the turn of the decade and the turn of the century. That is, unless you were a diehard believer that we still had one more year to go. Regardless, it was the time during which Gaia Wines, as a company, began to soar.

During mid-1997 we completed an expansion we called the "Birth of the Earth." Based on market demand, we doubled our space and added another five years to our lease arrangement. Technically speaking, the wall between the ends of the building got cut out and an additional production bay and three private tasting areas were added to

accommodate weddings, holiday celebrations and corporate functions.

As a project, it ended up being late in completion and a very messy
yet beautifully decorated dedicated space. Our part-time chief financial officer made us aware of a state program that we were able to tap
into for funding. A few projections encompassing corporate downtown access, convention business and the wedding market, and a
short stack of loan papers later, we assumed another five figures worth
of debt.

A specifications board hung outside my office to show the space,
and we began booking immediately. Over the early months, we had
modified our private-function policy to tighten the potential
customer's commitment to dates. Soon, we became a unique venue
for all types of gatherings. It provided our existing business another
avenue of service and drove new retail business in each time an event
occurred. Even though our growth rate was steady, it was amazing
how many guests were in for the first time during a private event. We
enjoyed being paid for marketing that private events garnered and
the increase in retail sales.

By early spring 1999, I had begun thinking about the turn of the
century: the millennium equals celebration, which equals champagne
and winery. As natural as the fit seemed, it hadn't been any part of
our long-term strategy. Still, it would assist us in making this a cele-
bratory and profitable year.

We managed the cost of a sparkling wine by acquiring the ability
to contract the manufacturing out, produce and bottle offsite to our
specifications in a custom bottle. We had to put something different
in to bring the "special" into play.

In what continued to be part of a long line of firsts, Gaia Wines
produced a Millennium Release sparkling wine for Indiana. Granted,
the big producers were way ahead, so it seemed less like a spectacu-
larly original idea. But with a little creative tweaking, we would make
it our own.

The label design for our original sparkling, "15 Big Ones," was
gorgeous; people were entertained and moved by the message. The
label depicted 15 life events that represented an opportunity to celebrate. It was a message that Angee continues to tell as a message I

taught her.

I believe you should always keep a chilled bottle of sparkling wine on hand. That way, you are prepared for the chance to celebrate whatever might come unexpectedly into your life. It prepares you for a celebration of the small events as well as the larger ones. It instantly provides you with an opportunity to enjoy today's triumphs.

My tradition started as a result of thinking I would eventually like to share a bottle of champagne with that special date. How romantic to be always that prepared. Yet it has a subtle and powerful message to it: Optimism! It provided the ability to create the reality that soon there will be a magnificent reason to celebrate. To hold glasses high, delicately clink and enjoy the reward and passion that would flow.

At once, this little act allows you to seem both anally over-prepared and wildly, romantically, optimistic. Right now, find that warm bottle that was a gift from the turn of the century and make room in your refrigerator. If, perchance, you started this book without an ample supply of your local labor of love, jot a note to find two or three bottles this weekend and immediately, and without passing Go, move at least one into your refrigerator. The best way to welcome a good time and special occasion is to be prepared.

Let's return to our story. The line-drawing simplicity of the "15 Big Ones" seemed a perfect way to create a local custom design. Having worked with this artist before, and knowing she could successfully complete my vision, I contacted her to discuss my plan. Together we identified the ideas that positively embodied Indiana: race cars, jazz, the skyline of the capital city, and of course, basketball. All were depicted through the talent of the millennium artist. With specially produced bottles, our not-so-original sparkling wine idea became the gift-giving success of that year. Bottles were custom etched and printed with the artwork in 14 karat gold. Against the black bottle, it was a breathtaking piece of art.

As I thought more about our efforts, I realized it created an opportunity for enhanced marketing. It would be a tribute to Indiana at the turn of the century. Even so, we found, it was a tough concept for the Midwestern market to grasp.

In order to make it more special, I contacted the city to request a day named for Angee and the artist. This brought nothing but concerns from the mayor's office. It was alcohol, after all, and the city could not possibly support that publicly.

My immediate thought turned to the fact that they had no trouble accepting the taxes that alcohol generated. I would have to learn to deal with this political discrepancy. Filling out the required forms and faxing them back to the city offices was the easy part. Our idea was, here are two artists, each, in their own way, adding to the celebration of the city and a remembrance of what made it special.

Still, naming a day after a winemaker and alcoholic beverage was simply not acceptable. It would have helped if I had accepted that. But Angee deserved a day, as do all people who create as wonderfully as she did. The graphic talent, again a typical artist, was a bit embarrassed about the attention. As we talk more about the marketing effect on her, an increased awareness of her art and the ability to sell it, she agreed to be part of it.

I continued with regular talks on how to propose a day. It was surprisingly easy to get, once we got over the alcohol issues. A couple of rewrites later, with the focus on the artistry of the product, and Angee and the label artist would share September 19, 1999, the Friday closest to the 100-day countdown to the turn of the millennium, as their day in Indianapolis.

Dawn had a huge banner made and it hung outside the winery for a month. Guests couldn't miss its oversized impedance, much to everyone's hassle; they needed to duck each time they walked by.

The media opportunity was fantastic. E-mails, postcards and faxes were sent out inviting guests to that day's events, the banner signing, a visit and private bottle signing with Angee, the artist and, of course, the chance to taste the new release. One employee had practiced and played "She" from "Notting Hill": people laughed, enjoyed and celebrated. It was a slice of what was great being a woman-owned business.

We were offered congratulations, and Angee moved through the gathering with her usual grace and style. While she vowed it was not the part she enjoyed the most, she excelled at the public persona that was so critical in this very public human-relations business.

Even amid the celebrations, it seemed that for every opportunity 1999 presented there were at least as many obstacles to overcome.

Nobody wanted to be far from home that final night, which made reservations for our annual Winemaker's Elegant Eve dinner crazier than any other year.

People changed their minds, the number of guests joining them, and all wanted questions answered that we couldn't, no one could, logically answer. Was it going to be safe to be out?

We got comfortable saying that if this day were, in truth, Armageddon, the best place to be would be in a cellar, full of wine! Most people relaxed at the humorous approach we took to the possible end of the world.

However, the night before New Year's Eve we were caught off guard. The caterer we had used for years called the night before the end of the century. They would not be doing the Elegant Eve dinner.

I took a deep breath and told Angee, as I simultaneously examined our options. In 15 minutes we were downtown to analyze the crisis de jour. I suppressed an initial impulse to call and yell, then threaten, then beg the offending caterer. It made no sense; why they had canceled? But what was more important, I surmised, it didn't matter. It was the approach they chose to take.

As familiar as they were with the way we operated the private events we hosted, I had to believe they had been offered a bigger, more profitable event, or had simply chosen not to work that day out of their own fear. You really never know what motivates a person: fear, greed, ignorance. But if they would not be motivated by the relationship we had developed and the business they had enjoyed, then I had little time to wonder what was really going on.

En route to the winery, we drove past a possible answer. Across the street was a well-received, locally owned Italian restaurant that shared our love for the growing area and the type of customers who were drawn to our respective establishments. I briefly talked of other solutions as Angee and I crossed the street. We gulped hard to swallow our pride at being placed in such a predicament, and stepped inside the restaurant. When we caught the attention of the co-owner and host, he smiled and waved us in.

"We need your help," I said. "Would you have a minute? Soon?" This was the night before the end of the century, and yet he never blinked or winced at our request.

Gently we explained our crisis, and he began to explore options. Ordering a different menu was out of the question. Deliveries on December 31, 1999, would be short and few in number. He also wondered aloud about quantity.

Neither issue turned out to be a problem. He would create three of the same menu items he had available. While he didn't have extra staff, we were convinced we could manage with our own, no matter how slim. We always had. He offered dishes and place settings as well.

It was done. In the 15 minutes since the crisis had begun, we had solved what could have been a disaster. He was gracious, calm and fair. We were grateful.

Elegant Eve, 1999, turned out to be one of our best. Staffing was tight, and Dawn, two part-timers and I fought in the back room about portions, serving style and timing. Yet our guests enjoyed a well-prepared three-entree dining experience free of hitches. Again, we had pulled answers out of thin air to succeed, just as any dedicated and passionate small business would have done.

That could have been a huge and expensive disaster. I am often asked what our biggest failure was. I can never really choose because it always turned out better because of the challenge.

Our sweet dessert wine, Muscat Canelli, was a perfect example of our knack at turning potential disasters to shining profitability.

As with all our wines, as part of an industry standard, we packaged in 750-milliliter bottles, the size you think of when thinking about wine. Not long after we began serving Muscat at tasting, we heard guests sing its praises verbally, but not at the register. We continued to listen.

Perception is reality. Our guests had the perception that, while they greatly enjoyed the Muscat, they did not believe they would finish such a special, sweet wine before it went bad. No one, except perhaps me, drank a full glass of the stuff. It was "liquid cake," as sweet as any treat. We dubbed it "dessert in a glass."

Without changing anything about the product, I set out to find the right package. We left the label as it was. We left the contents untouched. Soon I located supplier for an oversized tall slim black bottle. This bottle would offer preservation of the delicate product inside. More than anything else, however, was the fact that this new bottle was 375 milliliters. While exactly half the original size, more significantly, it was a size that two to four adults could enjoy after dinner without fear of waste.

With the same label, a more-than-half price tag of $9.95 versus the $15.95 for a full bottle, and a sexy, waxed, swirl-top closure, we sold Muscat consistently. Profitably! Problem solved! Again!

We were focused and proud of our quick, often creative solutions in the operations and marketing of the winery. The same formula would work well; we were sure, with the other functions within the organization, including securing capital and appropriate financial solutions.

It seems that nobody likes to talk about money—not the people spending it, not the people receiving it. We had to work hard to define our process to make the cost of service very clear and very painless for the guests, some of whom were often on limited budgets, or had not been able to work out their own process with co-hosts (or other payers). Often we found they didn't understand or were unable to execute their company's policies about how expenses got paid.

Our society has lost some sensitivity to money, with quick credit, a "Bill me" mentality, or "Charge it," or, worse yet, the option to say, "Bill my company."

Equally difficult, I have found, was getting our own employees to understand the importance of getting payment in a timely manner. No one had a problem expecting his or her check on time. But if it meant asking the customer to pay in a timely manner, it caused considerable conflict.

Money sensitivity is a national issue, not politely talked about for fear of judgment. Think about your closest friends. You most likely know more about their sex life, religious beliefs and politics than you do about their finances. You'd sooner go to bed with someone than have an intimate conversation about his or her income or debt. As we keep money and finance cloaked in doubt and confusion, so grows our discomfort.

Just so you believe I have dealt (somewhat) effectively with this issue, I'll share. I made $6,500 my last full year in the winery. No, it is not missing any zeroes. Keep that revelation in your mind the next time you walk into a small business and think that the owners are rolling in money and you request free services or better pricing just because you think you deserve it. I am not bitter (ha!), just trying to enlighten your perspective.

Most small business owners take very little out to remain flexible from a cash flow standpoint. If they take anything out to live on, that too must remain liquid in case there is an emergency that must be covered by good old-fashioned owner equity. Very rarely is there an unlimited amount of cash to run a business, particularly if the operation is growing.

One of our employees encountered an incident while hosting a small private party one night. Dawn, Angee and I went out to an early dinner with a potential wholesale account. There was always a lot of holding our breath as a function drew to a close. Tonight was no different, and no one at our table was surprised when the employee on duty paged me.

"What can I help you with?" I said only mildly irritated, knowing the questions could be answered quickly.

"The gentleman hosting the function says he does not have access to funds to pay for the function," our staff member explained.

"Were there any problems or a reason why he should not pay?" I inquired.

"No, it was all good," she replied.

"Well then, ask him to pay his bill." I'm sure that was easier said than done, or I wouldn't have been on this call. I could hear our staff member relaying the logical request. All I heard after that was mumbled conversation, as the phone was out of direct reach. She came back on the phone with his reply.

"He doesn't have a check from his company, and said that Angee said he could bill his company directly."

This was not an option, and he had made a critical mistake. He went too far up the ladder without the right information. Angee never handled any of the financial arrangements of private function guests.

Still, this guy felt he could misrepresent his way out of paying that night, and in the process cost us more money and time in collecting.

"Please put him on the phone," I requested.

"Hello?" said the customer hesitantly.

"Good evening, sir. How was your event?" I asked.

"We had a good time; everybody had good things to say."

"Is there a question about your charges, something we may have made a mistake on?" I continued calmly.

"No, I just don't have the check for the balance."

"But the balance is due at the end of the function, correct?" He must have panicked and thought he had an out.

"Well, in my conversation with Angee she said we could bill it to the company." It had not been set up as a billing situation, since we never did that; even Angee was aware of that. This was also a small, obscure not-for-profit organization that had recently formed. It was doubtful he would have never produced the information required to approve a billing status. But I continued.

"Setting up billing requires a lot of information and usually four weeks to get approved. I don't think that was done here."

"Well, Angee said…" Oops, there was his mistake. Never, ever, bull-shit a bullshitter.

"You know, I am here dining with Angee; let me go ahead and check with her…" I never finished my thought.

"Well, can you take a personal check and hold it for three days until I get reimbursed?"

"I don't think that would be a problem. If you put our employee back on the phone I'll explain our arrangements."

When he did, I simply let the employee know that the customer would be paying. She had heard the conversation, at least one side of it, and could imagine the other side. She was smiling; I could hear it in her voice. It was nothing she couldn't have done as well. She just chose, as so often many do, to pass the buck on up.

Perhaps the most expensive disaster we ever had, with little control over the end results, happened that same year. I was stepping out of the shower early one September morning. Angee had gone in to the winery to check the recent merlot gently fermenting, before we headed off to a state park to enjoy the fall day. Her voice on the answering machine was screaming as I headed to the phone.

"What the hell happened here?" Angee said, barely able to talk.

"What's going on? Are you okay?" I asked.

"There is merlot all over three production bays," she said in a panicky voice. "I'm up to my ankles in merlot."

All I could say again was, "What had happened?" I couldn't even visualize what had caused this to happen. We had often worried about disrespectful guests putting their feet up on tank spouts to use the expensive equipment and precious contents as cheap footstools. I dressed quickly and headed into the winery. In the meantime, Angee called the employee who had worked the party the night before.

Angee was screaming, "What the hell happened last night?"

Shocked at Angee's demeanor, our employee responded, "We had a great party, they paid, and we cleaned up and left. What's wrong?"

"And nobody touched or messed with any of the tanks? Everything was fine when you left?"

"Yeah, it was clean and there was no damage to anything. What happened?"

Angee went on to share her shock at standing ankle-deep in our most expensive juice. It hadn't even made it down the floor drains.

Without asking, after having worked late the night before, our employee headed in, and was there as I arrived.

When Angee had first arrived, she had seen a strange reflection from the three middle bays. Even with the lights out, the emergency lighting was causing a gentle reflection that told her immediately something was quite wrong.

When the overhead light came on, it showed that one of our worst fears had come true. Over 400 gallons of one of our best-selling and most expensive wines was bubbling up on the floor of three bay areas. It had gone everywhere, spreading out to the edge of the wall and under barrels and storage racks, making it impossible for us to get to it all.

I hugged Angee to try and calm her, realizing that we had a major problem on our hands. As was our usual method of operation, we quickly analyzed the issues and simultaneously devised a plan. We each took a phone and began calling employees to come help with the cleanup.

It was one occasion when I'm sure Dawn was happy she had no phone. The employee, who lived in the apartments upstairs, although not ready to face the world, was there the quickest.

The first thing we had to resign ourselves to was the fact that this was not going to be a day in the park, literally or figuratively. With only an hour to opening, we rolled up pants; removed shoes, and began to wade in the juice still bubbling with fermentation against our ankles.

Grabbing the wet vacuum, we began sucking up three inches of liquid. Old sewer pipes had actually become our friend on this occasion. Had they worked better, there would have been nothing left. Other folks grabbed whatever looked like it might help—buckets, shovels—slopping the merlot into a new, secure tank.

No one was sure what we were going to do, but saving it seemed like the first and best response. Angee walked back and forth from the tank, going over the possibilities with the employee from the night before. Occasionally there was a rant, and then tears.

Then Angee got mad, something she rarely did.

"Who wants it, this is such a fucking disaster, I'm selling, and who's got $20?" It was a rhetorical question, but someone felt obliged to answer. "Oh, I'll take it," the employee said. Wisely, everyone fell silent.

Angee had keys in hand, "Twenty bucks!" Luckily for us, the employee who spoke up didn't have any cash on her. It didn't seem like an occasion where Angee would take a check.

As the winery opened at 11 a.m., we let staff know there would be no tours today, since we were working in production. Two hours into it, it looked more manageable. But only slightly.

We took a break for soft drinks, kicked up the air conditioning and dried our feet, if only for a brief time. I tried to offer some comfort to Angee, convinced this was solvable no matter how "not easy" it seemed.

Toward the middle of the afternoon, we had gotten most of the 400 gallons into other containers and actually began cleaning up with high-powered hoses, mop and squeegees. At that point it smelled like a winery should: beautiful, fall-like and sexy, full of rich fermenting merlot wine.

Four hours later, we sat at TGI Friday's for lunch and lamented about the disaster. It was a "two Long Island iced tea" (our usually after-work power relaxation drink) afternoon for everybody involved.

After more reflection and investigation, we discovered that the power of the gas through fermentation had blown a bung out of place in the new tank. The out valve, unlike the other tanks we used, was at the very bottom and was not a metal close-off, but required a large plastic cork to stop the flow. With that much wine and a tenuous piece of plastic, we had all underestimated the power of fermentation. It was no one's fault, just one of the mistakes that happens and that you deal with.

But the smell was something we had to deal with for weeks to come. That wonderful wine smell soon turned rancid. The juice got into the very porous cement flooring and began to rot. An insurance adjuster and three chemical companies could not find anything to counter the smell and the growing yeast. It caused a stench throughout the building, and itchy noses, eyes and crotches for employees.

The encouragement we felt after 1999 was becoming the chaos of 2000. We did what every good group of growing business people should do: We embraced it. "Embrace the Chaos" became the mantra. We put it on jean jackets as that year's holiday gift to key employees. It's during this kind of time that you learn what you can and cannot do with relative success.

The three previous years of commercial acceptance, strong management, unique employee relations, creative marketing opportunities, growth and increasing profitability had allowed us the good fortune to be chosen as one of the finalists for the 2000 Ernst & Young Entrepreneur of the Year awards. It was billed as the "Academy Awards for Business." I knew about Ernst & Young but not of the grand stature of the designation.

By submitting a largely narrative application and limited financial information, we would prove to be considered among the best in our category for central Indiana. A film crew came in to shoot a video clip to show at the awards. The build-up was intense. Press releases and media provided welcomed free advertising and acknowledgment.

Days before the awards dinner, we attended an after-work cocktail party for the finalists. It was there we met our next banker and financial institution.

Well aware that the chaos of this next year would require resources beyond what our current bank had offered, I took the opportunity to meet another of the finalists. He was the vice president and one of the principals from the new financial institution in the state.

Boldly, Angee and I approached him and his partner at the bar to offer congratulations and make a wine suggestion.

As a part of our celebration of the recognition, we had sent everyone a bottle of our 1999 sparkling wine, personally signed by Angee. It got our company noticed and gave an additional air of class to what we were doing. I wondered why the bank hadn't sent out certificates of deposit to finalists.

As we made small talk, I asked if it made sense for two finalists to work together. The vice president agreed, and we set tentative plans to meet for dinner to hear more about each other's business and related goals.

It was also about this time that Angee was becoming increasingly sick in terms of both intensity and regularity. The previous fall we had made a merchandise trip to Chicago. Sweating, unable to urinate, and in pain, she collapsed in the restaurant bathroom. Before we made it to our room that night, she threw up outside the hotel.

I spent the night alternating wet, cold cloths for her head and trying to get her to drink something. She made it through the next day of the merchandise show, but on the way back we called the doctor, who suggested we go to the emergency room directly from the road.

The pain was consistent at this point, relieved only temporarily by the few doses of morphine she was given. Samples of blood and urine showed nothing. X-rays came back negative for anything that could explain her body's actions. But her pain and all the related symptoms were too intense to ignore.

The only explanation the doctors could give at that time was a possible kidney stone that had passed or was not showing up on film. We joked about it being lupus, a joke that we made from time to time, given Angee's often unpredictable symptoms and timing.

With a few successful bank meetings before year's end, we began to transfer our banking loan relationship. The financial institution's owner had moved our contact to his loan officer. The first service put into place was a line of credit to address our short-term needs. Then we moved the balance that remained on our original Small Business Administration guarantee loan over to the new institution. As part of the documentation process, I wrote an amendment to the lengthy banking security agreement.

Very simply, it stated that if we ever decided to close, the bank was aware and in agreement that our management and ownership was the best, and most appropriate entity to handle that activity. Willingly, they gave us 90 days to complete the process, without interference.

It was an issue we had discussed in great length and was simple to understand. With Gaia Wines and Angee holding the required permits to sell alcohol, and our established retail and wholesale channels, it made sense that the existing management be given time to initiate a process that would maintain value. Since all our personal equity was also tied up in inventory, the agreement made it possible for us to walk away with some cash for our years of effort. It was a mutual arrangement for the benefit of both the bank and us. The bank, through its loan officer, agreed without hesitation.

Through 2000 and into 2001, we continued to see steady growth in private functions and got better at creating demand and securing commitments from the guests. A 50 percent non-refundable deposit did wonders for the follow-through of guests planned events. At the same time, it provided us with cash to invest in the increased production of wines, as each wine quickly began to sell out.

Wholesale business, mostly through word of mouth, added credibility to our total picture. It did not have the margins we had come to enjoy in retail. It was terribly high-maintenance, between balancing a non-responsive distribution sales force and improper service by the same to our accounts.

Often, too much of our time was spent in trying to remedy their inattention and lackluster manner. We were aware going into those relationships that the products from Gaia Wines would never be a line item on their income statement, competing with major national brands. Nonetheless, we expected communication and the ability to fill orders in a timely manner.

Despite a lack of our own dedicated internal sales effort, we were skilled at finding good fits. That resulted in increasing the number of stores and restaurants that carried Gaia Wines to triple digits.

We became an international company on the heels of all this effort. One private-function guest so believed in the product and our entity that she educated herself on exporting, taking formal classes, and when they were completed, offered to handle Gaia products internationally.

Although it took massive hours of her time with meetings and e-mails throughout world time zones, in 18 months and with a prepaid order from a broker in Singapore, we became an international wine company. As we planned our growth, we targeted three other countries: China, New Zealand, and India. Each offered a separate opportunity to successfully grow the winery production in a balanced manner, because each had a different wine that was identified to be a well received, profitable fit in that country.

During a meeting with the Indiana export department, I inquired what they considered success in terms of dollar value within the export community. I was shocked and pleased at the reply. A sale of $1,000 through an overseas venture was considered a good effort. Our 12 cases to Singapore had already achieved that. We were on our way to worldwide acceptance, respect and success.

Chapter Six

Embrace the Chaos

"What would you do if you knew you could not fail?"
Unknown

"…in the little moment that remains to us between the crisis and the catastrophe, we may as well drink a glass of champagne."
Paul Claidel (1868-1955)

It was our bust-out year, 1999. There was no doubt that 2000 and 2001 would continue the forward movement of which we had consistently seen glimpses in 1999. It would require more time, talent and cash, more of us overall as a company. Resource management was my area of expertise.

Trial and error, as well as ongoing development, made me aware, early on, what would be needed.

After the first distributorship in Indiana, the next two states, Illinois and Kentucky, came relatively easy. There was a credibility factor that got the relationships flowing. I spent more time on the road. More often, I would travel to Chicago, Louisville and parts of Indiana within the same day or two, working with special events or the sales teams of our distributor partners.

Although we had legal relationships with distributors, I was aware going into it that Gaia Wines would never be a priority for the distributor's sales force. Securing a broker or sales person to actually represent the product and work with the licensed organization was first on my list. As well as sales talent, we would still need that other rare resource: capital.

During the quiet first quarter of 2001, I updated our business plan, including our private functions and wholesale divisions, two areas that were not part of our original plan. Both areas continued to serve us well, offering variety in cash flow cycles, production/labor needs, and profitability.

We occupied an incredible niche that had the flexibility to change market to market. In Indianapolis, we were the hometown favorite. In Chicago, we were able to play on the loyalty and originality of being a lesbian-owned winery. Chicago was a big enough and diverse enough market to be accepting. We were the only such player.

In Kentucky, it was as simple as being the chicks from up north that had some good tasting sweet wine. As we expanded, we found we were the women who were making the wine the market wanted. Labels, bottle style, taste and approach were all in sync.

Private functions had continued to allow us to increase our wine production during the previous year with holiday deposits alone. It provided cash up front, profitability and paid marketing. Each function usually brought in 80 to 100 predominantly new guests. Each function led to others, and with our refined pricing process, which required a 50 percent deposit to hold a date, it fit nicely into financing a portion of our growth plans.

Wholesale distribution to liquor stores and restaurants gave us instant credibility, even though it was the least profitable of our three areas of business. Of the 20 wineries operating in Indiana, Gaia was one of three that had secured a distributor. The other two wineries had been around for more than 30 years. That fact made people comfortable enough to want to join the bandwagon and add our product to their shelves or wine list.

Our labels were redone to include bar codes for the retail locations we served, and at the same time we added our history and expanded the educational portion to engage and entice the consumer.

I was well aware that the wine label, much like a cereal box, was immediately read while it sat on a dinner table, or when it was handed to a host or hostess. It often served to fill an early silence at a restaurant.

Each business segment drove our most profitable area, retail. From the 14 consumer-palatable wines to the 300 different wine accessories and five to eight monthly programs, it was all designed to co-mingle and drive increased marketing. The combination produced six years of steady double-digit growth.

Each segment of our business complemented each structural point of profitability, cash flow and marketing. But there was never enough cash produced internally to allow wine production to keep up with demand.

It seems a simple enough concept, but when making wine it's not enough to merely replace what sells that week or that month, or even that quarter. Every fall there are incredible cash outlays for not only the replacement of last year products but also the increases estimated for the coming one to three years. All of the processes demanded large, regular cash outlays. As long as we continued to grow, we would continue to burn through cash. The fact that it was secured by an appreciating inventory asset, like wine, made it a good use of that cash.

Turnaround in production is not immediate by any means. The shortest production period for wine was about four months for our mead (honey wine). Oak-fermented and aged merlot and chardonnay could take years. A winery is always playing cash flow catch-up if it chooses to continue to grow. Our plans meant we would always play catch up. Profits were always reinvested into our venture, displaying our commitment to long-term success.

The end result—with defined and growing market, award-winning, consumer palatable wines was always worth it, despite the painstaking cash investments. Margins were strong, and the demand for our unique offerings was often being pre-sold to our retail customers.

A business plan updated during a slow first quarter outlined the next three years of growth and stabilizing profitability. Detailed financial statements showed that the business would require $876,000 to move the company to the next level of operation.

The first meeting, after the plan was revised, was with our new bank. With a line of credit in place that we had yet to touch, the first quarter of the New Year was dedicated to securing the money that would take us from grassroots bootstrapping to consistent operational progress.

During that same period, Angee made a call to Dawn about coming back after a brief absence. Dawn was working at another small business down the street. I knew that Angee's call would at least get us the meeting. Dawn was distantly interested in, at least, meeting.

She stopped by two evenings later, and I laid out the plan for growth, the financial and operational needs, and our need for her. Very simply, we told her that we could hire someone from the outside, recruit someone new. But no one internally was ready or interested in the position. We were aware of the time saving she would provide. She listened intently, asked a few questions and came up with more than one objection.

"Well, I think you know my answer" was her reply. We were saddened, but tried to understand.

"Okay," Angee said. "Thanks so much for meeting with us; sorry we can't work something out."

"I can be here in six weeks-well, four-and probably start part-time in two," Dawn replied without skipping a beat. Three weeks later, much to our surprise, she became our first official full-time employee.

A few bank meetings later, we received a conditional approval from our new bank on the full amount of our loan request. It meant a couple of significant things. Angee could, finally, and with much excitement, move into the business full time. She would concentrate on wine production and maintaining quality as wine volume grew. She would assist in the tasting room as we geared up, and she would be more available for media and public appearances.

The loan officer had worked consistently to put the pieces in place from his side. But his bank was small and had its own growing pains, and decided to bring in an SBA loan servicing company. The representative seemed nice enough. The rep's family owned a vineyard in California. It seemed like a natural fit.

When presented with the final loan documents, I instantly had concerns. Information was partial, or in most cases just plain wrong. It was as if the rep had never listened to anything. About the fifth mistake in, I stopped the conversation.

"This says we have never been late in a payment, and we told you about the delay in getting the loan refinanced when the bank moved operations out of state. Doesn't that need to be explained?" I questioned, knowing the answer.

"Oh, it does?" the rep replied with hesitantly.

"Yes, we do not want the application to be false, and you have to explain the slow payments during that time." This was supposed to be the expert. The rep vowed to redo the paperwork and get back to us. It seems that they wanted it to go in as written, even if it meant not getting approved, or worse yet, being less than genuine.

Despite the issues being over two years old, the SBA requested that the bank seek another six months of payment history. At least that is what we were told.

During the interim, it was agreed we would use the line of credit to help meet short-term growth needs. When the new capital came through, we could pay down the line, with documentation of the use of credit-line proceeds. The purchase of bottles, juice, labels and corks could continue to help grow the inventory during the six months.

Before the six months had ended having made regular payment as required, we had a visit from the loan officer. He seemed stressed, or sad; it was hard to tell. Our information was all positive. We had again done everything we had said we would do.

We shared with him the news of the opportunity of the foreign markets, although we had not officially added it to the projections. Gaia Wines had, happily, become an international company with the start of business in Singapore, and was exploring other countries where production needs would be steady and high in volume.

"Things have changed at the bank; we are not going to be able to do this loan as we outlined. The bank is looking for more equity," the loan officer started.

We were shocked think this could have happened, especially since we were so close to the six-month "waiting" period. There wasn't much to say, so we continued to listen.

"The climate at the bank has changed, pretty significantly. It really has nothing to do with you," he said.

But it did affect us!

He went on, "You folks have always done exactly what you said you were going to do. You are one of my best clients. We had an executive that caused some problem loans, and even though he is gone, we are readjusting each of our loan portfolios and will need additional equity to do the deal."

The line of credit had been almost completely allocated during the previous six months. Every decision had been a chicken-and-egg scenario, deciding the most pressing use of limited funds at that time and taking great pains to anticipate other issues that might arise. We had foolishly not anticipated the bank's changing direction. Neither Angee nor I asked much about what had happened, since we couldn't change it, or the effect it would have on our expansion financing.

It was nice of the loan officer to come in and keep the communication line open. There was still time to raise a little equity; all our numbers were good and all our financial trends were consistently heading in a positive direction.

I went back to all my notes and began to update with venture companies and equity partners that had shown the most interest. Then I moved on to the companies that had never said anything by way of a response. I expanded our money search to regional and national companies, concentrating on those with a focus in consumer products, manufacturing, and woman-owned operations.

I made trips to Chicago funding meetings, lunches, workshops, and the closest Women Owned Business Development Cooperation, a division of the Small Business Administration.

I took every suggestion with merit, whatever was needed to more clearly outline our potential and the strides we had already made with so few resources. I added and deleted items to make the business plan concise and targeted, and explained any point that wasn't completely understandable to the potential investor.

There were visits to the Louisville Venture Club, with the thought that there was money in bourbon and whiskey and wine would be a natural extension of the investor mindset. There would be an understanding of the beverage market and production requirements.

The bank's loan officer suggested personal meetings with some of the more supportive members of his board of directors. He had often mentioned that many of the directors were incredibly encouraged by our progress and loved the high-profile media-worthiness of our venture. It was an opportunity to make the bank look progressive as well.

Over a short time, we met with two directors. The first had been responsive in setting a meeting, albeit on a Saturday morning. He came in with his wife and explained proudly how he had made his money and what his current investment strategies were. He and his kids had gotten involved in some of their spouses' ventures and they liked—no insisted on—complete control.

He bragged, in no uncertain terms, about financing the entire amount with his signature, based on his bank deposits and net worth. He and his wife walked around the winery and asked questions. We were honest and excited, yet cautious at the same time, and made a decent effort to ask the right questions of them to ensure a good marriage of efforts.

His background was in manufacturing, and that made it clear his focus would be on reducing the costs of that particular part of our process to affect the bottom line.

That suggestion in and of itself was not a bad thing. It became clear though, as we talked over the next few weeks, that he did not have a good grasp of our vision. While he claimed to be able to make Gaia a large money-making venture, his ideas on how to definitively do that never materialized. When we coupled that lack of clarity with his desire to have a majority interest, we felt that there was not a strong long-term match of strengths.

We had always known early on that any investor's vision had to match up with ours, and that there would be folks who would try to get something, mainly our business and dream, for nothing. If they were unable to add value and credence to what we had already built and created, it was easy to see that there would be no long-term pairing of resources. If Gaia was good enough to want a piece of (or control of) but not for a a fair price, there was no deal to be made. We had no problem turning down the wrong partner.

The second board member with whom we met with seemed more aloof. In both cases, the investment meeting was the first time either director had been to the winery. If commitment and belief meant anything, there was distance in their desire and support during the previous years.

The second director's approach was less about using his own money and signature, and relied on the thought that the bank could do it. Any assistance we got from him was going to be at an a arm's length. He had a difficult time discussing plans, since they had already been exposed to our financial information. I always found it cause for concern when potential investors displayed a lack of forward thinking and understanding for the future of the winery.

Another concern was that if they didn't know something about the business, were they able to ask the questions to clarify? Did they trust our answers, our knowledge, and again, our vision? If it wasn't clear at the questioning (dating) stage, we had little hope that it would solidify during the process.

This second director was able to share with us, during a strangely clandestine meeting, that he had concerns about the bank. In particular, we were told not to discuss anything with our loan officer, and that the service provider they had chosen to process SBA loans had been mismanagement and also downright inattentive in getting anything done.

Despite the fact the company and this officer remained a subcontractor with the bank, the bank had found that when resubmitting loans through the bank, previously denied or pending loans had been approved, even after those same loans had been rejected from the service provider's submissions. I was immediately concerned about how long they would allow this type of trend to continue.

While we were on a timeline, we agreed to this director's request that we not discuss the information he shared with the loan officer at this point. I defined a clear timeline for us to talk and move forward.

Weeks later, I couldn't get a return call from the board member. We had temporarily placed our trust of time and communication with someone who had been unsuccessful. It was not the basis for a relationship involving money.

As disappointing as it is to not have things work out, the rush of successful feelings overshadowed our frustration when something did work out. Such was the case when a previous contact called to say he had an individual interested in talking about investment.

After some disappointment with what we thought would be some natural fits, we were referred to a lawyer. Later that week, on another Saturday, Angee and I met with an a older gentleman from the area. He had made some money fighting a bank in his earlier years, and it propelled his firm into quiet but successful long-term growth.

He spent a great deal of time in Florida, and was getting ready to structure an exit from his firm. Again, there was a slight braggadocio in his ability to do the financing on his signature alone.

I began to find this attitude tantamount to that of the customer who says cost is no concern in purchasing. If someone makes a point that cost is no object, you should know that without fail it would be an issue. It is like they announce it to convince themselves it is not an issue.

This lawyer bowed to our expertise and gave credence to the efforts we had made. But like anyone engaged in a lot of life-changing activities, it would get in the way. He left with Angee and me convinced there was a reason to talk again.

Before we did, the gentleman who had referred him called to say that the potential investor would not be interested. I look to one's own ability to say yes, or no, as a strong indication of character. But it didn't make a lot of sense, so I questioned strongly. There were enough unanswered questions to warrant a call back to the proposed investor. The first line of denial had always been directly related to a shortcoming in our business. But the financial statements made sense and I surmised it might not have been communicated as it should.

Even after clearing up some of their confusion, the answer remained no. When I questioned the referral, off the record, the man was kind enough to point out that the the amount was slightly out of his client's range and the return time was too long for a retiring professional planning to live off his investments. That was fine; I just needed the real issues so we could effectively refine our process if need be and get better at how we presented the opportunity.

Why had telling the truth become about finding fault with someone else rather that admitting what were uniquely one's own issues? It wasted precious time, emotionally and mentally.

Then, while no one was paying attention, the dot-com technical bubble fueling investor net worth burst. Who had been holding the pin?

In the fall of 2001, I was on my way to the winery when I heard local radio personalities discussing a plane crash. I was concerned that it was local, at first. I worried about a friend who traveled often. No one seemed to know exactly what was happening, so they went back to music.

As I headed to the winery, the radio broadcast was interrupted again. Another plane had crashed into a building. I felt panic run through me and I had no idea why. As I drove, I called Angee at work. She was watching TV and sounded more concerned.

When I got to work, I adjusted the channel to the best reception and watched, like everyone else, as the tragedy unfolded.

The side effects of that day will undoubtedly forever ripple through our society. Every statement after that day came with the prefatory words, "Since 9/11..." Often it came as an excuse.

Private investors lost value faster than ever before. What little money remained in portfolios was going nowhere. That included the small, successful winery in Indiana. But I didn't stop.

With readjustments to the entry level, I continued to call on prospects and talk about the safety in our investment. I broke up the total amount needed—about $250,000—according to banks—into smaller $50,000 and $100,000 opportunities.

The Catch-22 we found happening at this time was that individuals who make money don't always make the investment decisions, and granted, maybe they shouldn't. They rely on someone else to handle their money and investments. This meant that most did not have access to funds in the amounts we were looking for without consulting the other liquidity of other investments.

In the market at this time, that was a deadly combination. Brokers often, and perhaps with some reason, aren't hawking the entrepreneurial investment. Beyond that, the relationship had been strained by the market flux and the incredible loss of value.

Lack of trust between broker and client meant no dollars were going anywhere in the volatile market. No broker wanted to advise clients to take dollars out of their already dwindling funds.

It made the high-net-worth individual without liquidity or with dependence on the broker an impossible fit given the economic climate.

Not long after exploring traditional methods, we went back to seeking grassroots financing. It's the kind of process we, like most entrepreneurs, are so good at. We are good at it out of necessity, not desire. During a regular staff meeting, I bit a huge bullet and explained our long-term growth plans and what they would require. I asked each employee to think about contacts, family, and supporters of the winery in an effort to raise money in smaller increments.

I am always amazed at the response you get when you ask the tough questions. After the meeting, an employee asked to talk with me privately. It turned out he was responsible for the investments of a family friend and unhappy with the returns her funds were receiving in the market. With her net worth, he felt comfortable with a $10,000 to $20,000 investment level.

Coupling that with the $50,000 commitment we could secure from the earlier interested attorney, we were on our way to nickel-and-diming it to the $250,000 the bank would require as equity.

The constant in this new economy of disaster, I was told, was that I was doing a good job in the absolutely worst time to raise funds. The pats on the back weren't moving us toward our goals, so I began looking at a subcontractor for funds.

There had to be someone or some entity that raised funds better and more efficiently than me. I had no ego issues about finding the right person. As serious as we were about our efforts, we had to make the financial commitment as well, and digest the bitter pill of the three to ten percent fees that would be associated with a professional's efforts.

Understanding the timeline, I contacted state organizations first. I began listing specific individuals and groups that could assist in moving us forward by way of referrals from the people I had already talked to. Every contact led to two or three more. Very soon into it, I started to get referred back to the people I had already talked with about a referral. That's how limited the resources were in the area.

As my efforts went regionally, I concentrated on organizations that were designed to help minorities and women, but usually focused only on racial and ethnic minorities. I never regretted not being Native American so much, since there were plenty of funds available if that requirement had been met.

Big investment firms requested $50,000 retainers for their efforts, and assured us that their companies would be successful. Even if we had had that amount of cash, I doubt that I would have paid retainers of that size. Instead, I offered higher percentages based on success. With little thought about the bottom line, it was always refused. That gave me a clear idea of their ability to succeed.

I had a few extensive meetings with a representative from CIT, a division of Tyco. He was known as the "go to" guy who could do less traditional or difficult deals. He said he could do nothing for the winery.

Apparently the size and business type made our deal undoable. That fact that we didn't want more than $1 million made it an unattractive and ineffective deal to do. That could have been it. Or could it have been that their own resources were busy paying for outlandish CEO parties and multiple residences?

I will remain wary of those who criticized too much over too little. It tends to cover up their own shortcomings, all the while making you feel confused and frustrated that your own best efforts fail to be enough.

There had been a number of bigger players in the local market. I explored them all before deciding on the one that had received constant coverage regarding its involvement and effort with other high-growth companies.

I made calls to the firm's references, yet I chalked up the non-specifics of their responses as a weakness in the company representatives rather than the service provider they had chosen.

Once I decided on a firm, I clearly outlined in our letter of engagement the three tasks they were to perform: secure three levels of financing, both within and outside of our current banking relationship; introduce our opportunity to their exclusive network of high-net-worth individuals for consideration; and maintain our accounting system and spruce up the executive summary to make it more "investor friendly," whatever that meant, as they had suggested.

With complete understanding of our goals, I still had to fire the service three months later. The quarterly tax reports had been sent in late; I could do that on my own. No investors had walked through the door or even picked up a phone, and there was no movement in the current funding structure. The firm still believed it had performed as outlined, and sent us a bill for thousands of dollars.

When we didn't pay, the firm sent a sheriff to serve us with a suit. I was surprised it had followed through on that process. When I got served, my first thought was to call the attorney we had dined with months earlier. I don't know why, since we had not met since the awards dinner and I had only recently seen her again with her father at a venture capital club meeting. Her offer to "watch our back" was reiterated, and she came on to help at a pretrial conference.

We stood firm in asserting that services had not been provided. At the pretrial conference, the firm walked out without resolving the issue, yet our new attorney had a call before the end of the week. The company would accept our lesser offer, covering only one month of accounting services.

Less than a year later, that firm let go the "no service" provider CPA that had been our contact. The next month, the firm disbanded entirely.

It became a common theme, one that Dawn calls "perpetrating fraud." Once fees have been assessed by big firms, they assume people will be unmoved by lack of performance and be so unaccountable themselves that bills get paid. Agreements for service, despite the lack of effectiveness becoming apparent, continued without review by the over worked small business owner.

The Indiana small business division tried to help by sending its newly hired executive director to counsel us. With no review and no discussion, he made what I found to be ridiculous and outrageous suggestions as to how to get the company "back on track." He suggested closing retail and going all wholesale, our smallest and least profitable business segment. He didn't like the private functions, nor did he understand that we were getting paid to market to new guests. He even warned that if we didn't do what he suggested, the results would be disastrous.

After careful, specific questions, we uncovered his lack of understanding about our business and the basic practices within our industry segment. We also uncovered that his defining success had been based on the fact that every company and division he had worked at had closed. Not wanting that outcome, we opted not to follow his directions. Less then 9 months later, he was gone from the state organization.

It seemed that I got to a point with each prospective resource quickly enough that I wore out their desire or expertise in helping us. Still, I didn't feel we were the worst business in the world that could be helped.

In what would become a last effort, we looked to friends and family. With $70,000 in pending commitments from an employee and a neighborhood professional, we felt confident that the balance of funds was within timely reach.

I had long since adopted the theory that we should explore every option. Between Dawn, Angee and me, we chose our top 10 very personal contacts. Careful to avoid securities issues, I drafted a letter outlining a request to discuss our opportunity. I passed it by our legal service for review and they were impressed with the structure and appropriateness, especially considering we were walking a thin securities line.

The people we selected would be able, without fear of homelessness, to commit to $10,000 to $50,000. With each unit of $10,000 investment, the percentage return would increase.

That return was far above what any of them were getting in private investments or stock portfolios at the time. The upside, we always knew, would be the investment secured in wine, since the bulk of the capital investment would go into production to keep up with demand.

That meant the worst-case scenario was lots of wine, and a tax deduction. The upside was a better-than-market rate of return. Only three of those people ever acknowledged the correspondence. Not one personal contact discussed an offer.

The possibility of $100,000 to $500,000 was gone as quickly as we had assumed it could come in. One potential investor even unhappily paid $30,000 in additional taxes that year rather than invest in a small business. The IRS was favored over our winery. That hurt.

CHAPTER SEVEN

CONSIDERING EVERY FACTOR

Critics are like eunuchs in a harem.
They think they know what to do.
They have seen it done.
But they have never done it themselves.
Unknown

No one ever erected a monument to a critic!
Still unknown

"We have considered every factor in making this decision." That was the phrase we would continue to market in our process of closing.

It was very true. It had become increasingly more apparent that, despite our best efforts, strong financial performance and market acceptance, local conservatism, the banking community, national climate, and international crisis were all factors that would materially affect our success.

The same village that raises a child must also foster the growth of small business. In one recent address, President G.W. Bush lauded the efforts of the small business sector as the future of America. Thanks for that responsibility! Yet within the same week, the president's office cut Small Business Administration funding by half. Was anyone asking the questions? Was anyone paying attention?

Sadly, the answer was: probably not. Granted, there were other things on our collective national plates: corporate cutbacks caused massive unemployment. It was big business cutting jobs, not small business.

Banking attitudes shifted from liberal 1990s dot-com financing to the thought that everything was undoable. It turns out that nobody asked any of the questions. Paperwork was completed and, I dare say, nary a banker read a profit/loss statement to look at forecasts much less, to analyze the trends. Forget about being proactively involved in solving problems before they become unmanageable. That's not a service included in your loan costs.

As a result, banks and the venture market quickly retreated. Suddenly, making money might take some effort, and an understanding of the market. It would require the need to be proactively caught up in the markets they served.

Oh, wait, I'm sorry, that assumes service. That was far too much to ask. As long as the payments came in and looked good to come in next month, "I need to move on" was the general banking attitude.

I always actively sought advice and assistance. Most people were kind but confused. Asking the bank officer about trends, requesting suggestions to improve or help identifying problems to be aware of, were met with blank stares and, again, kind words.

"We will have needs above our lending structure now," I explained in early 2000. "Hey, growth is great," "Keep it up," and "We wish we could help," were the standard banking replies.

Unfortunately, the success realized by a few, however short-lived, made it difficult for everyone else to be realistic. Venture capital had learned to be happy and expect 40 percent returns. Who wasn't?

At what cost? Did they ever know how the returns were made or how long it would last?

Banker became their own worst enemy by literally not being able to restructure deals they had made to benefit their existing clients-clients who had spent all those years paying fees and interest at the going rate. They were unrealistic with requirements in the newer climate. If every bank was asking their clients' loans to leave their portfolios because they didn't fit, weren't they all just exchanging problems rather than solving them?

Nobody was doing anything. It seemed that all the money people wrapped up their bats and balls and went home to wait out the storm. Were there no good deals, no valid investments to make? No, it would just take work. It would take understanding the business and asking the questions and caring about the answers, and no one had any time for that.

In June 2002 our small line of credit was to come due. Earlier, I had received a request from our loan officer to term it out. Instead of paying it all down at once, the bank would transfer it from a revolving line of credit to another term note with monthly interest and principal payments.

It made good sense, because without the full $876,000 package completed, paying it off was impossible. We had utilized the entire amount to stay slightly on course with future production needs. We had been comfortable with the funds being used for inventory and, therefore, secured.

After a couple of e-mails and ineffective phone conversations, we were asked to meet in the loan officer's office about the status of the line of credit. I was understandably confused as to why this was becoming such an issue. I had a letter from him asking us to opt for the term note in the event we could not pay it off in full. Since he was well aware that paying it off was not an option, I made the assumption that we were on the same page about terming it out.

Angee and I drove separately to the bank, and waited to go in together. I brought positive reports and was clear on our ability that a term note could be paid as agreed. Angee seemed more concerned, but I was comfortable with my data.

Wine assets had been created to secure the line of credit funds used, and a transfer to monthly payments allowed us time to continue to raise the balance of the equity the bank said was required.

The bank thought less of the plan. They would give a 30-day extension and then they would call in the note if it was not paid in full. Another banker sat in on the meeting with the loan officer and was strangely silent. I asked him, being new to us and to the bank, to explain the process, if we were not able to pay the note in full.

With a face of an emotionless cripple, he droned out the process of seizing the business, selling the assets and then coming after the house we lived in, which had been used to secure the SBA loan.

I looked at the loan officer, who was actually turning paler by the second and showing significant signs of stress. I clarified with his new boss. "You are going to seize the business and incur the costs involved in selling them for a $50,000 line of credit, which you will not take payments on?" It was an incredibly daft plan, even for a new bank. The boss sat stone-faced in a motionless pose that said he had done this before; that, in reality, this was his only job, he was the hatchet man.

He asked no questions, offered no mutual cooperation. If you have a mutual problem, I have strong feelings that the solution must be a mutual effort. I became clear on their lack of involvement in solving the issue; my help in resolving it didn't seem to matter to them.

The loan officer's boss went on to talk about the house as the asset securing the loan. After the business assets were sold, they would take the house. He figured we would have 60 to 90 days' notice in this process. Every time he made an announcement of action, I asked him to painstakingly clarify. I wanted to understand both his knowledge of the process and his commitment to the action. At the very same time, from a psychological standpoint, I wanted him to keep talking to allow him the opportunity to offer another option.

I saw him respond with a lack of common human emotion; he offered nothing but the rote of the dialogue he had obviously repeated before. In fact, that is what he did: killed businesses. I could see the stress on Angee out of my peripheral vision. I ached for the pain it was causing her. The finality of his words and the bank's process held no logic.

As we left the building in the evening dusk, in my mind I already had begun a plan of action or reaction. Angee seemed numb. Losing the house was, up to that point, her worst fear.

The next morning I called our attorney to explain the bank's outrageous plans to recover the line of credit. She offered a phone call in an attempt to meet with the loan officer. I told her about the letter with an offer to term out the amount and assured her that the monthly payments were within our cash flow abilities. We expressed mutual concern over the bank's reaction and inability to choose any other industry-standard banking option.

Within a week, she had a dinner date with our loan officer. While dinner had been her plan, I was surprised that he had agreed. If this was their irrefutable position, why sit over a long, uncomfortable dinner?

Our attorney was on her way home after the dinner meeting when she called. "I wasn't there twelve minutes when he caved. They will term it out. No worries."

I was confused and relieved. Angee was happy, but the damages of the meeting in the loan officer's office had already set well into her consciousness and begun to eat away at her mentally and emotionally, and most noticeably, physically.

I tried to understand, in the ensuing days, how our attorney had been successful where I had failed. She was kind in assuring me that I had set the groundwork and that the mere introduction of competent legal guidance gave the bank a different, convincing perspective of Gaia and the situation. She said I had done all the real work. She was kind, but clearly she had waylaid aggressive and erroneous bank action. Perhaps we did make a good team.

Before August rolled around, we had a term note for monthly payments on our line of credit. Just as we had earlier structured and, proactively, asked for. Why had it been such a drama fest?

As excited as we were about becoming an international company with our international broker, we were faced with the most volatile foreign market in American history. Rather than join the world together as a great leader would do, we had our leadership pissing everybody off in true "rich white man" tradition. Suddenly, America and its products began to lose the attractiveness and sexiness that had been vital in assisting small business overseas. Nations began hating America and therefore the products it offered.

Then there was something much more personal and important…us. No one was moved that I had no salary. I had long since ceased making it a point during conversation. The business was a hobby, and our commitments, instead of being viewed as good business sense, became described as cute. It shouldn't have been a surprising attitude in a time when a hefty executive compensation based on no results was the encouraged norm in corporate America.

No one cared that Angee was in year eight of balancing two full-time careers. A glaring example of the disregard was made apparent by one of our short-lived sales mistakes. After working a full day at her corporate job, Angee came into the winery at about 5:20 p.m. to start what would be the next job for six hours. As she made her way through to say hello, our three-day-old salesperson leaned back, smiled, and said, "Nice of you to show up." I was floored. In an instant, that sales person was history.

It highlighted a general attitude. This was a winery; how could it be work? It was the American Dream. While it wasn't their job to understand everything that was happening behind the scenes, it also gave no one the right to criticize the actions we took.

Both of us had continued putting everything we had, emotionally, mentally, physically, financially and socially, into the company. Angee's health was deteriorating rapidly in a fury of diagnoses that made it difficult to solve one issue without affecting two others.

Medication had caused significant side effects that were as painful as the disease. The 75-pound weight gain was hard to miss in pictures from our last Ernst & Young awards dinner, and managing pain was a daily challenge.

Without much talk, drama or fanfare, and with a good attitude, Angee was calmly over it: over the work, over the stress, the financial challenges; she was "over the winery."

It was the end of fall 2002, and we were heading into our busiest time of the year when cash flow and sales began to climb and grow larger as the holidays came into view. Parties and private functions had begun booking earlier each year, which made cash on hand a comfortable financial position. With the hopes of a profitable fourth quarter, we concentrated on maximum sales, reduction of debt, and no unneeded purchases. It was most likely a strategy that many companies were adopting, given the state of business in our country.

More wineries were putting off additional grape and juice purchases and trying, gallantly, to sell what they had. Very simply, the strategy nationwide was to increase cash on hand for some breathing room.

I stepped up the efforts to raise money, sure that the funds we had determined we needed almost two years earlier would still allow us to carry on and take the business to a more comfortable operating level. Every meeting had the same pattern to it: Identify the right company, then the right person. Next, lots of questions to qualify that they were actually investing and interested in our story.

By year's end, our thoughts of closing had become a regular conversation topic between Angee and me. We even shared our early plans with our attorney, who tried to convince us that there were options to take it to the next level, see it through and not close. She believed in the dream and our ability to make it all it could be. But she was not aware of all that it would require and all it had already taken.

Angee had erratic and unexplained illnesses that manifested themselves in somewhat changing symptoms. Each took us on a roller-coaster of possible diagnosis's and explanations. That fall she started to lose the weight she had put on over the past year because of medications and prednisone use. Without fail, every day, about 2 or 3 p.m., she crashed. It was like a dramatic drop in blood pressure that left her dizzy, nauseated and weak. Not just tired, but with severe muscle weakness. She had to be helped to the bathroom, and while baths helped with the muscle aches, she couldn't be left alone and needed help getting in and out of the tub.

We researched every drug interaction and all the possible medical reasons. It seemed much more than lupus, and still it was impossible to pinpoint or control the pain or symptoms.

Because of medications, and some symptoms of lupus going systemic, Angee began to be at a loss for words, at times even using the wrong words. Language impairment was a scary, progressive sign of a deteriorating process. The first few times I said nothing to point it out. Then, in a quiet moment, I asked if she was having problems thinking, with words. She agreed, and while I was happy we were able to talk about it and find a solution, in my heart I was pained beyond what I thought I was capable of.

I had always had in my mind the three years required to control lupus effectively. There was a high possibility that after that time period, the lupus could deteriorate into a systemic attack, progressing quickly. With no definitive treatment for lupus, we were chasing unknowns. But the end result would be the lupus attacking its own host body: kidneys, spine, tissues, and the brain.

Angee ate very little, but there was another reason for the dramatic weight loss. As the pattern of the mid-afternoon crashes continued, we looked for medicine interactions via the Internet-perhaps something that had not been explained to us in one of the numerous and increasingly common doctor visits.

It was not unlike the battles in business or with computer problems: Everyone pointed to something else. Software points to hardware and vice versa. Lupus doctors claimed it was another issue, and visits to frustrated family practice physicians pointed to lupus. While everyone admitted that there was something wrong, no one could define it or fix it.

I was angered by the lack of cooperation within the medical profession. A doctor would share with us later that in another time, as badly as her symptoms presented, Angee would have been hospitalized. But in the modern world of medical insurance, we bounced around among every doctor possible and followed every referral. Often it was months between visits while the pain and symptoms continued.

Out of sheer frustration (and, too often, the only way things get accomplished) I found at least one answer. Angee had more than 80 percent of the secondary side effects of a medicine given to her by a doctor. It was a new medication, which we knew, but only the primary side effects were ever shared via the doctor.

When we shared this info with the family doctor, she disclosed she had another patient on the same medication with the same problems. When I handed her the printout from the Internet, she asked if she could keep it. I grudgingly let her have it. It was there for all to see. I wondered what med students, interns and nurses had been so busy doing that they couldn't have run the drug secondary effects in any of the previous months of visits, or even asked or suggested that we do it.

No one had the passion to find out, to solve the problem; it was easier to just not do it. Why make the effort it took to punch a few keystrokes accessing the Internet as I had, and help not one but a countless numbers of patients who were being given the new medicine?

By the time we went to see the doctor who had issued the prescription, I was enraged. None of this was ever shared with us. Why? I questioned. He looked at the Internet page circled with all of Angee's symptoms; he smiled and shook his head. It was rare, but it was a new drug, and not a lot of people were on it. He didn't even seem concerned. But I was. One of the possible outcomes was a sudden and unexplained heart failure, likely resulting in death.

The holiday season that year was the worst financially we had ever had, including the first year we were in business. From a growing business standpoint, it made no sense. It put a perspective on the effects of the previous year's September 11 attack and just how long it would continue to affect business and our society. The result of the attack put the economy in a tailspin that had not yet begun to turn around. Since it had never happened before, no one could devise a plan that would provide assurance that there was a way out.

Our historically best season would offer no recovery to take us into the next quarter.

Because we had long been committed to proactive communications, in mid-January I let our lending partners know the loan payment would be delayed.

We had already begun to ask: Why continue? The personal quality of life and external lack of cooperation made looking at the big picture critical. Then the answer came, very easily.

Angee had set January, then May of 2003 to wind things up. I gave little consideration to hiring another winemaker, but acquiring the proper funding structures and partners remained a primary endeavor of mine.

Letting go came harder for me. I needed to understand the difference between circumstances beyond our control and my own ability to be successful. I struggled long hours, turning into days, with my own abilities and the ending of our dream. Without Angee, it was no longer our dream.

The decision to cease operations became easier as I sought out the pattern of involvement from every angle. No one cared. Not really. It was a nice little company with lots of potential. We had always done exactly what we said we would do. Still, none of that mattered.

Gaia Wines was a welcoming place for all wine lovers. It offered opportunities to be part of something unique to employees who relished in the challenges. The feeling that new guests had when they walked into the winery was still there. But, like a bad relationship, we had put it all at risk and no one was willing or able to help. I would ask myself the tough question.

Why are we doing this? Why are we risking physical, mental, emotional, and financial health when, despite the fact that we have a great product, wonderful services, and loyal guests, no one wants to join in the next step?

Once I realized that no one cared, it became easier for me to embrace the next set of challenges that would befall our small, but now internationally known, company.

CHAPTER EIGHT

THE FORCE OF TWO BREAKING HEARTS

"Whatever happens, I must not cry."
Puss 'n Boots
Shrek 2

"Looks like I picked the wrong week to give up drinking."
McCroskey
in *Airplane*, 1980

Shortly after Angee and I had resolved our process, how we would approach the end together, we prioritized the chain of communication to our close partners. We had already told three close friends, and Angee's mom and sister in their roles as investors. It was an effort to make it more real and a decision we would have to stick to, just like every other commitment we had honored in the growth of our business. We were determined to cease operations gracefully and elegantly, just as we had done everything else. It would be done our way, in our time, within our plan.

We would be organized and prudent in our communications, consistent in our message, upbeat and comfortable with the discussion of our decision.

It was a chilly Monday night when Angee arrived at the winery. It was now time to talk with our number one employee and close friend. Dawn was getting ready to catch a bus when we asked her to stay.

"I got thirty-five minutes before the next bus," she said. I assured her we would drive her home if need be. Angee grabbed some glasses and took an open bottle of sparkling wine out of the cooler.

We would celebrate the beginning of the end. Angee poured half a glass for everybody and sat down. I looked to her to start the conversation, to reference her position and out of respect. I would have plenty of opportunities to tell everybody else. Dawn had remained a loyal and uncompromisingly supportive partner in our venture and had as much emotional attachment as anyone.

Dawn's response was typical. "Okay, fine. You're sure? It's over?"

They were, all at once, questions of disbelief and statements of understanding. It had been hard on all of us and, good or bad, she had been a part of most every success and failure. She had experienced every "perpetrating fraud" experience that had walked through the door. She had waited for paydays, protected me while I was busy protecting Angee. Together, we had worked early for the morning press shows and late into the night for holiday celebrations and the start of marriages.

Dawn had taken the days when I couldn't physically go one more day, and a few holidays, so that Angee and I might have some semblance of a life. I had made her cry and she had often, when needed most, made me laugh. Without fail, she had challenged our choices while respecting each path we had taken. She was an employee who had become a close confidant and friend.

In the best sense of the word, Dawn had become part of our family. I turn to only half a dozen people to bounce off ideas and to gain perspective. She was always at the top of the list: whether a review of the week, a Friday wrap-up as we moved forward, or a social dilemma.

There were often times when she was the first one to hear a recent decision, opportunity or challenge, based not only on proximity but also on a strong and unique view she would offer of the incidents and details.

Dawn had embraced the chaos, found me for the important calls, and excused me when she was aware of other priorities. She had not yet begun to feel the sadness of our decisions.

February 28

We had a busy morning, with more medical tests, and a 1:30 p.m. appointment with the bank. Not knowing what would transpire, we asked our attorney to attend. She managed to come, although sick with strep throat.

Also in attendance was a representative from the company the bank had contracted to handle the Small Business Administration (SBA) loan. While the rep had a nice enough presence, I remembered from our bank's board member and from a previous employer that the company's and the rep's efforts were often ineffective.

I remembered the problem with our own application, from misplaced information to information that was downright inaccurate and could not be traced to any data we had given.

Joining us on their side was the newer face, the loan officer's boss, the hatchet man. He was your average sad, older white male. Immediately, it seemed apparent that he lacked basic social skills, not making any introductions or other socially acceptable offerings. During the conversation, he failed to display any significant knowledge about our company. I recalled his earlier talent. The skill he seemed to possess was the ability to tell a client how the bank would seize his or her house.

Our loan officer started with what sounded like childish whining. He felt I was using him against the SBA loan processor. It was amusing; as he went on to assert that I was playing them against each other, not communicating. I sought to clarify.

"Sir, I have an e-mail stating that communication about the loan should be directed to you alone, so when your processing company called, I simply repeated that my first communication should be with you. You can always copy the rep on what they need to know from our conversations or e-mails."

That sounded like he might have to do some work.

My attempt at comforting him came off as sounding condescending, I was sure. I continued. "I know you have never been through this and it is a totally new process for you." He shot a disgusted look to the processor, and they both smirked. I was unfazed; we moved on to the business at hand.

After thanking everyone for being there, I deferred to Angee. The room was silent.

"We have decided to close the business," she said simply. "We have decided to close the operation. We have given a lot of thought to what the best options are and with the current economic, banking and investment climate, we feel it is best." She was poised and calm. She had been over it since last June. I could only think that the words came easy and that this was a relief to her.

She turned back to me as I began to outline the plan of ceasing operations in an organized, logical manner.

"We will go to our most profitable customers first- retail-offering discounts based on volume. We have a unique opportunity in this business. The wine will not be available after we close. That means loyal customers will be looking not for 'close-out pricing' but the chance to get what is available, period. We will begin progressive discounting of merchandise and take the equipment to local, then regional, then national wineries, offering list prices and making all equipment available to the highest bidder with a deposit."

We were on top of our game knowing just what to do the next 90 days so that everyone would be taken care of. With the ratio that existed with assets-to-debt, our intention and ability of being able to walk away wholly satisfying our obligations was solid. Even a small remuneration for our eight years of effort would remain.

The bank asked for a budget of costs associated with the closing. Outside of a little more advertising, and decreased labor, which balanced each other out, we saw no significant change in operational costs. Marketing would begin immediately, and after e-mail, fax and direct mail had been completed, we would begin targeted ads over three to six weeks. Discounts on wine would remain consistent in order to avoid price discrimination, which was illegal with alcohol, but merchandise was "best offered" when customers walked in the door, since many items were one of a kind. Because so much of the winery was unique, we didn't expect to see much more than an average 25 percent reduction.

The strategy was one that left every debt satisfied. But it would take the full 90 days, we anticipated, making that happen. It was a time frame the bank had agreed to, through the loan officer, in the amendment to the security agreement, when the loans were established three years earlier.

That was a factor we didn't bring up at the meeting, feeling it was automatically understood. But then the bank asked an interesting question.

"Why didn't you do this last October or November?" the hatchet man inquired. There were two reasons this struck me as odd. Had they understood our business at all, they might have realized that this was an ignorant question. Why would a company that does 60 percent of its business during the fourth-quarter holiday season, including retail and entertainment, choose to close before that opportunity?

In fact, Angee and I had often talked critically of the closing of another winery that had gone out of business in early November, only days before what is surely every winery's best money-making occasion.

Next, I questioned, why did it matter to the bank when we closed? We had made payments in each month of the fourth quarter and, with the exception of the past due fees and January; the bank was getting money regularly as agreed. Any change we had ever experienced always warranted our quick communication, and a securing of their willingness to be reasonable, so there were no surprises.

When we asked why they mentioned those questions, and when we addressed the timing, which Angee did both confidently and calmly, they backed off the issue as if we might push too hard about why they had even asked.

As we wrapped up with their consent to begin the closing process, I asked how future payments would be applied to the loans, and in what order. The processor and the loan officer looked at each other, apparently having had no idea.

The rep began uncertainly, "I'll talk with the loan officer and we'll get back with you. I think it's the guaranteed SBA portion, interest, fees, and then the line of credit, but I'll check." This was the only job, to apply the proceeds to the loan as they came in, and there was still confusion.

I requested from them a guideline from the SBA on the process for closing. Everyone was unsure if it could be shared with us, the loan client.

"Let's ask anyway and get me a copy so I am aware of our responsibilities and can act accordingly and in a timely manner," I challenged the loan officer.

Before we ended the meeting, and as the loan officer was video-taping the winery inventory for the first time, we found out that Dawn's father, sick with cancer for the last few years, had died.

With Dawn in tears, I attempted to console her. At the same time, I informed the bank that given the reduced staff, the timelines for their information would have to change. Obviously, Dawn would be leaving and gone for at least one week, and maybe more.

Running the day-to-day operations, executing the closing plan and creating and running reports as requested, alone, would not be feasible.

Both the hatchet man and the loan officer offered weak, insincere condolences to Dawn. I reminded them that the timeline would change slightly but I would keep them up to date, and both agreed that would be fine.

March 6

Dawn's father's funeral was scheduled for Thursday. We set our disclosure of the closing plan to the next two creditors in line, the landlord and the Indiana business group representatives, for the same day.

At 1:00 p.m. the state reps came into the winery and seemed in great spirits. There had been verbally harsh e-mails between one of them and me when we let them know in January that the payment would not be timely. Yet today he seemed to have forgotten all that, and seemed genuinely glad to see Angee and me. Okay, maybe just Angee.

After some small talk, and as I finished up a phone call, I thanked them for coming and turned to Angee to take over.

"It has been a long, wild wonderful ride and after giving consideration to everything, we are going to close the winery," she said.

"Whoa, what are you saying?" asked one rep as both his and the other's faces dropped to the floor. "You guys are going to make it, you have done tremendous things. We are very proud of you and your business." They weren't even mad, just genuinely shocked.

My thoughts turned to just how supportive they had been, as individuals and as a corporate entity, during the previous holiday season.

Not one state party or celebration, neither of them, nor anyone from their office had been in to partake of holiday shopping or specials. No special offers from any of the government offices. Our governor still served California wine at the mansion. They were free to collect the taxes related to the sale of wine, but not willing to serve it as a viable state product. How proud they must be. I recalled asking one of them in one of the e-mails to inquire as to where his employees had spent their holiday money.

Overall, holiday spending may have been less than in previous years. Regardless, expenditures were still going to the big discounters. Here was a department that was supposed to promote Indiana commerce, and it was still spending state money with big chains and discount stores, ones without corporate headquarters in Indiana.

Like most everyone that previous holiday year, the bulk of gifts came from Target, Wal-Mart, maybe even Kmart. Holiday luncheons and business meetings were held at the local Olive Garden, TGI Friday's and the big chain hotels.

That previous holiday season, Angee and I had consciously given gifts from our local independently owned bookstore, the local spirits shop, and music from a local artist. It was as much a statement as a true desire to give what we thought was the best of local commerce. Sadly, the state didn't feel the same dedication to the business sources where income was generated.

Sure, they were proud, but not supportive. Still, their shock at our announcement was not what we expected.

The rep began offering other options, other solutions. "What about less space to decrease rent? Run it out of half the space…"

"That wouldn't do," Angee countered. "We are out of space now and we need to increase production to keep up with demand, not decrease it. Expenses are as low as they can go," she said, adding that every year we had managed to decrease expenses while raising revenue.

We offered the updated ratios with confidence. Total assets to debt were better than 2 to 1 and with our organized sales process we remained clear that everyone would be paid. As the plan was laid out, we asked for input to make it better.

"No, you guys know better than anybody how to sell this stuff," the other rep offered. They were still stunned when we asked what information or paper work needed to be completed from their end. Again, they weren't sure. A letter stating our intentions would help, along with possibly current financial reports. It sounded like they were stumbling.

"Do you want to tell them?" one rep said. Each looked to the other as we stood to say goodbye.

"Well, sure." He paused, "We are also closing…at the end of June, so maybe we can carpool to job interviews," he joked, as he talked about the dismantling of the state agency that had wanted us to remain viable. They had every resource in the world available to them as a government agency, and they, too, had to make hard decisions. It was easy to see that they would remain supportive of our plan and feel empathy for our process.

Shortly after they left, our landlord popped in, as I had asked, to set an appointment to talk. He was the last on our list to inform, and with Angee still there, it made sense to talk now.

One more time we recounted the decision, the process and the ratios. He, as usual, was understanding and supportive of our plan. He was happy to hear that the bulk of his money could be coming soon. He shared with us stories intended to make us feel better. He had just received five years of rent up front from a lessee. We were by far the best business people he had rented to. He wished us every success when we did it again.

As he left, we closed up for the night. What we had thought might be the worst of it was over. We were committed to closing, paying off debt and moving on with what funds would remain. It would be a tough 90-day process, but not as tough as the past nine years. Or so we thought…

March 14

Dawn had returned on the 12th, and we were getting geared up! Letters were sent out, and we began the process of informing the public and key partners in the business.

We had plans to go away on that weekend, and while we were used to working long hours, a little regrouping would be helpful. On this day, I received an e-mail from the bank. It included a forbearance agreement. A common bank document, it allowed a different payment schedule than originally outlined.

Even with everything that had been laid out in the hundreds of previous pages, the bankers seemed oddly committed to repeatedly getting additional documents signed that restated their rights and intentions.

This document had also been sent to Angee at her work. She called in a panic. It had to be signed and returned by 5 p.m. that day. It was an illogical request. That time frame gave no reasonable amount of time for us to read and understand the impact, much less time to get our attorney's valued opinion.

The most significant clause called for over 25 percent of the total loan debt to be paid in two weeks. It was an impossible item to agree to, and put us immediately in default and out of control of the process in 14 days.

We would need to think about its ramifications, consult our lawyer, and then say no!

Calming Angee, I told her I would call the bank and get the information to our attorney for review. Yes, we would still head out of town to visit with friends, as I didn't want to disappoint them, and knew there was nothing we could do about it before Monday. I felt it would still consume the weekend with worrying, planning and sending e-mails back and forth.

Before I could make a call, the loan officer was on the phone. "Will we be getting that document before the end of the day?"

My response was calm. "No, I need to get it to Angee and to our attorney. Surely, you understand that they have to review it before anything is signed." I offered. He seemed dumbfounded at my calm and logical response.

I spent the weekend trying to e-mail a strategy to our attorney. Constantly checking e-mails and long-distance calls cut into what I thought would be a relaxing weekend. Then, although I was removed from the area, the best thing I could have hoped for happened.

In the midst of everything, an obvious option came to the forefront of my thinking. You can't help but believe moments like this clarity is what makes people, and some of their deeds, great.

The bank seemed unwilling to admit that the process we had in placed was best for everybody. Everybody agreed to the 90-day closing process but the bank was now making new demands. Their forbearance agreement only set a date for a failure. Twenty-eight percent of the loan needed to be in their hands in two weeks.

We had two months of bank loan money on hand, but as quickly as the bank was changing its collective mind, we held off any payment transfer until it was clear what was going to happen.

While daily sales were increasing with the news of our closing, there was no logical way to commit to the amount the bank requested in two weeks. It did nothing but seal the date for bank possession.

Then I conceived a counter-offer. We would give the bank the business in its entirety. For a price, they could control the entire process from now until the end of the permit. I crafted the items I wanted in the agreement and e-mailed it off to our attorney. The rest of the weekend progressed nicely when I received her glowing response as to the logic of the whole offer.

For a mere $150,000, the bank would get everything: wine, merchandise and debt. They had the option, totally at their discretion, to hire no one or select people to help in the process. They could negotiate with individuals a separate fee for their assistance.

On Monday, driving back from our friend's house down south, we got a call from our attorney saying that the loan officer wanted a decision and the documents signed, sealed and delivered. We briefly discussed the merits again, and I promised to call as soon as we hit Indianapolis.

Back at the winery, I got hold of the loan officer. It was mid-afternoon.

"I understand you have left some messages. What can I help you with?" I said.

"You have the forbearance signed and ready for pickup?" he said.

"No, actually, Angee has reviewed it, but our attorney has been out all weekend." I ignored any further reference to it. "We think it would be a good idea to meet. We have structured an offer that pretty much gives the bank all they want, and we should probably go over it."

"We are not going to get the forbearance agreement?" he seemed confused.

I could tell he was losing what little cool he had left, and I wondered why the hurry on this timeline. Somewhere in the conversation, I began to realize, he had not shared with his new henchman or the bank's attorney our 90-day amendment to the security agreement he had signed. By executing the forbearance agreement, he would have made the amendment to the security agreement null and void without them ever finding out what he had signed and committed the bank to.

He continued, "I don't really think that another meeting is in the bank's best interest."

"Well, I'm not sure I understand." I said. "If you have the opportunity to get what you want, it seems it might be a good idea." Then I gently gave him an out and ended the conversation: "Why don't you talk with your attorney and your boss and get back with me." I loved staying vague and in control.

"I don't think the bank [as if it were some royal entity] would be interested," he said. "We are not going to get the forbearance?" he asked again. His persistence was cute yet ineffective.

"Not until our attorney reviews it, but you check with the bank about a meeting for our proposal. I'll talk to you later." I ended the call.

Two days later I received an e-mail that said a meeting was not in the best interest of the bank. They had neither the time nor the inclination to meet. Rather than respond to the e-mail, we took it to another level.

Angee crafted an e-mail to the bank's owner, the very man whose relationship we had started with and who we had been assured was very much on our side. She was exquisitely simple. We had been given a forbearance agreement, had no time to review it, and requested another meeting to make a proposal that would be in the bank's best interest. She expressed our concern that we had been told that the bank was not interested in a meeting.

The next day, the loan officer called to ask if Friday would be good for our attorney and us. We set 1:30, which had become our usual time for bank meetings. I contacted our attorney, who was more than happy to attend.

March 21, 1:30 p.m.

We set the table in the back so Angee could sit at the head, and the two bankers and their attorney sat with their backs to the wall.

Our attorney started with a general question. "What is it that is causing the bank to be so irrational in their actions? Because everyone we talked to says this just isn't right. What is causing the pressure? Are you selling the bank, or closing it?"

Everyone on their side of the table went white. It was a surprising reaction. The questions had clearly moved them. I feel it was clear we were mistaken to expect that there would be any honesty.

I saw the color drain from their faces. The bankers shot quick darting looks to the middle where their attorney sat, but no one was ready with a response. No one was ready for that question.

"It's the SBA," the hatchet man finally offered. "We have to wrap this up, and we're getting pressure from them." His stutter and delay indicated to me that he might be lying.

"That seems odd, because during my last conversation with the Small Business Administration, I asked them directly if they wanted to put us out of business as a result of your actions, and they answered with a definite 'no,'" I said.

There was a quietness that gave us a clear view that the bank was very unaware of the process. I continued.

"The forbearance leaves us with no chance of success, but we realize that what you want is control, so we have crafted an offer that gives the bank control." As I talked, I slid the offer in front of them, one copy they had to share. Their attorney grabbed it, moving it toward her. There was a moment of quiet. Then unforeseen anger began to surface. Faces tightened, and the pale white faces began to quite literally turn red.

I went on. "As you can see, this gives you complete control to dispose of the assets and pay off debts in the time frame you have in mind. We will keep permits in place and assist as you would like. You can negotiate with whomever you want to help in the process."

"We're not assuming the debt," the loan officer's boss interjected.

"Obviously, if you have all the assets, you'll need to take care of all the liability, but even with the payout to get control, you have plenty of assets to take care of the liabilities." I reminded them.

"The forbearance agreement puts in place what we need." The boss began changing physically as anger took over. His face got red, as he lost control.

Angee interjected clarity and logic. "As soon as I sign the forbearance agreement, I will be in default. Sales are increasing, but we cannot guarantee the time frame you have outlined. Basically, what you are saying is that in two weeks you have control. Our offer gives that to you now."

"We need to see a plan of how your closing process is going to happen," the hatchet man took the lead, and his anger was joining him in his irrationality. He started screaming his every word.

I repeated, "We outlined our process two weeks ago and you were in agreement that it made sense. I realize the loan officer hasn't been through this before. And, as his boss, maybe you haven't been through it with retail, and certainly not this type of business. It will require some of the cash influx to finish wine product for sale. Advertising is set to begin next week, and letters have already gone out to key customers. But we are really looking at our first true weekend coming up based on that marketing. But it doesn't seem like you want to take advantage of our offer, is that correct?" I attempted to get us back on track to something meaningful. I didn't wait for an answer. Seeing that the loan officer was not in a position to make anything happen, I stopped trying to be his advocate and protector.

Pulling out the 90-day agreement, I turned over a copy to their group. "We'd like to go ahead and start the 90 days we agreed to when the loan was arranged." There was only a brief minute to look at the document, but the resulting fury was amazing.

"I don't think you folks know how to do anything." The banker's boss addressed me and our attorney, still so red that he looked like a heart attack waiting to happen.

"I feel sorry for you," he said looking right at Angee, "because you are the one who is suffering." He turned to attack me, and I actually felt he would physically take a swing. "I don't think you know anything about business, and particularly how to run this business." It had started to get personal.

Remaining calm, I countered, "Well, Ernest & Young and six years of double-digit sales and income increases might mean something."

"That doesn't mean anything," the loan officer interjected, "The bank had that, and the sales increases don't mean it's successful. We need a budget."

"For what?" I inquired. "You have three years of profit and loss statements. We have an award-winning winemaker, an award-winning business and I have run this business in a financially and commercially sound manner. We have simply decided we don't want to do it any more, and want an organized, profitable closing."

The loan officer's boss then turned toward our attorney, while addressing Angee: "You don't have proper legal counsel and you lack sound business management. I feel really sorry for you."

Angee looked shocked at his irrationality. Our attorney jumped in. "You may want to take a minute and rethink your slanderous comments, and in the process may find that you owe these ladies an apology." It was a powerful, sincere, calm response to his outrageousness.

"Well, we need a budget…" he stuttered.

After a moment, I took a deep breath and ended the meeting.

"Clearly, you don't feel comfortable with me and so there is no sense for me to put together any information, as you would find it incompetent," I countered. "We will take our 90 days as the bank has agreed to in this document and move forward. There is nothing more to talk about. Gentlemen, this meeting is over."

Standing up, I pulled my offer back and arranged my notes and papers. Our attorney and Angee joined in standing as we waited for the bank people to move. They all stood, and without another word walked out of the room and through the darkened cellar toward the door. I started to follow them out, and Angee stopped me.

"Let them go…I am so sorry I didn't stand up for you," she said.

"I want to make sure they go out immediately," I said, but I think I just wanted to move. Dawn was coming toward us, and I asked her to make sure they got out without stopping.

I returned to the room, and our attorney tried to bring reason to the proceedings.

"That was some crazy shit, and he owes you and me a big apology for being the most unprofessional and obnoxious man on the planet," she said.

"Clearly, they are not being rational," I replied.

"I should have said something or ended the meeting right there," Angee repeated.

We were all in shock at how fast the tone of the meeting had deteriorated.

It was impossible to respond appropriately, although ending the meeting was a good choice. The fact that the bankers didn't try to bring it back around to something effective and businesslike spoke volumes to the level of people we were dealing with. And that level, we would find, we could not change.

March 27

At 3:30, an underling from the bank's attorney's office dropped off a package. There was certainly no shortage of paper when it came to the filings of these folks. About an inch thick, it repeated a lot of the same information. What was new was the injunction to seek a Temporary Restraining Order (TRO), effectively shutting the operation down if we did not meet their previous financial demand. I took a panicked breath and called our attorney.

"There is no way they are going to get that immediately; it's just putting a move in place," she responded. "What are they asking for?"

"Twenty-eight thousand and change by noon tomorrow, or we turn over the key to the winery. It sounds like a ransom note."

"It is, as a matter of practice. They are trying to convince a judge that you are selling their assets without their permission. Are you going to give them the keys?" There shouldn't have been any shock that she asked.

"No, I don't think that's in our best interest," I said.

The next day was as normal as could be. I had customers in the winery when the loan officer showed up late, at 12:15 p.m. The door was closed, but I saw him make his way tentatively down the stairs. He opened the door, stepped in and stood, as if he were a fire hazard, blocking the doorway.

Excusing myself from the guest's tasting, I stepped over to the area and said nothing. An uncomfortable few seconds passed before the loan officer asked if we had a check for him.

"No, we don't." He never asked for the keys as he shook his head to signify "okay" and turned to walk out the door. He hit only the first step before he was back in the door. I hadn't left the area.

"Is Angee here?" he inquired. What an idiot, I thought silently. But my response was professional.

"No, she is at her *other* full time job," I informed him.

"Well, because I'd like to hear it from her." I didn't say anything. He turned and walked out again.

I returned to the business at hand and was slightly amazed that it had been so calm an interaction. Dawn came in later that afternoon, and I headed home to work on the closeout process. Advertising would start next week, and I wanted to be as prepared as possible to maximize the returns of our efforts.

Mid-afternoon, I checked e-mail as I usually do. There was another threat from the attorneys that they would seek a TRO. I e-mailed and called our attorney simultaneously.

"It is 4:45 on Friday. They will never find a judge to sign off on it, and they are all off playing golf. Don't worry," she seemed confident.

After I hung up the phone, I checked messages on voice mail. There was one from Dawn. I called back immediately.

At 5:45, with guests in the store, a sheriff walked in and handed Dawn the Temporary Restraining Order. Angee and I jumped into the car; we were downtown in 10 minutes.

Angry and on an overdrive of emotion, I walked into the winery and grabbed the papers from my desk. As I read, it was clear we didn't have a choice. There had been at least one judge who didn't like to golf.

As I walked into the tasting room, Angee made out a sign to announce we were closed. Six guests, all ready to purchase, left with no exchange of money, not even for the tastings they had already received. We wanted no transaction to be recorded after the issuing of the TRO. I apologized and agreed to let them know when they could come back to purchase.

Dawn began turning out lights and asked what else she could do. Just secure the perimeters, I joked.

She went on to tell me what had happened. Angee posted the sign as I recorded the same message on our answering machine.

"The financial institution has obtained a Temporary Restraining
Order forcing Gaia Wines to cease operation. We are very sorry for
the inconvenience this action will cause. We fully expect to be open
on or around April 7, 2003. If you have immediate needs,
Please contact the Loan Officer at xxx-xxx-xxxx,
Or the bank president at xxx-xxx-xxxx. Thank you."

It turned out the bank didn't much like this message. I could not
have cared less. I didn't like their interfering with our legal process of
closing our business and it didn't seem like anyone was bothered
about that.

In the following days we remained closed, but I went in to get
messages and collect mail. Angee took off work two days before the
hearing, and we searched for a TRO legal expert.

By calling everyone I knew, we had three lawyer appointments in
short order.

One attorney had the right attitude but the wrong solution. Our
current corporate attorney accompanied us on that trip, and we had
a heated discussion about the options. The first new attorney was
ready to tell the bank to go screw themselves but that little piece of
informational attitude would cost $10,000 to $15,000 and a corporate
bankruptcy. It didn't seem like much of an option. While the assets
were present, the cash wasn't.

The second guy had a big office, big conference room, and a big
show for us. He got on the phone immediately, put the bank's attorney
on the speaker phone and told him we were not there as we sat at the
end of the long mahogany table. He appeared strong and confident, and
was, by all reports we had been able to gather, the local TRO expert.

As we left the third option, the one that read to us from the state
law book but rendered no strong strategy, we opted for number two.
Consequently, that's what we got, number two.

April 3

There seemed to be very little prep time invested in going to the
Temporary Restraining Order. The chosen TRO attorney told us to be
at his office at 8:30 a.m. for a 9 o'clock court hearing. Even though he

had been given the documentation, I was concerned he didn't have more questions for us. There had been no real concrete discussion of what was to be accomplished.

We felt that since he had come in as the TRO expert from the firm, this issue was as easy for him as Angee's making wine or my planning and selling. It would be second nature.

Angee and I went to breakfast, feeling that it was always good to have something on your stomach for these big events in your life. I don't know if that makes throwing up easier or if it helps settle what might be an upset stomach. Regardless, we would have initial strength for the day. We were still able to be at the TRO attorney's office by 7:30, and he seemed genuinely inconvenienced at our promptness as he moved through the expansive waiting area of the 29th-floor firm.

"I am finishing up on another issue and I will be with you in about an hour. Feel free to wait here," he said.

There was no warm and fuzzy feeling from his style. But he didn't have to be our friend or even our confidant; he had to win the case, and I took his focus as a sign of his legal prowess.

Shortly before the hour was up, the TRO attorney came back with his jacket on and ushered us to the conference room where we had originally met. He was brief in his overview. "This is a relatively simple case. I have talked with opposing counsel, and they have someone else who is going to try this."

"What does that mean?" I inquired.

"Well, basically they are spending the least amount of resources to defend their position. I don't know this attorney, but he is not a partner. So, probably a junior getting his chops wet. That is good for us; it ought to be an easy win. The idea is to get the order dismissed and get you back open, which I expect will be this afternoon."

I was surprised at the quick resolution, and I hadn't planned on going back to work to open, but knew that it would be done if needed. Dawn was standing by as well, wondering when she would work again. The time closed, we figured, would be nothing more than a small blip on our organized closing.

The TRO attorney said "We will go in and argue that they have the letter from October 2000 which says that they agree to let you do what you are doing and not interfere. The judge can remove the order immediately. They will probably get some required reporting to make sure the cash from the assets goes to them first."

"After regular expenses, correct?" I said. I didn't want the bank cutting off our ability to operate effectively as we moved through our process.

"Right." he seemed disgusted at my clarity. "I am going to grab something from my office, and we will head over to court."

It was surprisingly quiet on the 15-minute walk over to court. No pleasantries, even about the nice weather. I missed the emotional understanding of our attorney, and the ability to ask questions and continue to pursue information a strategy that would be of benefit. There was no way the TRO attorney could have known everything about the case, the answers to every move. But I expected him to be able to ask questions to become more knowledgeable, since the walk to court was time we were paying for.

As we arrived at the courthouse, the other side wasn't around. I figured it was cheap television lawyering tactics: showing up, presumably confident, at the eleventh hour. The very fact that it happened so much on TV would make it ineffective here.

Court was still in session from the previous case. We stepped into the courtroom silently and sat in the very last row with our backs to the wall: also, a good TV strategy. You avoid consistently turning around and looking nervous.

The TRO attorney leaned over to me as I sat between him and Angee. "This is a pro tem judge," he said.

"A substitute judge," I responded. He wasn't amused.

"Is that a good idea to go with someone else?" I asked.

"Not really. He is not going to be invested in the process, and probably does not have the background."

That became glaringly apparent as we watched the case in session. The judge wasn't actively listening, was asking questions that didn't lead to resolution, and he often seemed unsure of what to do. I mentioned my amateur observations to the TRO attorney.

"Should we be in front of this guy?" I asked again after witnessing his style.

"Not really, but we run the risk of pissing him off if we ask to reschedule. It looks like we don't trust him." We didn't.

As we talked, the loan officer and two attorneys walked in and sat three rows in front of us. The attorneys looked really young and small. But then so did the TRO attorney, sporting a bit of a Napoleon complex due to his lack of height.

He went to introduce himself, and they all stepped outside. We were already past our start time. I felt the previous case was moving in a slower pace than it needed to. There were no questions asked to move it along, and decisions were delayed, ones that I believed could have been called off the cuff. Much as we don't want to admit it, I can imagine most of the lawyering and judging is rote.

The TRO attorney returned as Angee left for the bathroom, but he had nothing to say from his meeting outside.

At 11:20 a.m. it became our turn. With lunch looming for the substitute judge, I imagined we would not get our allotted hour.

We waived certain introductions of evidence to save time as the TRO attorney moved ahead. The opposing counsel had to be coached from the sidelines by the attorney with him. Every question or move was initiated by a whispering between the two and a shuffling of paper.

The merits of the loan were discussed, and the bank put the loan officer on the stand to testify about the loan status. On cross-examination, the bank's TRO attorney asked about the letter dated October 2000.

The loan officer made a convoluted argument about it being part of a previous loan that had been paid off. The judge missed the laughability of the loan being paid off. We were in court, prevented from doing business, because the loan wasn't paid off.

There were key issues that were not getting clarified to the judge's understanding, and nobody seemed interested in reversing the trend. From the gallery, where I had been instructed to sit, I could not get the TRO attorney's or Angee's attention to help with the facts, or the issues that should have been brought to light. I felt we were at a disadvantage based on that alone.

While I didn't expect them to know everything, I was hopeful that when at a loss for the right question or answer, they would defer to me. All they had to do was ask.

When Angee got on the witness stand, she was brilliant. If she had been scared, nothing showed but resolve, capability and confidence.

She answered the bank's questions with accuracy, pointedly and simply. It was like a good moment from "The Practice," when the witness does nothing to destroy the position. I was proud, because I had imagined she was uncomfortable and scared.

Our TRO attorney rectified the bank's position on the letter from October 2000. "Ms. Walberry, have any of the loans to the bank been paid in full?" he asked.

"No."

"So, to your knowledge, this amendment to the security agreement signed by you and the loan officer in 2000 is still in force and a condition of the loan?"

"Yes, of course." It was a critical point to make.

"And that being the case, you are acting in accordance with the loan and this amendment to the security agreement in the operations of Gaia Wines?"

"Yes, we are." As brief as her responses were, they carried tremendous power and articulation to the strength of our position.

Finally, as the lunch hour approached, the judge had a clarification that the whole case would hinge on.

"Ms. Walberry, is the winery still in operation?'

"Yes, we are."

From my view, I could see what had happened. But apparently I was the only one. I tried to get the TRO attorney's attention, gently at first. No one was going to expand on this point. He thought he was done. I made a louder noise to get his attention, from my gallery seat, and although he looked over, he did not ask for a moment, or take the note I had scribbled out.

Both attorneys went into closing statements, and everyone was interested in wrapping it up. When the judge spoke, I was encouraged. He said, "The bank cannot argue that this letter of 2000 is not a valid amendment to the security agreement. It was signed on the same day as all the other loan documents and was never voided or revoked."

I looked to the seats for reactions, and then back as the judge continued.

"However, it does seem that the business is in operation and the assets are in danger of diminishment. I will keep the TRO in place until Monday, April 7, for the two parties to work on an agreement to resolve this."

Our case had hinged on the lack of clarification of one point. While Angee had correctly answered the judge's question about being open, our attorney failed to redirect the judge's question to allow him to understand that we were open and under operation only as part of the 90-day closing plan as outlined in the October letter and previously explained and agreed to by the bank.

There had been no forward movement, and the edict to resolve it on our own made no sense. The reason we were there was that talks had ended and action, legal and punitive, was taking its place. We were still to be closed.

It took every ounce of self-control I had as the bank and their attorneys walked by, smiled, and told me to have a good day. Old arrogance is one thing, but young snot-nosed arrogance coupled with a need to be coached in court was harder to take.

By the time Angee and the TRO attorney joined me by the elevators, all that anger was at its most uncontrollable pitch. Still, I held my tongue.

"We are not going to help the bank destroy our company. They don't know what they are doing." I said.

"This was a good outcome. What the judge did was split the baby down the middle, in that the bank has to work with you according to the security amendment," the attorney said.

"It's not going to happen. They can't sell the wine, they don't have the permits, and we will not allow them the opportunity to ruin everything. We're done. Give it to them and let them fuck it up," I was certain we had been wronged by this process. Everyone had filed out of the courtroom before noon.

April 11

Things calmed down ever so slightly over the next few days. When our attorney told the bank we were not interested in helping without giving consideration to the amendment, the tone changed.

Although the TRO was to expire on the seventh, we set a deadline of the eleventh to hear from the bank. Angee and I were well aware that they could do nothing with the wine and they knew too little about the general operations to actually put someone in place to handle an organized closing. We gave them the the time they needed to come up with their own plan.

Again, it was time wasted. They came back with a ridiculous request for us to go into the winery and handle the final bottling of the remaining wines. But, unlike most good counter-offers, and apparently without realizing the position they were in, they offered nothing in return for our efforts. They were acting like they were in charge, not that we were to be working *together*. Our goals were to be able to execute on our plan as it was outlined and as the bank had agreed to in friendlier, more reasonable times.

Without the ability to manage the closing, we had no way of guaranteeing payment to the other creditors nor would we have anything left for our efforts. The deadline passed without any firm agreement and we went back to our original stand. If we couldn't handle the closing as we had set out, then the bank could be left to their own challenge of handling the entire process.

Three days later, as Angee was on her way home, I received her panicked call from the car. She needed to go to the emergency room. It was a rare call, because Angee had always felt she was being more of a baby with her health and to have actually felt as bad as to go to the ER was a change.

I met her outside and we drove immediately to the local hospital. The chest pains were so bad, she could barely breathe, and every gasp caused more pain. It all seemed to be emanating from the left side of her lower back.

Two hours later she was being seen by medical staff, and I wonder how chest pains could be such a 'wait and see' option in an ER. A battery of test showed nothing remarkable although she enjoyed the morphine that removed almost all the pain immediately.

No set of doctors were working together to help move the diagnosis, or more importantly, the treatment, forward. If we were with a lupus specialist they pointed to general practice for an answer. When we'd get to general practice, they seemed to revel in blaming lupus.

It left us in a loop of treatments and tests that did little to relieve the pain, whatever the cause. That Friday, Angee went in for a CT scan in the hopes of finding something, anything. It was a weird feeling to actually want to find a tumor, a blood clot and cyst. We were looking for something that could be dealt with, rather then the volley back and forth in the unknown.

After the scan, I headed to the winery to check messages and pick up mail. As I entered the landlord's wife was mulling around.

"The bank will be here in an hour for a walk through" she mentioned as if we knew. We did not.

I had to catch the TRO attorney on his cell phone. So much seemed to be going on, and the communication from our own attorney was embarrassingly absent, if not teetering on carelessness.

"You know about this walk-through; what are they trying to do?" I questioned.

"There is no planned walk-through. Tell the landlord not to let them in; I will call over there." It seemed obvious he had taken the afternoon off. It may even have been that the bank's attorney knew, and planned for the walk-through in the hope that no one would notice. Both sides were at a high distrust level, and I was not going to allow any access that was not supervised.

Angee called back with the TRO attorney's response. Opposing counsel had claimed innocence, something like they thought we were aware, but their efforts to access without ownership present had been foiled. I waited around a while to see if anyone was going to show up. It turned out that no one did except customers wanting my answers to questions. Answers I still didn't have.

The incident made it clear to me that neither the bank nor its counsel was placing any trust or respect in our position and, more important, in our counsel. My concern grew, not so much about our position but the job that was, or wasn't, being done.

April 23

After my visit to the unemployment office, and a morning of substitute teaching, I received a call from Angee with an update.

"I talked with the TRO attorney, and the bank wants to meet tomorrow with the Alcohol, Tobacco, and Firearms Bureau (ATF, the regulator of wineries, among other things) and they think it would be best if you don't come." She was short and to the point.

"And what did you say?"

"I said that was okay."

"You said yes?" I was beginning to feel sick. As smart and capable as Angee was, she had an innocence and trust that could be detrimental.

"Yeah, I said yes, he thinks it would be..."

I couldn't even listen, as I felt my rage grow.

"What do you think they are trying to do?" I shouted. It was a question she hadn't had the time or energy to think about. "Never mind." I didn't-couldn't wait for an answer. "You go and do what they think is best." For the only time I could remember, I hung up on her.

I sat by the phone numb and cold, and started to cry. The fact that Angee had trusted our dream, what was left of it, to the very people set on destroying it was shocking. I felt sick and betrayed.

My only goal, my only job, in all our years together, had been to do what was right for us both, together. The fact that she had so easily agreed to whatever they had asked without consulting me shook my faith and love to its foundation.

I sucked down the sadness I felt and let it move quickly to anger. Anger at Angee, and her response in putting someone, anyone, before us.

What seemed like a long time was only a short few minutes and I was back on the phone, with every bit of rage I felt, lashing out toward her.

"What do you think is going to happen in this meeting, that I am the problem? I am the only one, including our attorney, who gives a shit about this company and gives a shit about you. You think the TRO attorney is going to know what he needs to move this forward."?" I was screaming and crying all at once.

"Well , he just suggested that something might be accomplished without you there, because of the problems with the loan officer," she said.

"So, is the loan officer going to sit this meeting out as well?" I already knew the answer.

"I don't think so." She was meek in her reply. It seemed like she was understanding, but that was short-lived. "I think we have to look at all the options to get this resolved." She seemed less sympathetic to my response, and that did nothing to make me feel better. It only appeared that she was siding more with them.

I continued, "I can't believe you didn't take a minute to discuss this with me and that you are going to trust the bank and our attorney, who has done nothing, over what I have been trying to accomplish, to protect us, you. You have made it clear what is important to you, or what is not important to you."

"I told the TRO attorney I wanted you there." She began to backtrack, but it was too late.

"But you agreed to not have me there, right?"

"I can call him back and tell him that."

"The fact is that you didn't think about it," I said. She was still more righteous than I wanted her to be, and I wasn't calming down. "You do what you want, it doesn't matter, and I'll stay out of it. Apparently nothing I have done has made a positive difference in protecting you or our interests. You made that clear." Again, I hung up.

I called my friend David, still in tears, which I wasn't proud of or comfortable with. But I felt it might be the only thing that would keep me on track. David did a good job of bringing me back down, and we talked out strategies.

Angee had always been my go-to person, the one I trusted without fail. Trusted to understand and be strong, and to keep our priorities, the priority of her and me. Without that, I began to feel like I didn't know who I was or who she was. At the time, I failed to understand this was what the bank wanted, to weaken our position by dividing us.

David came up with the idea to tape-record the conversation and to not have her agree to anything. It made wonderfully composed sense. It was the bank that called the meeting, allowing us to hear what its plan was.

I stopped crying and called Angee back, comfortable in the ideas that David had generated. He was and still is one of the few people who can successfully talk me back to the issues at hand. Down from the cliff and back to the strength it takes to accomplish whatever I am trying to accomplish.

With more peace, I recounted to Angee my anger and fear that she was being set up and that no one would be there to protect her. She again asked that I be there. I refused.

"We'll play it your way; I'll stay out of the meeting and you guys get something accomplished, some resolution," I said.

"But I do want you there, I'll tell the attorney that," she almost begged. I remained committed to David's plan had made so much unemotional sense.

I went out immediately and bought a tape recorder. So much had been said and misconstrued that an actual recording would add perspective and logic to this totally illogical turn of events.

The day of the meeting, our attorney didn't feel like there was a need to meet sooner than 15 minutes before the bank people arrived. He said it was the bank that had called the meeting, and we—well, he and Angee—would sit and listen.

"Who will be in the meeting?"?", I inquired.

"I don't know" said the TRO attorney, and I knew we were getting that answer way too often. He seemed unfocused and acted as if he didn't even want to be there, as he recounted why he thought it was a good idea that I not be there.

"Well, I am going to ask that you both do two things," I said, but I didn't wait for a response as he began walking around the shop, barely paying attention to me and my thoughts.

"First, we all concur that you are agreeing to nothing, correct?" I was direct.

"Oh yeah, this is just an informational meeting at the bank's request" was the attorney's response from across the room.

"And Angee, if at any time you feel like you are not being protected…" I offered.

"I'll protect her," the attorney quickly shot in, but he never turned to address me or Angee. I continued, unfazed by his bravado.

"If you need me, or if you feel it is not going right, productive, you ask for a break and come get me." I restated my strategy with the feeling that no one was really paying attention.

"I still want you to be there." Angee said again.

"I'm going to go with the thought that maybe something could be accomplished by my not being there. But I will be right here in the office; you can go to the bathroom, just excuse yourself, and come get me." I said.

She looked at me, understanding but sad.

"And tape the meeting, here is the recorder, it will keep the meeting civil and on the right track. Then we can review the ideas before we make a response." I said. With that, almost like it was timed, the bank officers and their attorney walked in.

Dawn was already there, and she and I disappeared into the office to go through mail and return messages. Mostly she was there to support me and hold me somewhat in control.

A fellow winery owner showed up unexpectedly to take a sample of the wine that had remained in bulk storage in the interim. There was a man from the ATF Bureau, looking around for reports and trying to make sense of the inventory. It looked as if this was the first time he had ever had to do this. We would find out that it was. The ATF had never had a winery go out of business with this much hassle from a banking institution.

There was a fifth guy, and I was surprised and encouraged by his presence. Although he was not introduced, I knew he was the president of the bank.

Clearly, I felt he had been moved by the lack of progress and his own staff's actions, and was here to make it move forward, logically. Perhaps even as planned.

I paced up and down constantly, and found nothing that distracted me as the meeting wore on. Dawn and I talked about the possible outcomes. I didn't know what to make of the time that passed. Was progress being made? What was being rehashed in such great detail? Would it be of any help?

As I headed out to the tasting room to get something to drink, I saw the tape recorder I had bought sitting in the middle of the table where I had left it. The TRO attorney and Angee were to tape the meeting and document offers and record the tone of the other side. I felt blindsided, that nothing we had discussed or agreed to was being honored. I couldn't believe that the meeting had gone on this long with no break, or what was more important, with no need for input from me.

The anger I felt at the loss of control was on the rise as Angee came into the office. I was not receptive to her request to find some piece of documentation. I inquired about the progress—what was happening, what direction was it taking, was there anything I could do to help, did she need me? She offered nothing but her own frustration and angst.

As quickly as she walked in, she grabbed some file and walked out. I knew that could not be good. The fact that she had been so unresponsive and had again rebuked my help was not encouraging. Dawn saw the tenor of the interaction and ushered me out to the street so she could smoke and I could breathe. Once outside, I felt free to talk and express my anger at the process.

"I need to get out of here, just leave. No one knows what's going on. No one wants my help." I said as I tried kicking the parking meter to relieve the stress. I paced back and forth between two storefront entrances. As I made the short trip back to our entrance, the bankers and their attorney were at the outside door.

They came through the door still talking and unaware of who Dawn and I were. The bank's attorney pointed to the sign we had placed explaining the bank's actions.

"This is going to come down too. We don't need this," he muttered. The bankers looked in horror as they tried to move him down the street to talk, at the same time making him aware of the fact that he should not be talking with such freedom.

I smiled at the obvious lack of awareness of his actions as I made my way past through the door and downstairs. Angee was busy documenting inventory on a stack of wine cases, while our TRO attorney mulled around in a seemingly purposeless way.

"What happened? The bank didn't look encouraged," I said. I was cautiously optimistic.

Angee turned to me almost without emotion. "We are going to auction," she replied. The TRO attorney paced back and forth against the wall and could not make eye contact with me.

"What?" I wasn't hearing it right.

"They just kept going back and forth; nothing was getting accomplished, so it was just decided to go to auction." She could barely speak as the words fell out, and seemed unaware of what had happened. I turned to the attorney, expecting some logical clarification.

"This was the best option you could come up with?" I asked.

He still did not meet my eyes, pacing with his head down, mostly facing the cinder-block wall of the winery. "There is the possibility of getting the value of the loan and some extra, and the process is the easiest for all." he said. It was essentially easier for *everyone* but Angee and me.

I don't ever recall being angrier. The feeling that I could have beaten him with a bottle scared me and seemed a good choice at the same time.

"And this is what you want?" I asked Angee.

"Just get it over"…she spoke in half sentences. "They will release the house and my personal liability…for the ability to take it to auction." I could only imagine that the bank's plan all along had been to wear Angee and the attorney down, into compliance with their wishes, despite the fact that the bank was actively breaching their contract.

The TRO attorney could not look at me. He was aware of his incredibly poor performance before I knew the half of it.

Was I seething? That was an understatement. Getting away from everybody was all I wanted to do. I turned to step into my office, grabbed my briefcase and walked out. I expected someone to stop me and explain it in greater detail, to have it make sense. Nobody did.

I had never wanted to be farther away from Angee and this mess. I jumped into the truck and drove, without knowing where I could go to calm down. I was set to leave the city, drive straight through to a friend in Chicago, someone who could talk me down, then get me drunk, and then help re-approach the plan for the next steps.

I glanced down at the gas gauge. I wouldn't be getting far. The winery's being shut down had closed off even the minimal income I had been able to garner from my efforts. I already knew there was nothing in our bank account; it was the end of the month and we struggled to balance a growing deficit of funds. Between paying attorney retainer fees and miscellaneous expenses, there was no money anywhere.

When I got home I was in tears, not from sadness but from an anger and betrayal I had never before felt. Eight years of being strong and doing everything we thought was right was gone, lost to the weakness and arrogance of a few who didn't care.

Dialing the number I had dialed so many times before, I was numb when the only answer was the pre-recorded voice mail. I would not be going to Chicago. The next number was David's. He had been helpful before, and he knew I shouldn't be here when Angee came home. I had no idea what she was doing, yet I didn't care.

"I asked them to do two things, just like we had talked about, and they are fucking going to auction. No recording of the meeting, no plan from the bank, just throwing in the towel," I told David, knowing he would understand.

He wasted no time talking. "Are you okay to drive?" he asked. Although I had already consumed the first whiskey and Coke, I was not feeling anything but rage. Of course I could drive.

"Meet me at our usual place, about ten minutes?" he offered.

"Sure," I replied as I downed the drink, feeling amazed at not having any desire to do anything but find an appropriate method to release what was boiling inside me at an outrageously fevered pitch.

I still wanted to be far away and two miles down the street didn't seem to be very rewarding. But my time with David and the four or five drinks while we talked served to numb the fury and resentment I was feeling.

We talked about the stress Angee must have been feeling, and how if she was healthy this would be a different challenge. I tried to understand what David was saying, but I desperately wanted to remain angry and do something damaging. He was too smart to let that happen. I still felt I needed to be far away. I was mad at myself for not having a way out.

Even in my frustration, I had thought of Angee, leaving a note for her so she would know where I was. She couldn't have wanted to be with me either. It was so easy to blame everything that had gone wrong, or been difficult, on my unyielding nature and demand for control. I was surprised when she walked into the bar area.

David and I had already talked about letting it go for a few days and that Angee and I should agree not to discuss it until we both calmed down. It was so against my need to over-talk each little point of an issue. I agreed anyway, figuring it would be an exercise that would make me even more invincible and full of resolve.

It was such a change that even Angee was surprised at my calm demeanor as she sat down. David was kind in sharing with her what a tough day it must have been for her. She was genuinely shocked at how composed and supportive we were.

"Let's just give this a few days to marinate, focus on something else, and then we can decide where to go from here," I said. I felt it would be a big discussion when it did come, and it was against every fiber of me to wait. The irritation began to meld into understanding before long.

Days later, I was eager to hear what had really happened in the meeting without me.

CHAPTER NINE

THE ULTIMATE SANCTION

"The problems that exist in the world today cannot be solved by the level of thinking that created them."
Albert Einstein

"Is it a bigger crime to rob a bank or to open one?"
Ted Allan

Earlier conversations with the man from the Indiana finance department ran through my head on a regular basis. "They are in real trouble over this one," he said about the bank. It seemed a cryptic yet telling message. At the same time, he and the landlord were convinced that pursuing it, beyond just the cost of legal fees, was wasting time, effort and money.

But I remember the look on the faces of the lawyers sitting across from us when our attorney asked what was causing the pressure and the "somewhat" (she understated) unreasonable actions.

"Is the bank for sale or going out of business?" she said. Almost at once, three faces turned white. The female lawyer looked like she would pass out. The bank employees quickly shot looks to the center of their side and back to us. There were muddled responses until the loan officer's boss' voice became clear and blamed someone else.

Between that meeting and the conversation with the man from the state via his "source" whom he chose not to identify, I couldn't sleep. At 2:30 one morning, I realized what an asset sat downstairs with access to the Internet. Had anything been written about the trouble the bank had dealt with from past clients? Were there any press releases from the company? Did anybody actually do investigative reporting any more, and would there be anything about how they were acting?

I searched newspapers, particularly from the local area. I searched business journals and banking at the state level. Still nothing! I went to "search" and typed "FDIC" and "The Bank."

About six pages came up, and I began reading the titles. Board selection, charter information, names similar but from outside Indiana, as well a fair amount of crap that makes you wonder how this amazing technology occasionally messes up so dramatically.

Page two of the listings: halfway down, in the dead of night, I had the start of clarity.

FDIC issues Cease and Desist to The Bank

I clicked on the heading and hoped not to lose the connection, sure it would not reappear. There was the document that began to explain what we had been going through and why.

It included eight pages of federal reprimands. Apparently rules and regulations, very clear to the FDIC, the institution had repeatedly violated.

My mind raced through the pages, hitting highlights before printing the document for further analysis. I started to wonder if they had done anything right. Everybody was included: the board of directors, the management—lots had been done wrong. This was the type of entity that we all think never makes a mistake. After all of their ridicule of us, they were a bank that was full of actions counter to government regulations. How could no one know? How could no one care?

I quickly cross-referenced the newspapers again. Not a story in print. I searched the company's own press releases. As a bank customer, I would have expected that our company would have received an annual report with information on status. We had received nothing. There was no mention of it anywhere in the entire Internet world, except for the complete report from the FDIC. It made for enlightening reading.

IN THE MATTER OF THE BANK, INDIANA

A cease and desist order was issued, based on findings by the FDIC that it had reason to believe that respondent had engaged in unsafe and unsound practices

[.1] **Management—Qualifications Specified**

[.2] **Management—Management Plan Required**

[.3] **Capital—Increase Required**

[.4] **Dividends—Dividends Restricted**

[.5] **Assets—Charge-off or Collection**

[.6] **Loans—Risk Position—Written Plan Required**

[.7] **Loans—Special Mention**

[.8] **Loans—Extensions of Credit—To Borrowers with Existing Adversely Classified Credits**

[.9] **Loan Loss Reserve—Establishment of or Increase Required**

[.10] **Loans—Concentration of Credit—Reduction Required**

[.11] **Loan Policy—Preparation or Revision of Policy Required**

[.12] **Growth Plan—Minimum Requirements**

[.13] **Violations of Law—Correction of Violations Required**

[.14] **Profit Plan—Preparation of Plan Required**

[.15] **Shareholders—Disclosure of Cease and Desist Order Required**

[.16] **Board of Directors—Program to Review Compliance with Cease and Desist Order required**

7-31-02

In the Matter of THE BANK   INDIANA

(Insured State Nonmember Bank)

ORDER TO CEASE AND DESIST

The Bank, Indiana ("Bank"), having been advised of its right to a NOTICE OF CHARGES AND OF HEARING detailing the unsafe or unsound banking practices and violations of law and regulation alleged to have been committed by the Bank, and of its right to a hearing on the charges under section 8(b) of the Federal Deposit Insurance Act ("Act"), 12 U.S.C. §1818(b), and under Indiana Code Section 28-11-4, and having waived those rights, entered into a STIPULATION AND CONSENT TO THE ISSUANCE OF AN ORDER TO CEASE AND DESIST ("CONSENT AGREEMENT") with representatives of the Federal Deposit Insurance Corporation ("FDIC"), and the Department of Financial Institutions for the State of Indiana ("DFI") dated April 15, 2002, whereby, solely for the purpose of this proceeding and without admitting or denying the charges of unsafe or unsound banking practices and violation or regulation, the Bank consented to the issuance of an ORDER TO CEASE AND DESIST ("ORDER") by the FDIC and DFI.

The FDIC and DFI considered the matter and determined that they had reason to believe that the Bank had engaged in unsafe or unsound banking practices and violations of laws and regulation. The FDIC and DFI, therefore, accepted the CONSENT AGREE-MENT and issued the following:

ORDER TO CEASE AND DESIST

IT IS HEREBY ORDERED, that the Bank, its institution-affiliated parties, as that term is defined in section 3(u) of the Act, 12 U.S.C. §1813(u), and its successors and assigns, cease and desist from the following unsafe or unsound banking practices and violations of law and regulation:

> A. Engaging in hazardous lending and lax collection practices, including, but not limited to, the failure to obtain proper loan documentation, the failure to establish and monitor collateral margins of secured borrowers, and other poor credit administration practices.

> B. Operating with an excessive level of adversely classified loans and assets listed for "Special Mention".

> C. Operating with an inadequate level of capital protection for the kind and quality of assets held.

> D. Operating with an inadequate allowance for loan and lease losses ("ALLL") for the volume, kind, and quality of loans and leases held.

> E. Operating with inadequate earnings to maintain acceptable levels of capital.

> F. Violating laws and regulations.

> G. Operating with excessive concentrations of credit.

H. Failing to follow the Bank's loan policy.

I. Operating with inadequate policies to monitor and control asset growth.

J. Operating with management whose policies and practices are detrimental to the Bank and jeopardize the safety of its deposits.

K. Operating with a board of directors which has failed to provide adequate supervision over and direction to the management of the Bank.

IT IS FURTHER ORDERED, that the Bank, its institution-affiliated parties, and its successors and assigns, take affirmative action as follows:

[.1]1. (a) Within 60 days from the effective date of this ORDER, the Bank shall have and retain qualified management. At a minimum, such management shall include a new senior lending officer with an appropriate level of lending, collection, and loan supervision experience for the type and quality of the Bank's loan portfolio. Such person shall be provided the necessary written authority to implement the relevant provisions of this ORDER. The qualifications of management shall be assessed on its ability to:

(i) Comply with the requirements of this ORDER;

(ii) Operate the Bank in a safe and sound manner;

(iii) Comply with applicable laws and regulations; and

(iv) Restore all aspects of the Bank to a safe and sound condition, including asset quality, capital adequacy, earnings, management effectiveness, and liquidity.

(b) During the life of this ORDER, the Bank shall notify the Regional Director of the Chicago Regional Office of the FDIC ("Regional Director") and the Director of DFI ("Director") in writing of any changes in any of the Bank's directors or senior executive officers. For purposes of this ORDER, "senior executive officer" is defined as in section 32 of the Act ("section 32"), 12 U.S.C. §1831(i), and section 303.101(b) of the FDIC Rules and Regulations, 12 C.F.R. §303.101(b).

(c) Prior to the addition of any individual to the board of directors or the employment of any individual as a senior executive officer, the bank shall comply with the requirements of section 32 and Subpart F of Part 303 of the FDIC Rules and Regulations, 12 C.F.R. §§ 303.100—303.104. In addition, prior to the addition of any director or the employment of any senior executive officer, the Bank shall request and obtain the written approval of the Regional Director and the Director.

[.2]2. (a) Within 60 days from the effective date of this ORDER, the Bank shall retain a bank consultant acceptable to the Regional Director and the Director. The consultant shall develop a written analysis and assessment of the Bank's management and staff needs ("Management Plan") for the purpose of providing qualified management for the Bank.

(b) The Bank shall provide the Regional Director and the Director with a copy of the proposed engagement letter or contract with the consultant for review before it is executed. The contract or engagement letter, at a minimum, should include:

(i) A description of the work to be performed under the contract or engagement letter;

(ii) The responsibilities of the consultant;

(iii) An identification of the professional standards covering the work to be performed;

(iv) An identification of the specific procedures to be used when carrying out the work to be performed;

(v) The qualifications of the employee(s) who are to perform the work;

(vi) The time frame for completion of the work;

(vii) Any restrictions on the use of the reported findings; and

(viii) A provision for unrestricted examiner access to work papers.

(c) The Management Plan shall be developed within 120 days from the effective date of this ORDER. The Management Plan shall include, at a minimum:

(i) Identification of both the type and number of officer positions needed to properly manage and supervise the affairs of the Bank;

(ii) Identification and establishment of such Bank committees as are needed to provide guidance and oversight to active management;

(iii) Evaluation of all Bank officers and lending staff members to determine whether these individuals possess the ability, experience, and other qualifications required to perform present and anticipated duties, including adherence to the Bank's established policies and practices, and restoration and maintenance of the Bank in a safe and sound condition; and

(iv) A plan to recruit and hire any additional or replacement personnel with the requisite ability, experience, and other qualifications to fill those officer or staff member positions identified by this paragraph of this ORDER.

(d) The Management Plan and any subsequent modifications thereto shall be submitted to the Regional Director and the Director for review and comment upon its completion. Within 30 days from the receipt of any comments from the Regional Director and the Director and after the adoption of any recommended changes, the Bank shall approve the Management Plan, and record its approval in the minutes of the board of directors' meeting. Thereafter, the Bank, its directors, officers, and employees shall implement and follow the Management Plan and any subsequent modification.

[.3]3. (a) Within 60 days from the effective date of this ORDER, the Bank shall increase its level of Tier 1 capital as a percentage of its total assets ("capital ratio") to not less than 8.0 percent.

(b) Within 30 days from the last day of each calendar quarter following the effective date of this ORDER, the Bank shall determine from its Report of Condition and Income its capital ratio for that calendar quarter. If the capital ratio is less than 8.0 percent,

the Bank shall, within 60 days of the date of the required determination, increase its capital ratio to not less than 8.0 percent calculated as of the end of that preceding quarterly period. For purpose of this ORDER, Tier 1 capital and total assets shall be calculated in accordance with Part 325 of the FDIC Rules and Regulations ("Part 325"), 12 C.F.R. Part 325.

(c) Any such increase in Tier 1 capital may be accomplished by the following:

(i) The sale of common stock and noncumulative perpetual preferred stock constituting Tier 1 capital under Part 325;

(ii) The elimination of all or part of the assets classified "Loss" as of December 3, 2001, without loss or liability to the Bank, provided any such collection on a partially charged-off asset shall first be applied to that portion of the asset which was not charged off pursuant to this ORDER;

(iii) The collection in cash of assets previously charged off;

(iv) The direct contribution of cash by the directors and/or the shareholders of the Bank;

(v) Any other means acceptable to the Regional Director and the Director; or

(vi) Any combination of the above means.

(d) If all or part of the increase in capital required by this paragraph is to be accomplished by the sale of new securities, the board of directors of the Bank shall adopt and implement a plan for the sale of such additional securities, including the voting of any shares owned or proxies held by or controlled by them in favor of said plan. Should the implementation of the plan involve public distribution of Bank securities, including a distribution limited only to the Bank's existing shareholders, the Bank shall prepare detailed offering materials fully describing the securities being offered, including an accurate description of the financial condition of the Bank and the circumstances giving rise to the offering, and other material disclosures necessary to comply with Federal securities laws. Prior to the implementation of the plan and, in any event, not less than 20 days prior to the dissemination of such materials, the materials used in the sale of the securities shall be submitted to the FDIC Registration and Disclosure Section, 550 17th Street, N.W., Washington, D.C. 20429, and to the Department of Financial Institutions, State of Indiana, Indiana Government Center South, 402 West Washington Street, Room W066, Indianapolis, Indiana 46204, for their review. Any changes requested to be made in the materials by the FDIC or DFI shall be made prior to their dissemination.

(e) In complying with the provisions of this paragraph, the Bank shall provide to any subscriber and/or purchaser of Bank securities written notice of any planned or existing development or other changes which are materially different from the information reflected in any offering materials used in connection with the sale of Bank securities. The written notice required by this paragraph shall be furnished within 10 calendar days of the date any material development or change was planned or occurred, whichever is earlier, and shall be furnished to every purchaser and/or subscriber of the Bank's original offering materials.

(f) The capital ratio analysis required by this paragraph shall not negate the responsibility of the Bank and its board of directors for maintaining throughout the year an adequate level of capital protection for the kind, quality and degree of market depreciation of assets held by the Bank.

[.4]4. As of the effective date of this ORDER, the Bank shall pay no cash dividends which would result in a Tier 1 capital ratio of less than 8.0 percent, without the prior written consent of the Regional Director and the Director.

[.5]5. As of the effective date of this ORDER, the Bank shall eliminate from its books, by charge-off or collection, all assets or portions of assets classified "Loss" as of December 3, 2001, that have not been previously collected or charged off. Any such charged-off asset shall not be rebooked without the prior written consent of the Regional Director and the Director. Elimination or reduction of these assets with the proceeds of other Bank extensions of credit is not considered collection for the purpose of this paragraph.

[.6]6. (a) Within 45 days from the effective date of this ORDER, the Bank shall formulate and submit to the Regional Director and the Director for review and comment a written plan to reduce the Bank's risk position in each asset in excess of $100,000 which is classified "Substandard" in the Report.

In developing such plan, the Bank shall, at a minimum:

(i) Review the financial position of each such borrower, including source of repayment, repayment ability, and alternative repayment sources; and

(ii) Evaluate the available collateral for each such credit, including possible actions to improve the Bank's collateral position.

(b) Such plan shall include, but not be limited to, the following:

(i) Dollar levels to which the Bank shall reduce each asset within 6 and 12 months from the effective date of this ORDER; and

(ii) Provisions for the submission of monthly written progress reports to the Bank's board of directors for review and notation in minutes of the meetings of the board of directors.

(c) As used in this paragraph, "reduce" means to: (1) collect; (2) charge off; or (3) improve the quality of such assets so as to warrant removal of any adverse classification by the FDIC and DFI.

(d) Within 30 days from the receipt of any comment from the Regional Director and the Director, and after the adoption of any recommended changes, the Bank shall approve the written plan, which approval shall be recorded in the minutes of a board of directors' meeting. Thereafter, the Bank shall implement and follow this written plan.

[.7]7. (a) Within 90 days from the effective date of this ORDER, the Bank shall correct all documentation deficiencies in loans classified "Substandard" and loans listed for "Special Mention" in the Joint FDIC/DFI Report of Examination of the Bank as of December 3, 2001 ("Report").

(b) Following the effective date of this ORDER, the Bank's management shall submit a written progress report on correcting documentation deficiencies relating to loans classified "Substandard" and loans listed for "Special Mention" to the Bank's board of directors for review and notation in the minutes of the meetings of the board of directors.

[.8]8. (a) As of the effective date of this ORDER, the Bank shall not extend, directly or indirectly, any additional credit to, or for the benefit of, any borrower who is already obligated in any manner to the Bank on any extensions of credit (including any portion thereof) that has been charged off the books of the Bank or classified "Loss" so long as such credit remains uncollected.

(b) As of the effective date of this ORDER, the Bank shall not extend, directly or indirectly, any additional credit to, or for the benefit of, any borrower whose loan or other credit has been classified "Substandard" or is listed for Special Mention and is uncollected unless the Bank's board of directors has adopted, prior to such extension of credit, a detailed written statement giving the reasons why such extension of credit is in the best interest of the Bank. A copy of the statement shall be placed in the appropriate loan file and shall be incorporated in the minutes of the applicable board of directors' meeting.

[.9]9. (a) Within 30 days from the effective date of this ORDER, the Bank shall replenish its allowance for loan and lease losses ("ALLL") in the amount of at least $750,000.

(b) Within 30 days from the effective date of this ORDER, the Bank shall make an additional provision for loan and lease losses which, after review and consideration by the board of directors, reflects the potential for further losses in the remaining loans or leases classified "Substandard" and all other loans and leases in its portfolio. In making this determination, the board of directors shall consider the Federal Financial Institutions Examination Council ("FFIEC") Instructions for the Reports of Condition and Income and any analysis of the Bank's ALLL provided by the FDIC.

(c) Within 30 days from the effective date of this ORDER, Reports of Condition and Income required by the FDIC and filed by the Bank subsequent to December 3, 2001, but prior to the effective date of this ORDER, shall be amended and refiled if they do not reflect a provision for loan and lease losses and an ALLL which are adequate considering the condition of the Bank's loan portfolio, and which, at a minimum, incorporate the adjustments required by this paragraph.

(d) Prior to submission or publication of all Reports of Condition and Income required by the FDIC after the effective date of this ORDER, the board of directors of the Bank shall review the adequacy of the Bank's ALLL, provide for an adequate ALLL, and accurately report the same. The minutes of the board meeting at which such review is undertaken shall indicate the findings of the review, the amount of increase in the reserve recommended, if any, and the basis for determination of the amount of ALLL provided. In making these determinations, the board of directors shall consider the FFIEC Instructions for the Reports of Condition and Income and any analysis of the Bank's ALLL provided by the FDIC.

(e) ALLL entries required by this paragraph shall be made prior to any Tier 1 capital determinations required by this ORDER.

(f) While this ORDER is in effect, the Bank shall submit to the Regional Director and the Director the analysis supporting the determination of the adequacy of its ALLL. These submissions shall be made at such times as the Bank files the progress reports otherwise required by the ORDER.

[.10]10. Within 90 days from the effective date of this ORDER, the Bank shall adopt and implement a written plan to reduce the concentrations in acquisition, development, and construction loans, in commercial real estate loans, and in high loan-to-value loans, as described in the Report. Such plan shall prohibit any additional advances that would increase the concentrations or create new concentrations and shall include, but not be limited to, the following:

(a) Within 270 days of the effective date of this ORDER, concentrations as a percentage of the Bank's Tier 1 capital shall be reduced to no more than the following:

Acquisition, Development and Construction:

Residential Construction – Spec	10 Percent
Residential Construction – Presold	35 Percent
Commercial Construction	50 Percent

Residential Lot Loans	5 Percent
Subdivisions	25 Percent

Commercial Real Estate:

Office Building	35 Percent
Strip Center	5 Percent
Manufacturing	5 Percent
Wholesale	5 Percent
Retail	30 Percent
Churches	5 Percent
Warehouses	10 Percent
Other Commercial Real Estate	75 Percent
Loans Secured by Multiple Collateral	30 Percent
High Loan-To-Value Loans—All Types	100 Percent

(b) Provisions for the submission of monthly written progress reports to the Bank's board of directors for review and notation in minutes of the board of directors meetings.

(c) Establishment of procedures to ensure the accurate reporting of all concentrations to the Bank's board of directors. Reports detailing commercial real estate concentrations shall contain information regarding the specific types of credits within this concentration.

[.11]11. (a) Within 90 days from the effective date of this ORDER, and annually thereafter, the board of directors of the Bank shall review the Bank's loan policy and procedures for adequacy and,, based upon this review, shall make all appropriate revisions to the policy necessary to strengthen lending procedures and abate additional loan deterioration. The revised written loan policy and any subsequent modifications thereto shall be submitted to the Regional Director and the Director for review and comment upon their completion.

(b) The initial revisions to the Bank's loan policy required by this paragraph, at a minimum, shall include:

(i) All recommendations detailed in the Report;

(ii) A demand deposit overdraft policy; and

(iii) Review and monitoring procedures to ensure that all lending personnel are adhering to established lending procedures and that the Bank's board of directors is receiving timely and fully documented reports on loan activity, including any deviations from established policy.

(c) Within 30 days from the receipt of any comments from the Regional Director and the Director, and after the adoption of any recommended changes, the board of directors shall approve the written loan policy and any subsequent modification thereto, which approval shall be recorded in the minutes of a board of directors' meeting.

Thereafter, the Bank shall implement and follow the amended written loan policy.

[.12]12. During the life of this ORDER, the Bank shall not increase its total assets by more than 3.0 percent during any consecutive three-month period without providing, at least 30 days prior to its implementation, a growth plan to the Regional Director and the Director. Such growth plan, at a minimum, shall include the funding source to support the projected growth, as well as the anticipated use of funds. This growth plan shall not be implemented without the prior written consent of the Regional Director and the Director. In no event shall the Bank increase its total assets by more than 12 percent annually. For the purpose of this paragraph, "total assets" shall be defined as in the FFIEC's Instructions for the Consolidated Reports of Condition and Income.

[.13]13. Within 60 days from the effective date of this ORDER, the Bank shall correct the violation of section 323.5(b)(1) of the FDIC Rules and Regulations, 12 C.F.R. §323.5(b)(1) cited in the Report. Within one year from the effective date of this ORDER, the Bank shall correct the concentrations of credit leading to the violation of Part 365 of the FDIC Rules and Regulations, 12 C.F.R. Part 365, in accordance with Paragraph 10 of this ORDER.

[.14]14. (a) Within 90 days from the effective date of this ORDER, the Bank shall adopt and implement a written profit plan and a realistic, comprehensive budget for all categories of income and expense for the remainder of calendar year 2002. Within 180 days from the effective date of this ORDER, the Bank shall adopt and implement a written profit plan and a realistic, comprehensive budget for all categories of income and expense for calendar year 2003. The plans required by this paragraph shall contain formal goals and strategies, consistent with sound banking practices, to reduce discretionary expenses and to improve the Bank's overall earnings, and shall contain a description of the operating assumptions that form the basis for major projected income and expense components. A copy of the plan shall be submitted to the Regional Director and the Director upon its completion.

(b) Within 30 days from the end of each calendar quarter following completion of the profit plan and budget required by this paragraph, the Bank's board of directors shall evaluate the Bank's actual performance in relation to the plan and budget, record the results of the evaluation, and note any actions taken by the Bank in the minutes of the board of directors' meeting at which such evaluation is undertaken.

[.15]15. Following the effective date of this ORDER, the Bank shall send to its shareholders or otherwise furnish a description of this ORDER: (1) in conjunction with the next shareholder communication by holding company, Inc.; and (2) in conjunction with its notice or proxy statement preceding the next shareholder meeting of holding company, Inc. The description shall fully describe the ORDER in all material respects. The description and any accompanying communication, notice or statement shall be sent to the FDIC Registration and Disclosure Section, 550 17th Street, N.W., Washington, D.C. 20429 and to the Department of Financial Institutions, State of Indiana, Indiana Government Center South, 402 West Washington Street, Room W066, Indianapolis, Indiana 46204, for review at least 20 days prior to dissemination to shareholders. Any changes requested to be made by the FDIC or DFI shall be made prior to dissemination of the description, communication, notice or statement. Disclosure by Bank Holding Company Inc. through Form 10-K and Form 10-QSB filings with the Securities Exchange Commission ("SEC") describing this ORDER shall constitute compliance with the provisions of this paragraph, provided that the Bank notifies the Regional Director and Director in writing of its intention to comply with this provision through SEC filings.

[.16]16. (a) Within 30 days from the effective date of this ORDER, the Bank's board of directors shall have in place a program that will provide for monitoring of the Bank's compliance with this ORDER.

(b) Following the required date of compliance with subparagraph (a) of this paragraph, the Bank's board of directors shall review the Bank's compliance with this ORDER and record its review in the minutes of each regularly scheduled board of directors' meeting.

(c) Within 10 days after each board meeting following the effective date of the ORDER, the Bank shall submit to the Regional Director and Director the board packet from the board meeting.

17. Within 30 days from the end of each calendar quarter following the effective date of this ORDER, the Bank shall furnish to the Regional Director and the Director written progress reports which have been formally adopted by the Bank's board of directors, detailing the actions taken to secure compliance with the ORDER and the results thereof. Such reports may be discontinued when the corrections required by this ORDER have been accomplished and the Regional Director and the Director have, in writing, released the Bank from making further reports.

The effective date of this ORDER shall be 10 calendar days after its issuance by the FDIC and DFI. The provisions of this ORDER shall be binding upon the Bank, its institution-affiliated parties, and any successors and assigns thereof. The provisions of this ORDER shall remain effective and enforceable except to the extent that, and until such time as, any provision has been modified, terminated, suspended, or set aside by the FDIC and DFI.

Pursuant to delegated authority.   Dated: May 1st, 2002.

It's not so much that there were problems—every business deals with that—and most of the time it either doesn't come out or it comes out and it's dealt with. Granted, sometimes dealing with it means broad changes internally and externally or total collapse, as was the case with Enron and WorldCom. With hope, someone takes a modicum of responsibility. Or someone takes the fall, with reason or without.

It was obvious that we had become classified as a loan to get rid of, regardless of the process. I guessed this little love letter from the Federal Deposit Insurance Corporation (FDIC) was enough motivation and pressure for them to screw up the entire process.

Still, we continued extending offers to make the situation, no matter how badly they were making it, better. Through our attorney, I offered to meet with the bank, though I insisted on it being with senior management. Someone at the institution had to care about our outcome and take a more professional stance. The owner of the bank-like us, I would have surmised—would have the sense to want to sit down and, with calm and rational thought, devise a better plan.

I am not sure the offer went beyond their attorney. No reply came. I could not make them stop the damage their folks were doing, if in fact they were even aware and chose not to respond. I took the lack of any response as another indication as to what level of common sense, professionalism and passion they had for what they were doing.

April 27

Angee and I sat down four days later after a long and uncomfortable period of not talking about the big pink elephant that had been the last bank meeting and the resulting action. I was calm and supportive as I listened.

The TRO attorney had not, in reality, gone in to listen. Instead, almost immediately, he had begun to force a plan on the bank that he had apparently agreed to with their counsel. He never shared that conversation with Angee or me. I was sure his total ignoring of his client and failing to secure her acceptance of the negotiations was plainly mismanagement. Angee had felt blindsided as well. The bank had nothing new to say, and the rehashing got to her after more than an hour.

She had realized that most of what they were saying involved conditions that we had already chosen not to agree to. We had no motivation at this time to change that cooperation. With considerable frustration, thinking it was the best she could do, and with release of the lien on her house and her personal guarantee, the bank would go to auction.

Angee had been completely misrepresented and failed to be

informed by her attorney. At any price, but most certainly the $225 an hour we were being charged, this was highly unacceptable. I began the search for knowledgeable counsel, again.

Some one had to be empowered to handle this mess with detachment but passion, competence and unyielding strength. Angee was too sick and worn out to do it. I gently suggested that she think about giving someone-her mother, our attorney, me, it didn't matter who-power to take this weight off her.

Regular updates only when she needed to be consulted would take a huge ongoing toll off her and reduce the constant stress to short executive reviews, if she would let it. Happily, she loved the idea.

I acknowledged what Angee was going through and reassured her of my love and support. I would handle everything, if her transfer of power of attorney was to me, and if it would help her mentally and physically.

CHAPTER TEN

LEGAL ROULETTE:
RETAINER, FIGHT, LOSE, INVOICE

*"Lawyers are the only persons in whom ignorance
of the law is not punished."*
Jeremy Bentham

Transcripts from a meeting regarding the Temporary Restraining Order (tape recorded)

With Angee, our attorney, myself (Margaret) and the TRO attorney:

May 2, 2003

Our attorney: So, where are we folks?

TRO attorney: I just got here three minutes ago. And they handed me something they found on FDIC's Website about how The Bank has been cited for lax collection practices and excessive number of bad loans, which may explain why they have been pretty heavy-handed here.

Margaret: They are under a cease-and-desist from the FDIC.

Our attorney: Meaning they can't lend any more?

Margaret: As of last May.

TRO attorney: Meaning they have…cease and desist is probably the wrong term, it's the one they use here, essentially it's mandating that they ratchet up their collection practices and lower their portfolio of bad debt.

Our attorney: Um?

TRO attorney: Is there a reason that tape recorder is running?

Margaret: Just so that I can look at my notes and listen and keep track of everything.

TRO attorney: Okay.

Angee: One of my concerns from last week, when we met with you prior to the bank, was that we said let them come up with a strategy, let's all get in the same ballpark. Your stance was (that) they called this meeting, let's sit back and listen.

TRO attorney: Right.

Angee: And so we really didn't get on the same page, and when we got in the meeting, you led the meeting, which surprised me when you started out, when I thought we were there to listen.

TRO attorney: Well, I had been speaking with the bank's attorney the whole time you guys were looking at the wine, and their position was exactly kind of what I set out, the bank's attorney had asked them, explain to the bankers where you guys are coming from. So they can put together a counter-proposal, so their attorney and I had actually been talking privately for about 20, 25 minutes. Over there, [pointing to the meeting place] trying to figure out what we could do once we got the clients back in the room together. So, then when you and I had spoken, what you had wanted to do was, it was my understanding of it was, you guys wanted to reopen and sell everything in the ordinary course.

Angee: That was a while back.

TRO attorney: I thought we had discussed that just over there, no?

Angee: No.

TRO attorney: Okay.

Angee: I kind of felt blindsided by hearing from the loan officer that they had filed a response [to the TRO]; I have not seen that, nor, did we file anything?

Margaret: Well, have we filed a response to the judgment of possession?

TRO attorney: You don't file a response to the judgment of possession. Here's what was filed with the court: After the hearing, what the judge said is that we have to either agree upon terms or they would be able to file an order which had set out what the judge had ordered at the hearing. We were unable to agree, so what they did, is they prepared an order setting out what the judge had ruled, faxed it over to me for what is called 'approval of as to form,' what that means is I don't agree with what it says but I agree that it sets out exactly what the judge ordered in the hearing. Essentially, what they do is they give me advance notice that they are about to file something, to give me an opportunity to object, to say no that's not what the judge said at the hearing. They gave that to me on, I think we met on Wednesday; they gave it to me on Tuesday. Then they sent it over on Wednesday afternoon. That's entirely how the system works. The judge gave us until the Monday before to agree on something, and we were unable to agree. So there is no response we filed to that unless what they submit to the judge misstated what the judge told us he was going to rule in the courtroom.

Margaret: And was there an extension on the TRO?

TRO attorney: Yes, the judge granted a TRO when we were in the courtroom.

Margaret: To that following Monday at 5 p.m., which is, normally, which is 10 days after it?

TRO attorney: No, what the judge did, in the courtroom, was he limited the TRO to allow you to come in, use the property, filter the wine, but he extended the TRO with respect to sale of any assets until such time as the immediate possession order was entered which is especially provided for under what called the replevin statue. So, again, entirely appropriate for the bank to get such order and possession order to be entered to protect the bank's collateral.

Margaret: And so what is your thought as to what happens moving forward? Because I guess what we're feeling is, we've done a lot of…nothing really has happened that has moved the relationship or our position forward in the last five weeks.

TRO attorney: Well, let's talk about that. Our goal was, my understanding of the goal, was to first oppose the TRO, back in April, [we] went into court tried to have the TRO dissolved and we tried to have the immediate possession order either eliminated altogether or curtailed in such a manner that they had to cooperate with you as a condition of that letter, that had been entered. The judge did not dissolve the TRO, but he limited it to allow you to come in to filter the wine and do whatever was necessary other than actually sell property. Then, in terms of immediate possession, he required the bank to cooperate with you, he found in our favor, in terms of saying, yes, that the letter of agreement modifies the security agreement and it's still in force, rather than their position that was the letter agreement modifies the prior promissory note, which was replaced. So it was a partial win for us, and what it got us was not the ability to reopen the business but it was a say in how the assets get liquidated. You have the ability to come in here and make sure the assets weren't diminished and you have the authority to make the bank cooperate with you and make the bank work with you to liquidate the inventory. Over the past three or four weeks since that hearing essentially, what we have been doing is going back and forth negotiating the terms of how that was going to happen. We lost about five days when someone at the bank had a death in the family and their attorney couldn't get back with me, but other than that it's been a fairly straightforward standard negotiation process. I don't think more than two days have gone by where I haven't heard from them or they haven't heard from me. So I don't think there has been a lot of time lost in terms of spinning our wheels; what we've been doing is a lot of negotiating. Now, the last full-blown offer that we sent to them by e-mail about ten days ago, they essentially choked on it, they thought it was ridiculous, it was entirely too much for us to be demanding. And that may have slowed things down a little bit, but we have it back on the table, so to speak. When we were able to have a meeting here last week, my understanding going into that meeting was that your goal was to try and reopen the business temporarily and sell assets, sell inventory to your customers, sell assets to other people that you had been able to locate. In fact, I thought that was the conclusion when we sat over there, beforehand. When we went in to talk with them it came out, 'Forget it, let's just liquidate the inventory now."

Angee: The other things they wanted were the things (previously) in the forbearance agreement...

TRO attorney: Well, I don't think so, forbearance agreement as I read it had economic triggers rather than performance triggers, [and] in other words, even if you tried your best and did everything you were supposed to do, if the numbers weren't justifying it, they had the right to pull the plug. Under the deal that the bank's attorney and I had discussed, the numbers weren't what mattered, what mattered was that you guys were doing the right things, that you were open, and that you were maintaining a certain overhead within the budget and that you reported to them daily on money in and money out. Now, the only economic trigger was that at the end of the June 30 window, whatever you couldn't sell on your own the auctioneer would step in and sell. So it was an economic trigger that would pull the plug and say forget it, you don't get to do this any more, whatever you can't sell...the auctioneer would sell.

Margaret: Do I understand correctly, from Angee, that they didn't want us to advertise as part of this?

TRO attorney: I don't think that really...we never really got that result. At the meeting, my recollection of the meeting was that we mentioned to them that we wanted to advertise and they wanted more information; I don't think they ever said yes or no. Either way, it was just a discussion topic, and that discussion got derailed once the focus shifted to getting the auctioneers and [to] liquidate right now.

Angee: But it seemed like since you and the bank attorney had some conversations that neither the bank nor I knew about before going into that meeting, it might have been helpful to have a five-minute recap. The loan officer's boss had started to say he wanted financial pinpoints. "We can't let them just sell $2 a day..." and to that effect, there had to be some financial triggers and so to me it was going right back to the forbearance, saying you have to sell five thousand a day or else you are in violation and...

Margaret: Did they ask that, for the banking relationship to be moved to the bank?

TRO attorney: They have asked for that, it was one of the last things they had mentioned at the meeting, which was something the bank's attorney and I discussed. It does not surprise me, but they can ask all they want.

Margaret: And, with this guy coming in [auctioneer], how do you know him?

TRO attorney: I have a personal relationship, um, not personal, business relationship, he is the best auctioneer in the state, I think, My partners work with him exclusively, um, not exclusively, yeah, I think he's the only auctioneer we hire. We also represent him and his company. He did the auction of a small firm that merged into our firm last year; he auctioned off all their equipment and assets last year after the merger. I think he's the best in the business, the bank's attorney knows him as well.

Margaret: Is he married?

TRO attorney: Is he married? That I don't know.

Margaret: Well, only because what I find is interesting, there is a female with the same last name at the bank's law firm.

TRO attorney: Okay.

Margaret: And it's a rare enough name that I'm wondering whether that's a good strategy, to hire the husband of opposing counsel's firm.

TRO attorney: I don't know if that's the case but even if it is, he's an auctioneer and both the bank's law firm and Gaia Wines want to bring the highest value for this inventory. So, let's assume he is related to a lawyer at the bank's law firm, I don't think our goals here are that much different.

Margaret: I don't see much cooperation, I mean, and again I feel like we haven't moved forward in one way or another…

TRO attorney: Okay.

Margaret: As I mentioned to you as we walked out of the TRO Angee's health problems are pretty much going to make her inaccessible, if fact, this will be the last meeting she will be in…

TRO attorney: Wait a minute, let me back up for a second, what you said when we walked out of the TRO was, 'Forget it that's it, it's over, give them the keys, we don't want to sell anything for the benefit of the bank, we're done, we're filing bankruptcy, tell them to not bother drafting the order,' so I called and told them that. Then you guys call back a few days later and say you want to negotiate and you want to reopen the store…

Margaret: No, no, no, they found out that they can't sell $250,000 worth of assets without our permit, and neither can the auctioneer…

TRO attorney: Well, the auctioneer can find a way to do it…but the point that I'm making is, I feel like I'm getting some mixed messages as far as about what you guys want to do, and I understand that because this is tough for you, but it makes it difficult for me to go back to them because our, your goals, seem to be changing…

Margaret: All we did was respond and, in good faith, we were, we were done with it, okay and obviously we're five weeks into it and that doesn't do anybody any good…

TRO attorney: This thing can't happen overnight, I mean five weeks, to liquidate this size business.

Margaret: But now see, our permit, there is time sensitivity to this…

TRO attorney: Okay, there is?

Margaret: Because June 30 [when the permit to sell wine expires], not only do they not have the right to it or the auctioneer, but we don't have the right to it. We can also turn in our permit early and walk away with the wine, which I thought was an interesting fact. We responded in good faith when we got the e-mail from you, from them, basically, saying, in a sense, we thought they were saying 'Okay, you guys were right; you're the best ones to liquidate this, let's do that.' We responded to that e-mail. We have not changed our position up to that point, okay?

Angee: We had a request from them for me to go in and do the wine, and bottle it… Have we received anything from them, in writing, saying what we had agreed to last week?

TRO attorney: I asked for that and they won't give it to us, my suspicion is it's because they got the lab results, and they asked someone, and that person said the same thing you told me, that the chardonnay is no good. I asked them well over a week ago to put that in writing, and my guess is they are not going to do it.

Margaret: So, a week ago they didn't have the lab results?

TRO attorney: Whatever day it was…

Angee: So I don't have the right to sell to the folks that want the chairs or the tank because we have nothing that says the bank allows me to do that, and the bank has possession?

TRO attorney: That's right. Absolutely right.

Margaret: And you asked for attorney fees to be taken care of, which I understand, out of the immediate sale of the proceeds?

TRO attorney: I had asked for that, and they said they were going to get back to us on that. It depended on what the auctioneer's estimate would be, the result of the proceeds, and that's typical.

Margaret: And did you ask that tax liability be paid?

TRO attorney: I…[stuttering] I had asked, but that was going to be up in the air until they knew exactly what they were going to be. I had estimated about $10,000, which I think was the number you guys gave me. And they said, show us something and we will talk about it again. Depending again on what the auctioneer thinks that property is going to be at auction. I'm sensing that you guys are having some real problems in terms of the confidence in me, and if you want to shift counsel, now is the time to do it.

Margaret: Right.

Angee: And we do.

TRO attorney: Fair enough, I will step aside, send you a bill, and you can hire a new lawyer. I don't see any reason for me to be present with the auctioneer.

Margaret: That's right.

TRO attorney: Okay, I'll send you a bill; I'll be on my way. [He walked out the door].

Our corporate attorney: What's going on?

Margaret: Well, I haven't been pleased since mid-March [after the TRO]. As you know, Angee and I talked and got the whole chasm resolved and got back on the same page. What comes first and foremost is her health; she is going to be basically out of commission for the next sixty days. She has generously turned over power of attorney, and I wanted to get something that I saw as inconsistent or not in our best interest. The TRO attorney went into that meeting saying, we stood right over there, and I said to Angee, if you need anything or if feel like you're not being protected, come get me. He didn't turn and look at me, but he said, 'I'll protect her.' If you go into a meeting and you're asking a bank to pay attorney's fees, and not asking them to pay the tax liability for your own client, I understand they want to get paid. Some of the things Angee told me, I didn't see him acting in the best interest of Gaia Wines.

Angee: He thinks I did a 180. He did a 180, we tried to get on the same page with him, and he was like 'They called this meeting, we're here to listen, there is no need for us to strategize because we don't even know what they'll come up with, the ball's in their court.' And while I'm running my ass off between Mark getting the wine [samples] and BATF's counting the bottles, and stuff like that, he and the bank's attorney are talking and I have no idea what they have talked about and he goes into the meeting and starts it.

Margaret: He seems more concerned with how his friend, or personal association, the bank's attorney and how the bank view him, than protecting our interests. I had a meeting with another attorney yesterday...

Our attorney: Who was that?

Margaret: A lady at ABC firm, where the bank's attorney used to practice. And she laid it out, albeit with limited, I don't want to say limited information, time, to analyze the information, looked at the security agreement. [She] looked at our amendment to the security agreement, looked at the TRO, and looked at the filing. They went and got all the filings. I mean, we haven't even gotten this from him.

Our attorney: Uh-huh.

Angee: The TRO was released on the seventh.

Margaret: The TRO was not reissued; we could have reopened on the seventh...

Our attorney: Stop for me for a second; am I to understand that he has misunderstood entirely the court proceedings? That you guys as lay people, who are not trained...

Margaret: Yes.

Our attorney: That you guys as lay people...

Margaret: Yes.

Angee: Yes.

Our attorney: Who are not trained?

Margaret: Yes.

Our attorney: ...Understands this better?

Margaret: Yes.

Our attorney: Than he appears to?

Margaret: Yes.

Our attorney: And what you're telling me, that as of the seventh of April...

Margaret: Of April, yes, ma'am. And we asked specifically and, you know, it wasn't even Angee or me or you, who are all very smart people. It was Dawn, who is also a very smart person, she's the one who brought it up to me at lunch, saying 'Margaret, the TRO was in place for ten days, can't we reopen?' I didn't even think of that. I e-mailed the TRO attorney and said I understand that the TRO was through the seventh, has it been renewed and can I have documentation of it? He said, 'Oh yeah, it's still in effect.' Well, according to the summaries that ABC [firm] got, it was never renewed, we had complete operational control after the seventh, [and] in addition to that, we were to file a response to the judgment of possession, it was to be our side of our plan, and that was to be done in twenty days, which would have been the 27th.

Our attorney: The response time.

Angee: Possession wasn't granted until the 28th.

Margaret: Which was a couple of days ago, and he missed the deadline, in addition to that…

Our attorney: I'm, um…

Margaret: I'm sorry, go ahead.

Our attorney: I…just a little shocked, certainly this is an avenue for what's called malpractice, there may be some avenue to compensation, so just duly note.

Margaret: According to the lady, the filing of the TRO was inaccurate and could have been dismissed because of the way it was filed. There is a breach of contract on the part of the bank, which she feels is a fairly significant countersuit and that the mere presentation of that issue that what had been done so far was not in our best interest, nor was it aggressive lawyering against a bank that was in trouble. She said they're going to push cause their under cease and desist…so I called FDIC.

Our attorney: Okay.

Margaret: See, I got a lot of free time, so I play lawyer…Called FDIC in Chicago and in Washington, the lady that handles the bank's case, all she kept saying to me was, 'They shut you down? They shut you down?' Yes, ma'am, we're under a temporary restraining order, I understand they're under a cease and desist; does it have any impact on the FDIC, and your proceedings with them, if we file a complaint? And she said, 'They shut you down?' Yes, ma'am, we announced that we were going out of business February 28, it was our best intention and our sole goal to take care of as many creditors as possible, with the bank being the first in position and being secured to take care of them first, we laid out the plan and less than thirty days later they placed us under a TRO. We can't make the loan payment. And she said, 'That's interesting, they shut you down?' She kept saying it over.

Our attorney: She couldn't get over it?

Margaret: No, she kept saying, see, you have to understand if they are under pressure to collect the loan, if we can't open, it can't happen. So she sent me around to a couple of different people, a couple of different addresses; in addition the counsel we met with yesterday said there is a significant breach of contract issue because the court has already validated the amendment to the security agreement, which is what gives us 90 days, the bank didn't allow us to do that, that's breach of contract...we are no more...

Our attorney: It's contemptuous.

Margaret: Yes, we are no more liable to execute on what Angee signed off on than they are to execute what they signed on...they say 'Yeah, we signed this, the court says this is a valid amendment to the security agreement,' and yet they didn't act under it, which she said is a breach of contract and a violation of the security agreement.

Our attorney: What are her thoughts?

Margaret: Her thoughts are, she used to work with a bank, so she understands the business, she says that not only should we be able to recover operation if we so desire, but she also believes there is a case to not even have to pay the bank and we can counter sue for these other things that happened.

Angee: She said we should have never gone in front of that judge.

Margaret: When our attorney walked in, she said the judge, who is in Court Five, would have never let this happen.

Our attorney: I agree.

Margaret: This was a substituted judge; we should have said, look, we have some issues here which you probably don't have time to brief yourself on, very nice...

Angee: I could have been sick, gone to the bathroom to throw up, something, so we had to continue it.

Margaret: And I said, this isn't the regular judge, and I said, do we still want to meet in front of him? And the TRO attorney said, 'Well, if we tell him we don't want to meet in front of him, then we've pissed him off. But no, he's not really the judge to see.' So our own attorney acknowledged this was a substitute teacher, I know, judge pro tem, but in terms of knowledge, the judge was running late, we had a 10 o'clock court time, his 9 o'clock ran to 11:25 am, we got in at 11:25 a.m., he wanted out in time for lunch, so we didn't have a full hour. So there were just a ton of things that happened from the start, she didn't dismiss him personally, because she didn't know him and the firm's good. I don't understand why all these mistakes were made; this guy's a rookie? I said no, this guy's a partner. And she said 'What?' He's a partner there, and she says this is…she was starting to get furious, she says you guys are getting raked over the coals, you guys are getting screwed up the ass, and none of the things that should happen from a competent lawyer standpoint. I mean basic stuff like telling your client you can go in after the seventh because they have not issued another TRO, and the guy I originally talked to was so sweet, he went and got all this, and I asked the TRO attorney a week ago, do they have possession, have we filed our counter? And we…

Angee: He said you don't need to do that.

Margaret: No, you have twenty days to do that.

Our attorney: It's all just hanging out there…

Margaret: All our requests are here in e-mails here to meet to strategize, this is the third time, we've been dealing with him for five weeks, this is the third time we've had a meeting, it lasted 20 minutes, the total cumulative meeting time with him face to face, you know, he says, I'm getting confused I'm getting mixed messages. How about showing up to a meeting and staying longer than 20 minutes to really put together a strategy that we can all stick with instead of just jumping through the hoops that the bank gives. And of course this is very typical, our meeting last week was at 1:30, he wants to meet at 1:15. Is 15 minutes enough time for us to be on the same page? He walked around, he looked at stuff [in the winery], I don't know what's going on, [and] I don't know if he wants to jump ship [or] impress the bank's attorney…

Angee: Or he just has bigger fish in…

Margaret: [with] ABC, can't even touch their retainer... they want $2,500 and she said it could go $5,000 to $10,000.

Our attorney: If she saves the assets.

Margaret: What I did was call three or four firms, I said I want your bitchiest female attorney, and they were like, 'Excuse me?' This one lady says, 'Well we have a couple of them.' I want a ball buster...

End of transcript

Right after that meeting, we had been scheduled to meet with the auctioneers. Although it was no longer part of the plan agreed to by the TRO attorney, we had no time to cancel the meeting. As our attorney and Angee left, I waited for the loan officer and the auctioneer.

For a brief moment, we had no legal representation. Our attorney would have to play catch-up as we waited to bring on our new powerful, attorneys from the big firm. I asked and received permission to record the meeting for the benefit of our legal representation.

AUCTIONEER MEETING, May 2, 2003

[Transcribed from tape recording]

The auctioneer (TA): I only brought one packet with me. Basically, our company is a 12-year-old company, my prior life I was in industrial manufacturing, and the last ten years of that were sales and marketing, so I have a lot of sales and marketing experience, and that is basically the main function of our business, we are marketing people. The auctioneer is important, I mean, anybody can get up there and say five-ten-fifteen-twenty, bid calling, the most important aspect is the marketing. If you don't have people standing in front of you when you are selling, you are not going to get anything worth what you are selling. And the number of people that attend the sale directly corresponds to the dollar value; the more people, the more dollars. Very basic. We do not specialize in one area of business or another; we sell everything from ostrich farms to large manufacturing, retail and everything in between. I brought one marketing packet which gives you examples of advertising we do. I like to do full-color brochures because that catches their eye better, two-color is not too bad, we do take

digital photos, I write the advertising myself, I determine the marketing, the target market we're going to mail to; we use a combination of
purchased [mailing] lists, which I will buy, which for this specialized
list by standard industrial codes, SIC, and will pick out SIC categories
in this area, we will do a nationwide, if there are 2,700 [wineries] we
will mail, depending on the value of the whole deal, we mail about
3,500 brochures like this to make sure that we reach the industry for
the higher dollars, and we'll do some newspaper advertising locally,
we have a Web site that gets a lot of action, um, people check our Web
site all the time, for the local, regional types, they will be the most
likely buyers of your light fixtures, tables, chairs, and a lot of your gift
items. The combination of all that, these forms of advertising, will
result in the best opportunity to recover the maximum for the bank or
whoever the beneficiary of the sale will be. We conduct a lot of bankruptcy sales, a lot or working sales with banks, we work for most of the
banks in this area at one time or another and I have a reference list,
which I'll be happy to provide. I believe that's basically what we do. I
would like to know a bit more, and the good thing about not special-
izing is that we don't get lazy. Every deal is new, fresh ideas, fresh mail
list, so you don't get a mail list I used a year ago, which is probably
half out of date, the mail list changes so quickly, so we use that, we
use a fresh purchase list and we augment that with our own customer
database that is customized by the things they buy.

The loan officer (LO): How much time would you anticipate
needing to get a sale like this together?

TA: The normal is four to six weeks, if you require it done faster, the
longest lead item is the brochure. I would need, saying you want to
move this along quickly, I mean this is all money that's just sitting here
doing nothing, and naturally, we like to turn it into cash…as quickly
as feasibly possible, and reasonable. The timing in general, it takes
me a week to week and a half to get all the marketing determined, get
a listing, get photos, get on our schedule, then I get it to my printer,
he can turn these brochures around in four days. Have them in the
mail, so that's two and one-half weeks. So we can have a sale in four
weeks at the earliest.

LO: Would you be opposed, or would you be open to consideration, if we…if you were to only look at certain items, like just the gift

shop inventory, versus the winemaking equipment and table and chairs if we were to split it up? If we asked you to handle one bulk sale pertaining to gift shop, is that something that is too small?

TA: We would do it; is there a reason why you're asking?

LO: Well, there seems to be another winery, another gentleman in the area that buys and sells used wine equipment throughout the Midwest, throughout the country, and he's been in several times looking at the equipment and he's been able to give us a ballpark on certain items, and I think with his contacts, and that's what he does for a living, with his contacts it might be more beneficially, potentially, actually, to use him for that function; maybe not, I don't know…

TA: I would say, generally speaking I would disagree with that.

LO: Okay.

TA: Because we will market to end users, because the end user will pay more than dealers, the dealer will pay just a small fraction of what the on-the-street market is, 'cause they got to make money and they got to buy it as cheap as they can. Where we, our marketing, is going to be geared to the end user, instead of the dealers, we will invite the dealers. However, I says 90 percent plus of the time [we] sell to end users.

LO: Well, I don't think he'll want to buy, and then resell; with his contacts he would point us to the end user, the other local, mom and pop, wineries…

TA: Well, that may be good if you can sell to the end user, if you can sell and get a good return.

LO: What are your thoughts about the wine…are you allowed to…

TA: I'm looking into that, in fact. I was talking to your lawyer about it, and I think he said he was checking with some people, um, but why couldn't… and is this business still licensed?

Margaret: Yes.

TA: …Is the business able to sell it? And we just auction it on behalf of the business?

LO: Yeah, possibly, yeah.

TA: I don't think there'll be a problem with that, but I can check with my attorney and find out if that would be reasonable. Now, would this be a court-ordered sale?

LO: Probably, it will be, I think we're still striving for a mutually agreed-upon sale, but I think it will be court-directed.

TA: 'Cause, I know the court, they have a lot more clout than, you know, just to sign directly with the seller. Court-ordered sales, generally no one is going to question it.

LO: Okay. Well, from what you've seen here today, I know you just did a quick walk-through, I know with table and chairs, fixtures maybe just excluding the wine, tanks, barrels, equipment what do you think the success of the sale would be?

TA: It's always better to have to the entire company, the entire package, because the wine-making equipment is going to draw people, and as long as they are here to buy winemaking equipment, they may buy some of the inventory and may even buy more, because they already sell it or stock it in their businesses, where Joe off the street, if he was just buying to get a cheap deal.

LO: Okay.

TA: So I'm thinking if the whole package was together it would do more success, if it, the wine-making equipment...but I still believe the auction sale is the best way to sell it rather than have a garage sale.

LO: Okay.

Margaret: What fees are associated with your services?

TA: Um, usually our fees consist of commission and expenses, and it varies depending on the size of the deal. Generally speaking, our fees range 10 percent plus or minus commission to the seller; we do tack a 10 percent on to the buyer. If the deal is sizable enough we will work out our commission, but really I don't know what we have here, but I'd say it would be in the 10 percent range. Depending on what the value of the winery equipment is...

LO: Okay.

TA: And expenses would be advertising and the labor to get the sale ready and conduct the sale.

LO: Would you suggest that that take place here? At this location, or somewhere else?

TA: Yes, absolutely, I think here is the best place.

LO: Why is that?

TA: It's just a phenomenon; I don't know what it is, if you take...whether office furniture or retail items out of the place where it came from, the value seems to go down, that's just how it is. I don't know why, it's just how it is. We have had businesses where we had to move the furniture, computers, to a warehouse setting or an auction setting, and they are out of place. And people don't pay as much for them.

LO: Okay, would you look at this as a weekend type sale or a week-night?

TA: I'd say the business assets are best sold during the week, because business people generally don't want to go to auctions on the Saturdays.

LO: Okay.

TA: The retail crowd might be a little different so if we were doing just the retail, but even if on Saturday you're competing with a lot of garage sales, estate sales, there are a lot more auctions on Saturday that are for the general public. It depends on what we have, you know, the tables, chairs, lighting; they'd be better during the week. The inventory, it could go either way…

LO: Okay. How far in the process do you get before you could tell us a value, a potential value? I guess I assume we have to come in and do the inventory, do the research, to find out what it goes for, to give us a ballpark figure, I know there's no guarantee.

TA: Sure, I can give you a ballpark figure. What would help me greatly is if I can get an inventory listing, an assets listing if those are available, if they have costs on them. That's better, it just makes things a lot faster, otherwise I'd be starting from scratch, and basically trying to inventory everything, and that would take a lot of time and may be unnecessary.

Margaret: When you talk about expenses, what are those normally…turn out to be?

TA: It varies from sale to sale, but I'll be able to ballpark that for you and get you a written proposal spell those out in the written proposal.

LO: The bank's attorney has a copy of the inventory…I'll send him an e-mail and ask him to get those to you; I think he's out of the office. It'll be Monday.

TA: Okay; it'll be a fun sale…

LO: Like, the chairs, the folding chairs, we got someone interested in them at 20 bucks a chair. The folding chairs in the back, padded…is that something you could do better at, at a sale?

TA: I can look at them.

LO: Padded.

TA: That may not be bad.

LO: I thought that was a decent price…

TA: Now these [looking at tasting-room chairs] are nicer chairs.

LO: This is what the guy bought, right? Okay, 'cause, as people, as Gaia got the word out about selling some stuff, there were responses to that notice, so people are calling the bank, calling me, and I want to put a list together of what people are interested in. I'd just as soon…some of these people we can possibly get a premium off of as opposed to an auction sale. But I don't want to let a twenty-dollar chair go if you think you can get thirty.

TA: Right; I'll be glad to look at it. And if there are opportunities, and I look at it, if you hire us we're partners, we're here to achieve the same goals, and that's to get as much money as possible, and if someone comes up prior to the sale and offers us a great deal, on whatever, I'm not opposed to selling it if we all believe it's in the best interest of the seller.

LO: All right.

TA: All I need…if I could get a listing of the assets and inventory, and I'll take one more walk through and try to ballpark what the labor might be and I'll operate on a pretty firm proposal of how we would approach it, the timelines and so forth. Is this something where you're pretty ready to proceed?

LO: Yeah, from our standpoint we are.

TA: Good.

LO: I think June 30th is when the license, alcohol license, expires, so from that standpoint that's hanging out there.

TA: Okay, so we'll be getting you a proposal, you'll review it, decide if we're going to go ahead, get a motion filed, twenty days notice, but we can work during that notice period, as long as we don't anticipated anybody, throwing us off. [To me] And if you're on board I don't think we have to worry about anybody else. I'd be comfortable getting started, and having the sale within a week or so after getting the approval.

LO: Has your company ever handled a going-out-of-business sale, as far as staffing it, and running the register, and all those kind of things?

TA: Yes.

LO: Okay, so that's a service you offer as well.

TA: Most recently we did a flower store on [inaudible] street. We sold out of there, the gift shop. We had a lot of collectables; we came out with over $100,000 that we sold for them.

LO: And on that you still handle the advertising and the same thing...

TA: Hey, we handle everything, spell it out in advance what that would be; we handle the labor, we'd spell it out, the labor, the commission. That may work out a little better, especially if we can do it in a short time frame, maybe there's two weekends we can do it.

LO: Yeah, that's a possibility.

TA: If you'd like a proposal on that, I can outline that for you.

LO: Yeah, that would be interesting.

TA: That'd be a good way to get a little more net out of inventory because...

LO: This kind of inventory.

TA: Well, actually...

LO: March 19 they're showing a retail inventory of $118,000.

TA: Is that including the wine?

LO: No. Well, it might include the stuff on the retail floor... [To me] can you comment on that? [I shake my head no]. No, okay. There are boxes and empty bottles as well, wine bottles, and not bottled, not filled or corked or anything.

TA: Okay.

LO: There is a discrepancy as to the value of the wine itself. We can't offer you anything firm on that as to what's here, what's not here.

TA: Okay, because that could be a real good draw, selling that wine, wine and gifts, get a little cheese [laughing] you know have a pretty good sale. If you could find out more about that, 'cause that'll make a big difference in the response we might get.

LO: I will do that; I'm waiting on our attorney to get back to the office.

TA: Okay, what we've done in a couple of cases with going-out-of-business sales, we may have a going-out-of-business sale, um, like Thursday, Friday, or Wednesday, Thursday Friday, whatever makes sense, and then have an auction on the next day. On whatever's left…because on this kind of auction, we may not tag every item like we normally would; we just put them in lots. And have seating and just bring it up in front of the crowd, and show it to them and have them bid on it. And just keep shuffling the merchandise around, that's probably the best way to do this kind of…type of merchandise as far as an auction goes. We'll be glad to help you in any way we can, any questions you have. Thank you very much. Many types of sales large and small… [Walking to the back to look at chairs] Are these all separate shops?

Margaret: Upstairs? Yes.

LO: There are 124 chairs left.

TA: These might bring more, we have a restaurant and equipment store also, that my brother runs, and we sell chairs like this, we would probably sell these chairs for closer thirty bucks than twenty; you put them in auction, you're taking a chance basically. You know what the cost was? [I shake my head yes].

TA: Well, would you tell me?

Margaret: I'd have to look it up.

TA: The artwork, is that for sale?

LO: Is that something you get a lot of interest in?

TA: Um, sometimes, it varies depending on the sale; we've had sales where the artwork brought big money, others where they brought very little. But I think the type of people that would come to a sale like this, especially if we have that wine, we're going to get a lot more affluent people, than if we don't.

Margaret: Thank you.

LO: Thanks, Margaret. [I lead them out].

TA: Nice to meet you.

Margaret: Nice to meet you; thank you for your time.

Chapter Eleven

What Asset Destruction? Destroyed but not defeated

*"When you are getting bitch-slapped with a fish,
you got to say something smelly."*
MEJB, January 2003

"Banking may well be career from which no man really recovers."
John Kenneth Galbraith

May 6

Our attorney was not comfortable taking the lead in this case, and thought she would do us a great disservice by delving into an area with which she was not familiar. Had we been dealing cocaine instead of wonderful wine, she would have been our "go to" gal. On more than one occasion, however, she chose to bow to someone else's expertise.

After the rush job with the TRO attorney, I felt that looking for an attorney was much like looking for capital: You never stop the search. I called the next three top law firms, knowing that the bank had the number one ranked firm by size and our recent problems with number two left us to move down the list of top law firms list.

My message was received as odd at first. I called each firm and said I wanted to be put in touch with their bitchiest female litigator. One receptionist laughed with confusion.

"Is there a problem?" I asked.

"No, it's just that we have more than one female attorney like that," she said through her laughter.

After checking any conflict of interest, and a nice phone conversation with the head of litigation, I was meeting with a woman from a high-ranking firm.

She was a larger woman, and clearly not a people person. I had dropped off the loan documents and a $500 retainer before the meeting. Whether there had been a lot of time spent was unclear, but after I recounted our TRO outcome, she seemed well prepared to respond to the issues.

"There were a ton of things done wrong here, and in very basic terms, you got screwed," she said.

"It does feel like that, that nothing is going as it should," was my enlightened response.

I was encouraged that she practiced law in the banking arena and knew the bank's attorney, one who had left her firm some years earlier. She was not impressed with his abilities, and intimated that he had left their firm under a cloud of uncertainty. I took it all with a grain of salt, assured that she was just trying to impress a potential new client.

She went on to systematically outline where the TRO and banking process had gone wrong. With our security agreement amendment and the bank's unwillingness to honor it, the bank had instantaneously put themselves in a breach-of-contract position. Based on that alone, she felt there was good reason to void our obligation of loan repayment. She also felt we had a significant breach-of-contract counter-suit pending for damages. Our dim circumstances began to look like an opportunity that could turn out better than past months had indicated.

She was equally amazed with the outcome of the temporary restraining order hearing. On the filing status alone, she was confident it should have been tossed.

"I don't like to speak badly about another attorney," she started. Of course, I thought as I let her continue her train of thought. "But this was procedurally filed wrong, and even a junior attorney like this should have been able to catch it; it's one of the first things you look for."

"It wasn't a junior attorney; it was a partner in the firm's corporate law division," I responded.

"What? You are kidding me, right?" she asked. Sadly, I wasn't.

"That is inexcusable. Who did you go before?" she asked, turning to the head of her litigation team.

"A judge pro tem," he quickly responded.

"A substitute judge," I repeated under my breath.

"The judge would have never let this happen; you should have never gone in front of this other guy," she said.

She was getting the picture into focus and confirming things that should have never happened. Yet it had all happened right down the line.

The retainer was way out of our reach, but I knew Angee had thought her sister might be willing to help out. Even though the attorney thought the fees could go as high as $10,000, she agreed to just wanting $2,500, maybe $5,000, to start. I wanted to see what she could do, in short order, before I issued a check. She agreed to call opposing counsel and have an initial conversation.

I asked for a follow-up meeting with our attorney the next week, before she did anything. A second opinion from a legal mind that was aware of our side would be valuable. It also allowed time for meetings I had with other attorneys set for the rest of the week. I wanted to take what little time we had to make a better decision this time around.

May 7

I received an e-mail from the woman at the firm after she and our attorney had bonded. I was more impressed with their take on our attorney than with their stuffy paneled walls and large conference areas. She did have a conversation with opposing counsel and had obligated me to a walk-through with the loan officer and a contacted buyer, according to her. This other winery was apparently ready to hand over $100,000 for their choice of inventory.

With my agreement to walk through on Friday, she saw a quick end to the bank's control and the required TRO action.

I wished I wasn't so pessimistic, but I couldn't believe there was a winery with access to that kind of money ready to spend it on Friday. It couldn't be that quick a done deal. Nonetheless, I agreed to meet with the loan officer and his winery contact at 1:30 on Friday.

May 8 the next attorney

Our attorney and I had always maintained that procedurally, the bank must have failed to do something significant. It was the cover-up that was motivating all these fumbling counter-moves.

Happily, the next attorney at the 4th largest law firm could not have been nicer. Again, he had come from the banking arena, and he spent two full and painfully long hours organizing and reviewing the loan documents.

His assessment was not encouraging. Based on what he saw, there had been nothing done wrong, no bad filings, no lack of securing the collateral with the state through a Uniform Commercial Code filing.

The Uniform Commercial Code (UCC) allows for a state-filed lien on assets, which is common practice when a bank makes a loan. But there was some doubt as to how often that had to be updated and whether the bank had even filed it with regularity. I was discouraged that I had not walked away with something substantial, but thanked him for his time. He promised to come to the auction and help by buying things at basement prices.

When I got home, I was convinced that I had to call the bank's buyer contact and confirm what I thought was going to happen.

My call to the potential buyer was short but telling. She was not, in fact, going to buy a large amount. Basically, she wanted a walk-through prior to auction. I asked directly what kind of budget she had to work with.

With her answer, I wondered how attorneys could be so bad at asking questions when so much of what they do is reaction to the answer. She had no more than a few thousand for trinkets, maybe a fermentation tank or two. But she had no intention of spending $100,000 to relinquish the bank's position.

I said nothing more, and confirmed to see her at 1:30 p.m. and ask her to call me if she felt she would not be able to make it, or if what she thought she would be getting was any different, anything more. She agreed.

May 9

I arrived early and went through messages and mail before anyone got there. The potential buyer and her husband showed up before the loan officer did. I took his lateness as another sign of his indifference and lackluster view on how to handle the issues pending with Gaia Wines.

In the short time I was there, no fewer than 10 people came to the door wanting to purchase, some from out of town. As kindly and calmly as I could, told them we remained closed. I asked them to check back later, certain that many of them never would. I watched despondently as more sales opportunities walked away.

When the loan officer arrived, he was even more embarrassingly disorganized than I had thought. My impression was that this was his meeting and he would be anxious to get the loan off his books. But he was without the inventory sheet and did not know pricing or what terms he could agree to. He did manage to blame it all on his attorney.

The phone continued to ring, and as I walked the husband-and-wife team through, I handed the phone questions to the loan officer. He took more than one message to call people back regarding sales and other business issues. But I knew it would never happen. With the loan officer unable to close the deal with the potential buyer, I sped along the process with the need to get to another meeting. The woman and her husband left 45 minutes later and with no purchases. I was upset at the waste of time, and happy to see the bank and the loan officer, in particular, failing so badly at running the closing of our business. But being right was no comfort to the damage they were doing, not just to the value of the assets but also to the value of what we had built and our reputation.

Somehow I found the ability to hold out an olive branch to the loan officer, in an effort to save him and the business from what was a fast, massive downward spiral. I made him aware of the issues that they were not dealing with.

"You have a security issue with the back door open and access to the wine and merchandise. I have been here more than once, with it open," I continued, so he would understand. "People are coming and going with no one to watch what is leaving. It creates a license issue with the ATF and the state. I am sure you are concerned about the bank's assets."

"Oh yeah, I will talk with the landlord about that," he said as he jotted a note.

"Also, the wine here was set to be bottled when you closed us down; it is at risk. It needs to be stabilized and bottled," I said.

"Right," He seemed glazed over. "What will that take?"

I was vague, but I made his job seem what it was, something he couldn't do. "Well, you need the supplies, then the labor to do it, someone with a permit, and chemicals," I answered.

The loan officer was changing colors as we spoke, red with embarrassment and white with fear. In a moment of compassion, I did the adult thing and held out another olive branch. I was standing behind our large custom-made copper tasting bar as I spoke.

"You know, this may have gotten out of hand very quickly with the lawyers and all," I said. I too would blame the attorneys. The loan officer was about three feet away from me at that point.

"I think we could probably get back to a logical process, if it was just you and me. We had a good working relationship at one point," I said.

"Well, yeah, but your lawyer, at that meeting, that got nothing accomplished." He was missing the point.

"Neither lawyer was effective in getting anything done. Yours was not even aware of the issues, but that's not what I am talking about," I replied.

I was not going to say that anything bad about our attorney, because she did exactly what we wanted. It was just was not the "rolling over" the bank had wanted and had probably come to expect. Another strong female was more than these boys from small-town Indiana could handle.

Another thing was happening as we talked. The loan officer began slowly, and with noticeable fear, moving back from the tasting bar, or more correctly, from me. I continued anyway.

"I think if we sat down and went over the issues logically we could get the winery reopened and get the process going. It has been six weeks and nothing has happened. You are not getting your money any faster than what our plan outlined," I offered.

"But we need to know where the money is going; I mean the land-lord tells me you haven't paid rent in a year." Now, he was falling back on lies and misinformation. Before it had even begun, our commu-nication was breaking down. "And there have been no loan payment; where is the money going?"

"You have three years of financials, and you are misstating those issues; we have paid rent monthly. Sometimes we were not able to pay the full amount, but he always got something. And the bank is current until you closed us down," I said. He moved back again, and I tried to redirect our efforts.

"Well, you think about it." I continued to back off on whatever was threatening him. "I'll be around this weekend; you can e-mail me if you want to get together on Monday. If I don't hear from you, I will assume you are not interested in resolving any of thisinterested."

He stepped back again, and now was not at a realistic talking distance. I moved from behind the bar, as he mumbled while moving backwards.

"I'll talk to our attorney, and see what he says," he said. It was a poor attempt at a stall, and I knew I would not hear from him. "Where is the landlord's office?" he inquired on his way out the door. It was the only place he could continue to back into.

"Go to the corner and turn, he is on the other side of the build-ing," I offered. He thanked me for opening up, and I knew it would be the last "one to one" conversation we would have. I was also painfully aware that he was no longer an advocate for our business, nor inter-ested in doing the right, rational thing. It followed that he did not want to accept help to rectify the damage the bank continued to generate.

As he had walked away, so did I, from any desire to help make their mess better.

The next week, Angee left for a long weekend of rest and relax-ation at her sister's home on the East Coast. She and her mother were driving to New Jersey; to what we had all hoped would be a peaceful time away. When she called the first night from a hotel, as always, I could tell in her voice how she was feeling.

She was in serious pain and in the middle of nowhere, a hotel in Pennsylvania, at about the midpoint of the drive I could tell she was frustrated by the inability to turn back and be home. The other choice of a long drive to the Newark airport was no better option. If she didn't feel noticeably better, which was unlikely, she would hop a plane home the next day.

I did a terrible job at hiding my anger and disappointment. Without a doubt, she was in a lot of pain, and I could do nothing to help her. I offered to drive out and meet her, but as much pain as there was, another long drive only meant another thirteen hours of pain.

I was angry at a disease that was controlling our lives with such unpredictability and that plans were never set. Even dates with the simplest tasks were often broken. I was anger that I would lose the first weekend in a while where I thought I would only have to take care of myself. Of course I would pick her up at the airport, but I couldn't shove any more anger down and pretend that time, for and about me, wasn't important. It was just one part of the weekend that would not be about me.

May 16-18

When I found out that the deal to resolve the whole mess was a sham, I lost faith in the attorney who had set it up. But the woman was able to remove herself, much like so many of our salespeople.

It was a surprise to receive an e-mail saying that they could not represent us due to the unlikelihood that they would recover their fees. I had never told them about the ability to pay the retainer, and instead had chosen to see what they could do and how they could do it before they sat on a huge (at least for us) chunk of cash.

I received my deposit and all the information back before I could share with them how the meeting had gone. I would find out that they had asked opposing counsel if attorney' fees would be paid from the assets' proceeds. Did they really expect the bank to say yes? I wondered what had happened to the conviction of the cause and the huge countersuit that was possible. What had become of the legal right we had to defend ourselves, and the right, as it was explained to me, that the bank could not stand in our way regarding a defense?

Again, I had mixed feelings-anger at the legal process, and at the same time, relieved that they had shown their own lack of ability to believe in the cause before there had been an investment made. The investment in a retainer, at that point, would not even have been ours. As conservative as I could be with our money, I loathed using others' money ineffectively.

Our corporate attorney had agreed to be back on the case the week before. What she may have thought she lacked in legal experience with this type of case, she compensated for a thousand times over in her passion and belief in us! I was convinced that would get us where we needed to be. She had a history with us and was a part of the early struggles with the bank. She was the pit bull we were looking for.

Her own struggles with cancer, law school, and a difficult family made her a strong female presence, and together, as she had often said, we made a team to be reckoned with.

Still, I was surprised when I returned home that Friday to not one but three of her calls.

"Get to the winery now. Open up and SELL, SELL, SELL!"

"Where are you at? Go to the store, open the doors and do some business."

"Call me; you're 'on' to open."

She had influenced opposing counsel that we were the best to create and retain value. The weekend was a big "avenue" event that I had mentioned was a good chance for us to make some money. Our attorney had taken that idea and turned it into a chance to prove us right.

Without hesitation, I headed into the winery and was open by 4:45 p.m. In my haste I had forgotten to get money for the cash drawer, but it didn't hinder our sales. People were happy to use credit cards or checks and seemed extremely happy that we were open. In three hours, with no notice, we had done better than on most regular business days. I was cautiously optimistic.

The next day, with cash in hand from our personal account, I opened up and began e-mailing and faxing guests to generate traffic. The sale was still on, and traffic remained steady throughout the day. At the end, we again had a solid sales day.

Even though there were closing sale prices with decent discounts, all but a few people did not take advantage of the volume purchasing. It was still a tough economy and people still were holding onto most of their money. But almost intuitively, most felt the urgency of the closing and the uncertainty of our business hours.

Dawn took over on Sunday. We doubled the sales from Saturday. Overall, the weekend was on par with a slow January-the whole month of January! We had, as our attorney had hoped and I knew, proved our point to the bank. We were the best people to handle the closing sales. In two days we had generated more cash than the bank had done in eight weeks under their control.

Based on the terms of the deal outlined by the bank, outside of expenses, the money from the weekend was to go to the loan. We were to stay open and continue the closing process, albeit an accelerated process. Our permit would run out in six weeks. After that, selling the remaining wine would not be legal. The bank had used this weekend to gauge our success, and no one could argue that it wasn't exceptional, even amazing, given the short notice.

Waiting for a bank meeting was a painful four days, four more days that we could have been selling-a time frame that I am sure did more to damage our value and reputation. Anybody who had received e-mails or heard of the weekend's "last minute" opening would be coming in during the next few days. Seeing us not opened would show us as unprofessional and cause for valid concern. And I was concerned.

Our attorney asked me to bring the receipts and a check to the meeting with the bank attorney that Thursday. I wondered, as did our attorney, what had taken so long. At the same time, we had become used to their "hurry up and wait" attitude. The only emergency was their lack of planning.

May 22

Fighting a bit of a cold, I grabbed some tea and went outside the Starbucks to wait with our attorney. We talked briefly about pending issues. She mentioned that opposing counsel had been having problems with his clients, that there might be a change in attitude. I must not have been paying attention, because I didn't understand the statement.

The bank's attorney arrived as we were sitting down. He had a "typical attorney in a big law firm" look to him-power tie and a nice suit-still, he looked a little nerdy. He grabbed some coffee and made a big production of taking his time, cleaning his sunglasses with his tie.

Our attorney made introductions and began discussing our success with the weekend sale.

"I have a question," I said to the bank's attorney. "Who was the third guy in the meeting about a month ago?" No one had ever introduced the bank president, and I found his presence at the meeting and his lack of involvement interesting, if not questionable.

"That was," he replied, "was the bank president."

I knew before I asked, having seen his picture in the paper. I had never met him personally, and since I had not been in the meeting a month earlier, I would probably miss the pleasure altogether. I had thought his attendance had meant progress. Unfortunately, it did not.

"And why was he there?" I inquired.

The bank's attorney stumbled a bit, and I again wondered how he justified his $350-an-hour fees while being so ill-prepared. Why did they never expect us to ask questions? Did they really think this hit-and-run was going to take place without witnesses? Without any questions?

"Well, as I understand it" (lawyer-speak for "I am making this up,") "he was between meetings with the other guys and just tagged along to observe."

A less involved person might have believed him. That's how he made his money. It was doubtful that the bank president had time, or should have time, to attend a meeting for this size of loan. With the problems the bank had created, the bank president took on a greater level of arrogance by not becoming involved in what was obviously a huge miscalculation on his team's part.

We went over the receipts as I left the president attendance at the meeting alone.

The bank's attorney asked for a full inventory update. The computer program didn't allow for just those days, and I would have to run the entire report again. The weekend didn't leave us time to do that, but I offered to get it done the next open day. Then, the bank's lawyer turned to address our attorney. "The bank has had a change of heart about this" he said.

Our attorney looked as shocked as I did, and I felt blindsided. We had gone in again and generated cash to improve their position, yet they were changing course without reason. I was finished saving their asses or to put it nicely, trying to help.

"I don't understand; can you explain that to me?" our lawyer asked.

The bank's attorney answered uncomfortably, "They don't want to incur the costs associated with reopening. They felt it would be too much money, expenses" I could feel the rage as it consumed me from the inside out.

The bank would pay an auctioneer and sell for pennies on the dollar, but an electric bill and hourly wages were out of the question.

In that moment, our agreement had changed. When it did, so did every plan that had been laid out. The bank's attorney moved into the request for funds. I interrupted without apology and addressed our attorney. "Could I talk to you for a minute?" She politely excused herself, and we walked around the corner for privacy.

"Unless you order me to, with good reason, I am walking out of this meeting and he is not getting a check for the balance of the funds," I said. Our attorney looked as shocked at me as she had been with the bank's attorney's announcement.

I persisted. "I am sick of this crap and game playing. Is there a reason he should get a check?"

"Well, they may consider it conversion, not handing over money that is theirs," she replied.

"No, when they change the rules, everything changes. Will I go to jail for this?" I said.

"No, it's more like white-collar stuff."

"Are you going to order me to give him a check?"

"No."

"Then I am out of here." I said. I was seething, but with resolve, as I walked back around the corner, cool and in control.

"Sir, it was so nice to meet you," I choked out to the bank's attorney. "I need to go, but thanks for your time."

"Bu... well, what about the check?"

"Yes, you can all talk about that. I have an appointment." I was short in my reply.

He went on, "The bank is right across the street; we can go over there." I ignored him.

"Thank you so much," I thanked our attorney for nothing really. "Call me."

The bank's attorney must have caught his breath long enough to formulate a threat. He directed it to our attorney. "I hope your client realizes the consequences of her failure to turn over funds, and you have advised her to do that now." What would his clients say when he called to tell them he had nothing?

"You all have an enjoyable afternoon. Thanks," I said. I disregarded his threat gaily. I headed to my car, the blank check with me.

The bank, as well as its attorney had experienced one more sign of our resolve and perseverance. It left him speechless and out of control. I am sure that must have been a rarity for an attorney.

May 23

Since our attorney was definitely back on the case, we had a Saturday morning strategy session. As Angee and I pulled up to our house after errands, the lawyer was getting out of the car.

Angee stayed outside and tended to gardening while our attorney and I began our discussion. It was commonplace for us to talk it out and get all emotional about theory versus reality, law versus right and wrong, and then give Angee the condensed update. We both hoped it would reduce the stress and effect on her related sickness. While she said it helped mentally, I don't know if the knowledge that we were still fighting the issues helped physically.

Our attorney started off with bad news for our case. "The state has filed a petition to deny the jury trial. They claim your loan agreement with them provides for no jury trial. Which is common, you know."

"But they are not the plaintiff here, they were simply named as co-defendant; we are not arguing the issues of the loan with them." I argued. I thought it was a ridiculous pretense to object to. None of their paperwork was part of the court case. Why introduce clauses within it as a reason to object?

"Are they doing this for the bank's benefit?" I said.

"That makes some sense. Then the bank doesn't look like the worst of the bad guys, but at the same time tries to avoid a jury trial. They may very well be letting the state do some of their dirty work."

"And what is the state's reason for helping?" I questioned. This was the very agency that had told us to forget fighting it and give up, because after all, it was the bank.

"They are probably hoping to be treated fairly by the bank after the auction of assets in the hopes of getting something, knowing full well Angee is judgment-proof," she said.

"There is nothing we can do?" I asked.

"Not really, they have a right to object." I didn't completely agree, but I could sense it was a battle our attorney didn't want to pursue.

I had no answer, so we moved on, and I figured I would research and re-approach, fight it at a later time. Since their document was not subject to the proceedings, I found it illogical to assume they had the right to evoke terms.

After a review of the conversations with attorneys, it seemed a counter-claim was in order. When our attorney responded to the last motion from the bank, she included some damages we wanted to detail officially to the court. The motion was simple but powerful, and concisely summed up the essence and reality of the bank's actions to this point.

Our response came with the following claims: First and foremost, the bank had breached their contract to give us ninety days to close. That action was quick and damaging. Next, it had sought and received wrongful possession. Our security amendment had put their rights to seize and do anything with any asset on hold. Finally, with the actions so far, it was clear that they were failing to act in a commercially reasonable manner. This was something that every person we talked to and every document we were able to access clearly stated had to be part of any bank's action.

From destroying the wine that needed to be bottled to refusing to allow us to continue the business we had pending and the plan we had laid out, nothing was reducing value faster than their inaction initially, and then the thoughtless actions that followed. It was a move that granted us a response to all that was happening and what was continuing to happen despite our best and continuing efforts to make it right. Soon, not even our best efforts would be able to save the assets from the damage of the bank's actions.

That weekend Angee and I worked long hours cleaning up the yard, planting, burning brush, designing the large area that had suffered from our eight years of efforts in building a successful business. It seemed an appropriate use of our energy. Instead of destroying, we would create.

Busy summer months at the winery had left anything but basic mowing to chance. Yet here we were, in front of a fire pit, burning uprooted wood and branches as we cleaned the back of our three-lot yard.

On Monday of the holiday weekend, I knew I needed to head to the winery to recover, at the very least, my phone book, to invite people to the upcoming fire-pit birthday celebration.

Midday, I bounced over to the winery. I was suspicious when I saw a note on the door that wasn't ours.

The locks have been changed.
Any questions should be directed
to the bank's attorney at xxx-xxx-xxxx.

Along with anger at them, I was pissed at myself for not assuming this would eventually happen. Now access to personal items was being denied. Even with no one there, I sensed their desire for a reaction. Perhaps they imagined or hoped we would beg for access, offer repeated requests to reconsider, any action that might give them the upper hand.

Instead, still angry at myself, I resolved to believe that their complete control would absolve us of further responsibility and leave the bank struggling for cooperation.

June 22

Even when you know something is coming, it can be a surprise. The entire ordeal took a significant change on Sunday.

By any standard it was a regular day. Angee woke up earlier than me. We enjoyed the paper together, sitting on the porch, relaxing, doing our best to relish the day despite the pressure and uncertainty of the future.

I stepped inside the house to get something. Angee couldn't wait for my return as she yelled from the chair outside, while making her way inside with the morning paper.

"The former Gaia Wines auction will be June 26 at 10 a.m." she read out loud. As shocked as I shouldn't have been, I was devastated. I grabbed the paper and read it three times before I responded. Then, as I had often done, I picked up the phone and called our attorney.

"You busy?" I hardly waited for an answer, "Why is there an auction ad in Sunday's paper to sell Gaia Wines assets?"

"We knew that was coming." She was too calm.

"It's in four fucking days. What happened to six weeks of public notification, as required by law? Did anybody tell you?"

"No, but they don't have to," she replied.

I couldn't cry. I couldn't yell. But I was sad and furious. And yet I was numb.

"There is no cooperation after this, the way they are treating us, the whole issue," I said.

Our attorney could have said "whatever" and I'd have felt more compassion. Apparently there was nothing to do but attend the auction.

June 25—The day before

For the sixth time, the bank asked for our assistance by way of a meeting the day before the auction. I had requested that we be able to get our personal items and the computers for corporate records. Six months into the year, nothing had been filed in a timely manner —or at all. My agreement to meet with the bank's attorney was a last effort to explore other options.

As I had advised all along, the bank and the auctioneer had no ability or intention of selling wine legally the next day. Not because they didn't want to, but because they couldn't.

Under the guise of advising on the wine process, I still thought something, anything, would bring a human element to their actions and a better option would prevail. Of the many things I was wrong about, I continued to be ill-prepared, internally, about the actions they would take.

I grabbed money out of the register when I first walked in. It was personal money used for change the weekend we opened in May. The bank's attorney wanted an outline of what to do with the wine, still in tanks.

One more time, I recounted what he needed in terms of staffing, capital and time. It would not be done in time for the auction tomorrow. It could not be done if they planned on selling the equipment, which they did.

The people from the auction company I had met with during the loan officer's last visit were packing and moving everything around. They had boxes, what they thought were the business files, all sloppily stacked on three pallets in the middle bay.

Our attorney asked about the computer information and the business records it contained. The bank, through its attorney, would allow nothing to leave. Our attorney weakened in her presentation, and rather than making a case, started to beg. I couldn't watch, so I made an attempt to stop it.

"You know what?" I said. "The state and feds already know the bank is not allowing us access to the information. I will simply restate that we made an effort and they refused to give us access. The bank can be held responsible for the amounts and reports due. Those computers also contain confidential and proprietary corporate information. Not having access to that can't be right. Are you not giving us access to the files?" The bank's attorney smirked and shook his head no. Our attorney gave me a quick panicked look, and the bank's attorney remained silent. It was the wrong time for him to do that.

He should have been active in his resolution. He was still worried about the wine, which wasn't going to be sold at the auction, or ever, by any of them. He refused to believe it, as he tried again with me, arrogantly, after he refused our access to the computer files.

"Why don't you put together a proposal, outlining what you see as being needed, so the bank can look it over?" he said. He was a bad negotiator, even for a lawyer. The time for looking things over had ended.

I addressed him directly and without compliance. "Sir, you need to have a talk with your client. I am not going to put anything together until you can ensure their cooperation, and nothing against you, but I don't think you can. There have been way too many changes, and we are not going to waste our time making proposals that they refuse."

"What have they refused?" He was asking because he either didn't know or he didn't remember. There were probably bigger issues he was dealing with, and his indifference to our deal made him look insensitive and incompetent. Regardless, I recounted the last four attempts we had made to help and the bank's response each time. He failed to understand how much over a barrel his client was, particularly without our assistance.

The auctioneers, who everyone was sure could sell the wine, couldn't. The bank, which was sure they could sell the wine, couldn't. The bank, which was sure we would fold into fear and compliance, was finding out we wouldn't.

Three guys from the local shelter, whom we had used often as quick paid labor, continued to load up my truck with a pallet of boxes. Although the bank's attorney followed me around the winery like a puppy, he wasn't as cute, and given his attitude, he received no further cooperation from me.

I walked out without the computer files. He let our attorney hold the $200 from the cash drawer in escrow, until they could settle the bank issue. Big deal. That was how petty his case was. Half a million dollars of assets and he was worried about the $200 from Angee's personal account as collateral for the debt. It was a pathetic display of his abilities. The fact was I could live without the cash. It appeared that, his clients couldn't. One couldn't help but wonder which business was the better entity.

As I stood in the winery for the last time, it was among the saddest sights I had seen. Our beautiful, vibrant winery, full of life and love, was reduced to tables of items that would be sold in bulk the next day for pennies on the dollar. I would not attend the auction. I couldn't be there and guarantee I could handle the emotions of the devastation that would be central to the day.

June 26

Angee, Dawn and another employee attended the auction. Angee felt a strong desire to be there. I did not. The rage at the deconstruction of such effort, pride and passion was too much. I could not watch it die a slow, illogical death.

I busied myself with house projects, preferring to be productive rather than destructive. Angee called throughout the day to ask about what I had wanted and what prices items were bringing. She gave regular rundowns on who was there, and by every calculation it was poor attendance. Not surprising, with less than four days notice and no direct mail piece as the auctioneer had told the bank was commonplace and commercially reasonable auction marketing.

I reveled in the auction failure, as we estimated that eight, possibly 10, percent of total value had been realized. I called to relay the progress, or rather the lack thereof, to our attorney, but she seemed detached. It seemed like forever to me, and must have been a nightmare for Angee and the employees there, despite the great deals they were receiving on merchandise. No wine was being sold. Another employee got there before Dawn had to leave, so Angee was never without moral support.

Late in the afternoon, Angee called to say it was wrapping up. She and the employee would come back and unload the haul. She had spent just over $400 for almost $10,000 worth of product.

Four-thousand-dollar oriental rugs were bought for $120 each. Two custom pieces of artwork which had cost $700 and $2,400 were ours for $60 each. I tried to feel good about the bargains, yet I died for the damage and finality that had been done.

As I helped unpack, I checked over Angee's invoice, then our employee's. I was confused and surprised at the date on the documents: June 16, 2003. Why was an organization that was responsible for the competent handling of other people's assets so negligent in their documentation? That invoice date would never reconcile with the event date. No one had notices and no one had any answers, but I filed it among the thing I would need to find out about.

Chapter Twelve

Holding Court: Trials and Tribulations

*"I am not afraid of tomorrow, for I have
seen yesterday and I love today"*
William Allen White

*"Almost all our misfortunes in life come from the wrong notions we have
about the things that happen to us. To know men thoroughly, to judge events
sanely, is, therefore a great step toward happiness"*
Henri Beyle Stendhal (1801)

"The state is out" was our attorney's short message.

"What do you mean?" I was confused.

"They're bailing; said they know it's going to get ugly. They want no part of it, from the time standpoint and the liability standpoint. As a result, they're dismissing their objection to jury trial. And they're writing off the loan amount, and releasing Angee from her personal liability."

All of it was good news. Still, I wasn't sure how to react. "So the bank will file an objection to jury, right?" I said.

"No, they can't do it; time has passed for them to file." This was truly good news.

"You're kidding me? Do I understand this right? The bank tries to have the state do their dirty work and the state bails, leaving the bank on the hook for a jury trial?" I inquired.

"Pretty much; that's how it went down. I'll have the papers from the state's attorney by the end of the week. They don't want to put any more money into the fight, and feel they're exposing themselves by staying involved."

"So, we got a jury?" I said. I was actually excited by the stroke of good fortune that had come from doing nothing but letting the big boys duke it out. In the same instance, I was surprised that with the state's resources and attorneys, most likely compensated with ongoing retainers, they weren't going to pursue the bank or us. Whatever deals the bank may have thought it made with the state for help; they probably had nothing in writing. The bank's lack of attention to detail seemed to me to concern even the state.

Within a week, our attorney had the motion to withdraw the objection to the jury trial and the release of Angee's personal guarantee from the state loan we had secured to expand in 1997.

Shortly after that, the bank filed its motions: for the abandonment of the wine assets, the right to sell assets (which had already been sold), the right to apply the proceeds of the sale to the debt, the right to release the surety bond (in place since the temporary restraining order) and the right to foreclose on the last remaining asset securing the loan—our home. In the interim, the bank's attorney even felt compelled to draft a letter saying that our counterclaim was frivolous and would cause the bank to take further action against us and our attorney. But with everything gone and destroyed, it seemed an empty threat.

There are certain things you remember from great and traumatic events in your life. Even if you can't reconcile the reasons, they are the types of occurrences that stick in your mind when you recount it all.

The way the industry responded to our closing was one of those events. Dawn had asked pointedly how I thought the news of Gaia closing would affect other wineries. I calmed my ego, and even though we had made an impact that was positive, I was not about to say that anyone would have had any reaction other than morbid curiosity.

I was both right and wrong. Some customers and partners were sincere. The restaurant partner who saved us in 1999 for our New Year's Eve event was among the nicest. His voice mail message was simple and heartfelt. He realized how tough business was, found us to be the best of the business people he had dealt with, and said we had always been helpful to him. If there was anything he could do to help, all we had to do was call.

The bigger wineries in the state were noticeably silent, offering nothing either positive or negative. Yet neighboring winery personnel were in tears, both at the auction and later that week when we saw them at a theatre function. They were truly sorry for what had happened and at the same time appeared a little scared at the fact that it had happened at all.

As Dawn had said, it brought the reality of what could happen: that despite anyone's best efforts, everything could be destroyed. If we were subjected to such wrath, how would anyone avoid it?

Other wineries, I had heard from Farmer Dave (a close colleague in the industry), had inquired indirectly, hoping to get the inside scoop. It seemed more like fear from their own perspective, he said, than being nosy.

Seven months later, we were still seeing people around town, even from other states, who were expressing concern and sadness for the loss. Most surprising to me was a man from Nashville, Tennessee, whom I came across during one of my interviews for employment. He was familiar with the industry as a whole, being a partner in a wine brokerage operation, as well as a friend of a vice president at our distributor.

I was filled with satisfaction and sadness as he talked about how well respected Gaia Wines was in the industry and community.

"Everyone I talked with was always amazed at the brand equity Gaia Wines had developed in such a short time. It was incredible, the reputation, the quality, they way people felt about the brand," he told me.

Filled with pride, I shared his sentiments with Angee and Dawn. Let's remember him when we go to trial, Dawn responded. Can he be a witness? She only half joked. Angee had a small moment of sadness and pride, and probably didn't feel the full impact on what that meant, most likely because it was coupled with dead silence from so many other partners, including our three wholesale distributors.

The entire economy was in the toilet, and distributors were losing major brands faster than at any previous time. No one had the time to inquire about our condition, much less offer condolences. Still, it hurt. Reaching out when it is most difficult to do so is what makes us better people.

I was still receiving e-mail requests to hold birthdays and weddings, and getting orders for wine that had long since been sold out. Now, without access to what wine was left, every e-mail response brought about a new sadness regarding the loss. We were even getting job applications, intern inquiries and expressions of interest from foreign distributors.

I had taken a job painting an ex-employee's newly acquired home during three months over the summer. It was the best job I had ever had. I worked my own days and hours, making it possible to go to Angee's doctor appointments and also interview for new employment when opportunities arose.

When the expedited hearing date arrived in mid-September, my eyes were burning from the start of an early day, too many hours of wearing contacts, lack of sleep, and stress. I struggled with what would be the best use of what little energy I had left. There was an unrelenting and continuous frustration that had built up inside my chest, forcing every breath to be a reminder of what had happened and what was still happening. I had often felt it was similar to being raped, with everyone standing around, saying this shouldn't be happening. Yet it continued, and no one seemed to be able to stop the devastation and harm.

Almost in an instant, an outlet came into focus. I decided to write this book. Angee and I joked about possible titles. But the result we wanted was clear: to tell a story about how passion can be damaged by arrogance.

Earlier in the month, while we were out of town, the bank's latest motion came. It was a legal request to seize the final asset securing the loan: our home of 10 years. Throughout the negotiations, we had always focused on our residence as the one item we wanted to save. What was actually happening, though, was that as every asset of value flew through our hands and passed the timelines imposed to save it, we realized the lack of control, and, ironically, the lack of the importance of each hard won asset.

"This is organized pressure, and by design, is specifically to make you cave," our attorney said. "They had the right to take your home six months ago. The fact that they didn't is interesting. The fact that you are unmoved by it is a beautiful thing."

"But it makes no sense," I argued.

"Listen, you have to understand what you are dealing with. The problem the bank has is that 99.9 percent of the people they deal with would have caved decades ago. They don't know what do with you."

Chalk up one heck of an experience to my ability to say no!

Trial in Courtroom Five—September 16, 2003

I wanted to call someone who would understand what we were going through, and listen. I had two problems. Did I understand what was happening? What would I say, and who would understand?

Dawn called early in the morning, before our scheduled 8 a.m. meeting time. She had dreamed about her father. I had slept uneasily that night, most likely unable to get comfortable with what was about to happen. Angee could have slept the day away. We all reacted as distinctly differently as the strengths that had made us an effective team during the previous eight years.

But at 7 a.m. it seemed too early to think about the breakfast we had agreed to start with the day before. Court was always unpredictable and always based on someone else's schedule. It was doubtful that we would be able even to determine our own eating times.

"What are you doing? I'm up and hungry; call me." Dawn shouted to the answering machine. Angee was almost dressed as I returned Dawn's call. I understood the variety of response I was getting that morning from everybody. All at once and in different ways, there was anticipation, anger, fear and sadness. I had spent much of the night reviewing in my mind answers to questions that would never come. I would find the exercise a waste of my time and energy.

Angee was on her way to pick up Dawn while I got presentable. I felt reassured by the call we had received the night before from our attorney, who sounded confident and ready.

During breakfast, Angee was quiet, reflective and sad. I laughed, joked, and acted silly to avoid any feeling of fear. I was determined there would be no fear. Dawn was nice enough to pick up the tab, a subtle show of support and a sign of how much had changed and evolved during our times together.

After a high-security check-in, we headed to Courtroom Five of the City Building. Three sad-looking African American women sat on a long bench outside the courtroom as we approached. I wondered why they were there and even how I might help or be reassuring. My confidence was high, having surrounded myself with people who knew, could understand, and could be of assistance with the process we were about to go through.

Our attorney's heels clicked down the tiled, empty hall. She greeted us with a loud "Hello, ladies," in her usual style. She was dressed in open-toed shoes, a long tan suede skirt with a white blouse. I found her appropriate and powerful, not the brash vixen she had been described as in the past by her less confident colleagues.

She fumbled for the papers releasing us from the state's claim. I handed Dawn the complaint du jour, since she really had not been advised of the recent motions the bank was requesting. She shook her head, laughed and winced in pain as Angee read over her shoulder. It was then I realized that Angee had not seen that day's complaint. Our attorney handed us the state's document. Angee and I signed, releasing us from the debt to the state. One the state had been all too happy not to pursue.

We moved into the hearing room, which turned out to be a much smaller room than the one for TRO hearing. It put everybody in the room very much on top of each other, physically and emotionally. We headed to the far set of seats, which meant the bank would contend with the bright, sunny day from a bay of windows at our backs. It turned out that that was the least of what they would contend with that day. I sensed it was a good move, and ushered Angee into a seat next to our attorney. Dawn and I sat in the remaining two chairs against the wall.

Attorneys began to speak, comments flying back and forth with little direction or purpose. The bank's attorney sat down and spread out his papers and files as he asked who was in the courtroom. I introduced him to Angee.

"I remember her from when she turned over the assets," he replied. I laughed out loud.

"You remember her from what meeting?" I said. It wasn't really a question, only a negating of his assertion. He was there to ask a judge for permission to sell assets that his client had already sold through the June auction. He probably assumed that we would not have read the motion. How could he still underestimate us so? He never responded to my comment.

Our attorney introduced Dawn. The loan officer looked at her and smiled weakly.

As our landlord and his attorney entered the room, our attorney jumped up and asked to speak with the landlord. His attorney didn't follow until the landlord and our attorney were both out the door.

When our attorney returned, she leaned over to Angee, smiled, and whispered something. I waited to hear from Angee as she repeated it. I turned my head to Dawn so no one in the courtroom could read my lips.

"We have confirmation on the deception," I said. Dawn tilted her head but still looked perplexed, so I continued. "Assets were sold before the auction, and it is not right." She leaned back in her chair and looked across the room.

With confidence, our attorney grabbed the state document we had signed and addressed the bank's attorney. "I've got this release from the state for your signature," she said.

"We're not prepared to sign that now," he responded. Again I laughed out loud. To me, his actions came across as tacky television lawyering. Yet I would remember his line for my own use later.

We stood as the judge entered. It's odd what crosses your mind during stressful times. He was wearing a conservative blue shirt. I should have worn a blue shirt, I immediately thought, knowing that mirroring people makes them feel comfortable. Everyone threw around introductions at the judge's request.

The judge recounted the issues for the day's hearing: abandonment of assets (the wine that remained uncared for at the winery), permission to sell the assets (already gone), use of the proceeds (money that had been received from the auction), the request to pursue foreclosure of our home, and the release of the surety bond (which, as required, had been posted at the time of the TRO).

The bank's attorney seemed confused and ill-prepared as he started. "We ask the court for permission to sell the assets," he said.

"Haven't they already been sold?" asked the judge. There was a timid "yes" response.

"We ask that the proceeds from the sale of the assets be now moved from escrow and applied," the bank's attorney continued.

What were those proceeds? I was surprised that no one was thinking of asking that question. The bank had rushed to auction $250,000 of assets from our eight years of toil. I motioned across Angee to get our attorney's attention, to have her ask, but the action only served to allow me a small break in the confusion of the courtroom.

I turned to respectfully address the judge. "With your permission, may I ask what those proceeds are?" The question was out before I got permission.

The room went dead. The judge looked over at the plaintiff's table and waited. Our attorney and Angee didn't move. I couldn't see Dawn from the side. I caught the landlord's eye across the room, but fixed my attention on the loan officer as he wrote down a figure on the back of a motion paper and slid it—one inch—over to the bank's attorney, who looked at the paper and then up at the judge. "Eight thousand," he said. I let out a strident laugh at their failure. I wasn't even angry.

The first thing I noticed were the landlord's eyes widening as his mouth dropped open. Then I saw Angee with her face in her hands. I didn't know what she was hiding. A gasp came from Dawn that turned my head; she was in tears, shaking her head and wiping her eyes. I reached out to touch her arm to comfort her, saying, "it's okay."

I saw Angee's head move up, and she was also in tears but somewhat more reserved in her crying. I placed my hand on her shoulder, reassuring her that it would be all right. I just knew. Our attorney looked over at Angee, but didn't seem to know what to do or say.

The landlord seemed a little paler. Neither the loan officer nor the bank's attorney looked over at any of us at the defendant's table.

The judge asked for a complete accounting of the proceeds. Anyone could deduce that would be an interesting submission. The arguments continued. The judge asked whether dumping the wine would be the best answer, then patiently waited for a response. The bank's attorney said nothing.

Our attorney voiced our concern. It was not in anyone's best interest, she said, but without the bank's cooperation little could be done by her clients. Everybody continued to talk over one another in a process that seemed counterproductive to any of the specifics being heard.

I passed a note to Angee saying that I would go into the winery and help inventory the wine for the landlord's benefit. Our attorney continued to argue against the possession of the wine being back on the company. "Permits have expired, and the plaintiffs have sold the equipment required to finish anything not already in bottle form. There is no capital to purchase supplies," she argued.

I looked across the room and saw the loan officer mouth the words "Do we have to pay for that?" At least it was an option in his mind. His disorganized fear became clear. The bank's attorney mouthed an answer, while shaking his head to indicate that he would not allow that to happen.

"Well," the judge said, "I'll go ahead and release the damaged wine for disposal. See what can get done in sixty days to sell the bottled wine, and resubmit your abandonment motion." The gavel went down, we stood up and the judge walked out.

Our attorney started the wrap-up by asking when we should all get together to inspect the status of the remaining wine. Everyone seemed available now, but I thought giving Angee and Dawn a break and an opportunity for us all to regroup would be important. But in the mass confusion of disorganized, unprepared voices, it was decided. We were going now.

I stopped the landlord on the way, to say I would help with his issues. Gaining his cooperation and mending fences could be important at this point.

Our attorney stopped at the door. "We can get this stuff moved and everybody paid off and out of it." She seemed happy.

"The one thing we didn't want was for possession to be transferred," I replied. "We don't have the time, money, or permits, and taxes will not allow us to do anything. It's the one thing Angee didn't want."

The quick look on our lawyer's face said what I could sense. I was pushing her, but I failed to understand why attorneys walking away from a hearing thinking the exact opposite of our intended purpose served as a victory for us. I did not expect her response.

"*So, fire me,*" she yelled, and turned to walk away. I prayed that everyone had already left the hallway. We watched her move toward her office elevator. She never looked back. I controlled my first instinct—to run after her—figuring that giving her time would be best.

Angee, Dawn and I got on the elevator in some shock, wondering what had happened, both good and bad. As soon as we got outside, they both lit up cigarettes as we walked toward the car.

"We can take Dawn to work and head to the winery," Angee recommended. "I'm calling to take the day off."

"I don't even want to do this today," I responded. It felt like shock as we began to process what had happened. Dawn broke the daze we all seemed to be feeling. "Eight thousand dollars? Margaret, we were getting 97 percent of the value, not three," Dawn said, almost in tears again.

"It goes a long way to support our claim of commercial unreasonableness. No one can say three percent of value was the best option, not while there was a functional operation getting 95 to 97 percent," I answered. As I fell back on logic and numbers, I wondered at what point I had gotten so ridiculously anal-retentive.

On the car ride over, I asked Angee if she thought our attorney was mad at me. "Oh, hell, yes," Angee replied.

"Can you be 'good cop' and go make sure she's okay when we get there?" I pleaded. "Yes" was Angee's sympathetic reply.

A few short blocks later we were pulling up, two spaces away from the loan officer and his attorney, parking next to what seemed to be the loan officer's new car. He was on his cell phone.

"What would you pay to hear that conversation?" I joked. I was chewing the gum Dawn had given us to wet our mouths, and although I was done, I waited to get rid of it.

Approaching the entrance like kids, we pressed our noses to the window to see what had been happening to the previously empty space upstairs.

For some reason, it felt good being back. There was something peculiar and empowering about our return. Our attorney was not five minutes behind us as she parked. I excused myself to go grovel, fearing she was going to quit this battle.

I bent down and tapped on the window. "Don't be mad. Are you quitting us?"

She laughed. "You goof; it's all cool, just blowing off. We do that, you know."

"No, we… don't scare us like that."

"It is way cool, we're good."

We moved toward the door as the landlord motioned us in from down the street. The bank representatives got out of their car, and with great purpose I turned toward them standing in the street and spit my gum. It landed a foot away from them. No one said anything, but I felt good.

Angee and I led the way down the stairs into the cellar. As we passed a double sink turned upside down at the end of the stairs, I said, within earshot of all, "Hey, the bank didn't sell the kitchen sink." There were uncomfortable giggles.

"It looks like a war zone," I verbalized. It did. Broken bricks, dirt and rubble were cluttering the floors. Stuff, even valuable assets, hadn't been sold. I stepped around an Oriental rug and turned to our attorney. "There's three grand right there."

Two desks were still in the office, which was odd. In an auction, selling office furniture is typically one of the easiest things to accomplish.

Inside, Dawn, Angee and I all headed in different directions. But I stayed close, within audible range of both our attorney and the bank's.

"So what are we doing?" I asked for directions.

"We need to know what the status of the wine is," the bank's attorney countered. Pretty bad, I thought.

Although there was no smell, the landlord was quick to point out all the gnats and bugs that had been destroyed by his recent chemical bombing. It was a war zone indeed.

I looked at the 55-and 60-gallon blue plastic drums that were in two general states—bad and worse. Three drums were sucked in so badly that the drum shape looked like a big tripod. The other three were bulging so tightly that the next swell might mean the end of the plastic seams.

There were notes written on top of the drums. I turned to address the loan officer.

"Who moved this wine from the oak barrels to the blue drums?"

"Uh, I forgot his name… the consultant for the potential buyer."

"Okay, you don't know his name. Is he bonded?" I didn't wait for an answer.

"Sir," I said as amiably as I could, "we're going to need his permit information, his ATF reports and his chemical reports."

I'd have bet my life at that moment and the lives of three of my best friends that he didn't have any of that. "You want to write this down?" I started to repeat.

The loan officer had become such a pawn in all these activities that one could almost feel sorry for him. He was going it all alone at hearings, without the support I had.

He most assuredly was going to lose his job after this was all over. Although he was noticeably uncomfortable, he had no idea of the extent of his ability. That fact would most likely cause him to lose his once lauded "golden child" status at the community bank. Perhaps banks everywhere would be disillusioned with his capability.

He jotted down some notes. The bank's attorney began to address me about the information needed. Something he said made Angee laugh. He turned toward her, annoyed. "Now, just wait and listen."

He was very easy to arouse for a partner in the city's largest and presumably most prestigious law firm and someone who was supposed to be in the assumed driver's seat of this nightmare.

"It looks like we should have Angee open and inspect the product…test and taste it," I offered.

Dawn moved toward us with the umbrella that had been a prized personal possession, and I went looking for the ladder we loved. The landlord's wife was off on a search for tools to open the drums. None of the movement was necessary, but not much was happening anyway. It seemed more a reaction to nervous energy.

The landlord stood attentively as I moved back toward the drums to be inspected. I put my arm on his shoulder in a friendly, team-like manner.

I said, "See, what you all forgot was, I was your best mother-fucking friend." He smiled uncomfortably yet knowingly. I continued, as I placed my other hand on his arm until I stood squarely in front of him, "Now it's too late for them to come to 'Jesus', but you still have an opportunity to see the light."

He laughed; I dropped my hands and moved toward the business at hand because, quite frankly, nothing was being done. I was getting hungry.

"May I borrow a piece of paper? I need to record all these quantities" I addressed the bank's attorney. He made a small huff and tore a sheet of his legal note pad. I moved to the back drums and recorded the type of wine, amount and dates. I asked Angee questions to answers I already had, just out of respect, and to balance out the power we were demonstrating for the bank.

The landlord's wife made her way back to the first set of drums with a large wrench and an extra-long screwdriver. I met Angee back at the damaged wine in the drums. She had also gotten to a zone in being there, familiar, comfortable and at peace with the process.

I grabbed the screwdriver and began twirling it in one hand like a drumstick. Dawn was not far with a long pointed umbrella. Angee was holding the wrench. We looked like the black, lesbian, and, okay, really older version of "Charlie's Angels." At that moment, it felt like we could take them, all of them.

The attorneys were standing just off my shoulder as I watched Angee attempt to get the drums open. The bank had sold the specific fitted tools at the auction, so the wrench had to do.

"Is it going to explode?" the landlord asked, most likely because he was in his good "going-to-court" suit.

"Oh, yes," Angee responded.

Then, in what I believe was the stupidest move of the day, I heard the bank's attorney address ours: "Once you open it, you are liable for it."

In a moment that was less than a split second, I leaned over to Angee, softly touched her arms and said, "Wait."

She did just that. It was a beautiful moment, being so together, so trusting of each other and so responsive. It was why we were together. It served as evidence of why Gaia had achieved all that it had, under our direction, in such a short time.

"They are saying we're liable if you open it." I repeated to Angee. She looked at me only briefly as I turned to the bank's attorney.

"What did you say?" I requested his repeating.

"Once you open it, it's yours, from a liability standpoint," he repeated.

I looked hurriedly at our attorney, but didn't wait for her cue and turned back to Angee. What happened next was one of the most beautiful things I have ever seen.

Angee threw the wrench on top of the plastic drum. She looked strong, sexy and passionate. She had removed her jacket, looking ready for work in the winery, even though she had on a short black knit skirt that gently hugged her hips and a sleeveless red V-neck sweater. She looked healthy and so incredibly beautiful. It was the only thing that day that left me breathless.

The wrench hit the barrel with a thud. Angee faced the bank's attorney defiantly. "I don't have to open this to tell the wine is bad. I've had wine in poly drums over a year without them looking like this. You have 40 gallons in 60-gallon barrels. They are not supposed to buckle like this." She didn't need a breath as she continued, "I have been cooperative with you. I have told you what I needed, how much it costs and the labor and time required. I am done trying to help you."

The room was silent. All eyes were on Angee. It was a "Norma Rae" moment that proved to confound the bank and counsel yet again with the conviction of these two women from the winery. In a brief moment, it seemed like a lot of time passed. The bank's attorney looked to ours with a plea for help.

"I wish I had known there were offers to help," he responded arrogantly.

"There were," our attorney said with equal disdain.

"Oh, well, for $400,000..." he replied, inaccurately referencing information I had given him as to the value of assets after the loan was paid off. That is going to be a bargain by the time we are through, I thought. Could they get nothing right?

Angee and I returned to documenting the wine status, and I saw both attorneys move to just outside my old office. I was sure I would hear about their conversation soon.

I promised the landlord that as soon as I had letters from the regulatory agencies, as required, I'd be in to dispose of the wine that had gone bad under the bank's watch. Dawn walked out with the umbrella, her sign of defiance. As I walked by our attorney, I remarked what bullshit this was. We were done trying to help the bank out of the messes that they, with increasing ignorance, were continuing to create.

Our attorney said, "Cha ching" in an attempt to sound like a cash register.

I wrapped it up with a bit of levity by saying, "Thank you and good night." We had indeed just performed some serious drama. It had moved us miles with our counterclaim. It was time to eat.

"How about going to lunch?" I offered as we gathered outside to decide where.

It was quickly decided that there was a need for a martini lunch. As Angee, Dawn and I waited at the restaurant, I mention the "cha ching" comment our attorney had made.

"What's the deal?" Dawn said as our attorney sat down to join us.

"Cha ching" she responded. Give us more, please, I thought, but I let her remain in control of telling about the interaction.

She continued, "After they saw the drums, there was some significant sweating. The bank's attorney pulled me aside, asking what he could do to get out of this. They are so incredibly aware they are screwed. Today was good, we got information on deception and we proved commercial unreasonableness. It was a good day. We also pierced the corporate veil with the deception issue, which means going after directors, their assets, and bank officers."

I was aware from general consensus that the deception issue added one more zero to the damages almost automatically. The state allowed three times damages on the unreasonableness, which had easily begun to put us at seven figures. I hoped we weren't celebrating prematurely.

It had been a tough day, and an even tougher year. Nothing had gone as we had expected. Small incremental victories brought joy through all the insanity.

Lunch continued with debriefing and strategies. Our attorney suggested that the bank would offer the surety bond the judge had passively not released. We could probably also have the wines. We still didn't want to attempt to handle that. No one had the time or desire, or, now, the legal ability to sell the bottled wine.

"Can you handle a few more months of battle, or does that kind of offer sound interesting?" I said as I could tell our attorney was still looking for a quick end. Yet tying everything up prematurely meant leaving money on the table. It was simply too much to walk away from at this point.

"You can avoid bankruptcy, keep the house, and walk away with something. I want you to sleep on it," she said, speaking directly to Angee.

"Hell, no," Dawn cried out, even though it wasn't directed at her. Once again her support, her belief in us and the alliance in the cause was tremendous.

I did the math in my head. Too much cash would be going out for what would likely result in about $35,000 for eight years of work. I was in for the long term, including our court hearing, but held my judgment.

Angee asked for a sidebar, and I leaned in to hear what she had to say: "Should we seriously look at this deal now, cut our losses…?"

I whispered back to her how significantly events had changed today. I would be talking to the bankruptcy attorney and our financial planner about the ramifications this week. There was more to be had to cover the damage we had experienced, I was sure of it. She smiled confidently. I didn't skip a beat as I turned back to our attorney.

"So, what I've got to ask you is how you feel about sticking with it? Can you, already working a full-time job, stick it out another four to six months? Is your percentage impacted by doubling, maybe tripling the award for damage the bank has done?" I said.

"Oh, yeah." she didn't wait.

"I want you to sleep on it," I smiled. She admitted the dual with a return smile.

Our attorney went on to explain that the landlord had been able to confirm that he had been told that the bank had sold the items to the auctioneer before the public auction. It was an act that we had become aware had a familiar and distasteful element to it. That very act made it possible to go beyond the bank as an entity, to the owners and board of directors, if needed.

Lunch was finishing up as Dawn and our attorney flirted with the restaurant's proprietor. I truly wished each of them some good love, although not the same love. I wished them something as good as what I shared with Angee. Even through all the trials, we continued to support, believe and trust in each other with no reservation. I felt saddened by what they were missing in their own lives.

At 3: 30 that afternoon, I called our attorney to give her the value of the damaged wine in the drums. Sixty-two thousand dollars and some change had been spoiled from poor care while in the bank's possession. It made us sick. It was the best chardonnay Angee had ever created. People had begged for it to be released, and never balked about the price, even in Indiana. Now, due to the bank's impatience and arrogance, it was gone.

It was about 6:30 later that night, when I noticed that our attorney was calling.

"Okay, got home, dog is walked, and I'm on the couch. It is just hitting me. Do you have any idea what went on today? The significance? I ran it by my supervisor, told him I was out of here in 30 days," she said. Her ownership of the case had changed. It felt like she was in and on-line for the value of the whole experience.

Three days had passed since the hearing, and I fully expected at least a weak, interim offer. At the same time, I was not surprised. The bank's disorganization and self-importance were evident. No one was really running things, and decisions were more pressured by time. We decided to take the last issue out of the equation: the personal guarantee of our home.

Angee and I had begun looking casually at rental houses and apartments and even including Dawn, in the excitement of getting out from the hassle of the house and in preparation for the year of travel to support this book.

Through foreclosure research, I found out that we did not have to pay the mortgage during the process. Eventually we would most likely be able to purchase something else. Voluntarily turning over the house to the bank would have no negative effect on our credit ratings.

The auction on the house would put unpaid tax liens at the forefront, the first to be paid. Exhibiting our passion and poise, our decision came peacefully and painlessly easy.

We would give the house to the bank. No drawn-out foreclosure process. All that we had done to fix up the house during my free time was encouraging. However, there was still more money that had to be put in to get it up to repair standards. And this was during the worst period of foreclosures ever, especially in Indiana.

It was also, in a remarkably healthy way, pulling out our dicks, displaying nothing but zeal for our position. Angee relished being able to toss the keys to our house and related problems in the bank's general direction in front of an audience.

After the second mortgage two years earlier, there had been a lack of equity. The house was most likely flipped in terms of value to the remaining debt. Drug dealer activity across the street made us laugh at the posture and arrogance of the bank thinking that there was any cash value to be had by seizing it. At least it kept us from crying.

Did they have the right to take the house? Most definitely the house secured the loan by the documentation we had signed. Yet we would prove our maturity and responsibility in not mounting a defense to the evident claim. Hopefully, it would not be lost on the court when it came time for our countersuit.

Telling—more like convincing—our attorney about our decision was a little challenging. She had always been protective, and rightly so. Our challenge had become an act of love. Keeping the house had always been a huge concern. It had been what Angee had always negotiated. She wanted to save a place to live, save what little security was left of a very insecure situation.

With the release of the personal guarantee, the house could not be seized. Although that release had been promised many times by the bank, nothing legal had materialized. We doubted it ever would. It had been what the bank had repeatedly offered as compensation for our assistance. But as their abuse and inconsistency continued, that offer never took the form of a document. It became easy to feel that it was not worth saving.

Within a week, our attorney was on board with the logic and strategy of giving the house to the bank. She would use it when it seemed most appropriate. I set out to prepare the players needed for documentation of our counterclaim.

"You know, this really is whipping out your dicks, and leaving them with nothing," she commented. Yep, if everybody was thinking the same thing, it must be right.

The next conversation with our attorney was enthusiastic. She was noticeably excited.

"I talked with the bank's attorney today and he asked, 'So, "the girls" filed bankruptcy, right?'"

She went on. "No, as a matter of fact they are going to quitclaim the house to you. Just let us know when the sheriff's sale is, and they'll be out. No sense arguing personal guarantee. Now, with that out of the way, let me know when you're ready to discuss our counterclaim." By her tone and enthusiasm, I could sense that it was a legal moment she truly treasured.

"WHAAAAA?" with no "T" was articulated in the bank's attorney's response our attorney said. Evidently, it didn't seem like our response to their aggression was expected. Their attorney continued, "Well, it just seems like we're miles apart on this."

Actually, I thought, miles apart was months ago. We were now operating in different time zones. The bank and their attorney continued to be 60 days behind what we considered acceptable, and I imagined that would continue up to our trial date.

Our attorney had a response to the court on the foreclosure and the bank's conversion allegations towards me for holding the money from our weekend sale on Friday, without the opportunity for me to review them. I wondered if it was procrastination or just a clever move to not allow me to comment.

As the tide began to turn, our attorney was calling to update us. She was convinced there would be resolution by Halloween if not, Christmas.

"The bank really can't get anybody to come in as an expert to test the wine," she said.

"What about Mark?" I asked.

"He's not interested." The fellow winery owner had come in for the first round of testing, but after seeing what happened at the auction he was no longer willing to be part of the bank's plan.

"Good for him, he and his wife were very upset about what went down. His father was a lawyer and Mark goes to auctions all the time. He knows how bad it was." I told her.

"Maybe we should add him to the witness list," our attorney replied.

"Beautiful." Our witness list now included banking, winery, auction and business experts. We listed and had agreements from 12 witnesses to the bank's three, if size was to count for anything.

In October we didn't make the mortgage payment. I couldn't help but wonder if the mortgage team at the bank might bring up the non-payment at the next banking meeting. At the same time, I realized they were too far gone for it to have an impact.

The following Sunday, we toured the city to determine what was available in our price range. It was both exciting and tragic. To ease the pain, we joked about being able to have all our clothes in one place, with the hope of bigger closet space. At the same time, I looked around to see what stuff could be sold. Other possessions would be carefully and lovingly moved.

It seemed a hassle more than anything else, having been there 10 years—eleven for Angee. It was all us, from the bold wall colors to the flow of the sometimes hectic mess. Motivation for cleaning became nil. With great sadness yet conflicted joy, we began the search to find our new home, at least for the next six months, while I finished this book and mapped out plans for the tour to tell our tale.

Everything seemed very much out of control, laced with an under-lining calm. There was a peace about our decision and our control of what at most times seemed like an unmanageable series of events. I was proud of our attitudes and emotions, even as events seemed to cause everything to crumble around us.

Obviously there was little left to do but ride the storm of indecision and screw-ups that would continue to flow from this apparently incompetent banking bunch.

Chapter Thirteen

Entrenched in Inaction

"No Problem is Insurmountable, with a little Courage, Teamwork and Determination a Person can overcome anything."
B. Dodge

"Any woman who chooses to behave like a full human being should be warned that the armies of the status quo will treat her as something of a dirty joke."
Gloria Steinem, 1972

A month past the hearing of incredible disclosures and little has happened. Farmer Dave suggested that the lack of response from our attorney was due to the possibility that she had another job. He was convinced she had an offer from the law firm associated with a member of the bank's board of directors. While I had a hard time believing it, I also had a hard time sleeping, thinking about it.

I had questions, and waiting for weeks was one issue, but failing to get a response from our attorney other than a quick "You're on my radar" provided no comfort. In another 30 days we would be back in court, filings would have been made, and we would have failed to be as proactive as possible.

Knowing that foreclosure was an option, we did not make that month's first or second mortgage payment. At first what seemed like a good strategy made me begin to wonder about what damage might have been caused, at least with the first mortgage. What if the bank failed to go through with its threat?

Had our attorney ever made contact with the expert in California? Was Mark willing to test a sample, or had we been duped again and the bank had gone in without our knowledge?

The landlord was understandably upset that he had not seen any movement, and our attorney had made it clear to his attorney what we were waiting for. The landlord laughed out loud at the fact that the bank wanted testing of clearly diminished assets. He had to understand the bank people's attempt and desire to rid them of any liability. In their awkwardness of banking and lawyering, they would again find themselves stacking the deck on commercial unreasonableness. Time had allowed documentation to mount.

The morning would bring another doctor's appointment. Angee and I were struggling with a decision. If nothing was found, it felt like we had to choose between the experts taking us down a laparoscope's trail, or to pursue one of the three national clinics known to treat lupus, which would take more of a team approach.

The Mayo Clinic, The Cleveland Clinic and Johns Hopkins all had programs that dealt with autoimmune systems in a more aggressive way than some others. Although we had been seeing the best in Indianapolis, much like our experience with best of the city's attorneys, it felt like good money after bad and weeks turning into months with no relief on the horizon.

Angee hesitated to make the appointments. I was sure that week and those tests would bring her to the motivation to finally believe that she did not have to live like this. Still, any clinic choice would be a three-to-six month appointment wait, and something had to get on the calendar soon or we were looking at another year of health struggles.

She had been better than the previous year, we agreed one night. But there were still untimely episodes of pain, mostly around her monthly period, that drained her. It was counterintuitive for us to be going to a new doctor and a new set of labs, hoping and praying that they would find something, almost anything, a tumor and cancer, a lesion, something that could be tied to the pain and related symptoms and then quickly corrected, removed, drugged, or destroyed.

I was reminded of the strong emotional conflict of the pain Angee had experienced during her vaginal ultrasound, so clear and so immediate. As she squeezed my hand in wrenching pain and turned white. I was sure we had, quite literally, hit on something that meant it could be addressed and fixed, once and for all.

At the same moment, the thought of a tumor or cancer was horrifying, and I tried to adjust and reconcile myself to the battle that would be ahead, as I always had done. A few short tears and deep breaths, and we were off to another struggle that seemed so wholly unfair, yet completely manageable with a plan of action. We had become creatures of habit in dealing with our struggle, and we were good at it. I could only wish that we had the chance to be really good at something else, soon.

It was almost six weeks past the hearing, and very little had transpired other than more delay. The bank demanded to have the wine tested, then became aware that there was nothing to gain by that report actually being in black and white. Subsequently they refused to pay for testing.

I finally tracked our attorney down for a brief Friday phone call to discuss the option of paying the first mortgage, keeping that in good standing and simply holding back on the second one due to the bank. She felt sure that the bank people had no intention to pursue the foreclosure, but we had to be ready. She committed once again to talk with our California expert. Still I knew that she was busy, controlling and doing everyone else's job of lawyering.

It would be frustrating to walk into court again, in fewer than 60 days, with no progress. At the same time, I wanted to have the judge smack the bank's incompetence with something, almost anything, that would shake these people awake from the disaster they were drawing out.

Mark, a fellow winery owner, was on board to draw the testing and send it off on our behalf, but with no one to pay for the cost of testing, the results hung in evidence limbo. It wasn't going to be tested locally, but out of state at a wine-analysis lab.

As the plot thickened, prospective players got more concerned about being called in, because everyone from this point on was a potential witness. Amazingly, most of them sensed this and declined to be involved.

Recalling the feelings of people at two other wineries, I realized folks didn't know the danger of possibly being next, given the volatile economic climate. Nor did they understand that there was a benefit to going through the experience before it was yours and yours alone. It was that very attitude that made our resolve so valuable at this time. But you can only lead the winemaker to the barrel; you can't make him or her taste—particularly if it might taste bad.

Dàys later, I received an encouraging e-mail from our attorney about how the California expert was the guy to make the bank move. We discussed options to come up with his fees.

Without a job and with mounting medical bills, we were running a monthly deficit budget. There was nothing extra for fees. I resolved that I would adopt a Zen attitude about it. If George W. Bush could be calm about the budget deficit he was running, why did I have to worry? We'd figure something out; we always did.

I was also convinced that if the diminished assets didn't cause a strong motivation to settle (at something we considered equitable), an expert report was going to do little, at least until we got to trial.

The only option that seemed plausible was to get involved where it could really impact or hurt. To involve the bank's ownership and the board of directors remained the only hope I saw for getting movement. The risk of being responsible and on the hook had to make an appeal to the millionaires who sat in their newly acquired homes while the grunts at the bank evicted people under the actions of dishonesty and commercial unreasonableness. But it was a strategy that our attorney seemed reluctant to explore at this and every other opportune moment. Yet she was convinced that a document from the expert would motivate them.

We had time to wait on securing that expert, and since no one else was taking a stance that this had to be solved, I left it to our attorney. She was busy with trying to get samples to testing, and authority to remove the product that had gone bad under the bank's watch.

Additionally, the landlord wanted to move to get judgment on back rent, and said he had another interested lessee who wanted the space. It struck me as doubtful, given that the access was now limited by the new business upstairs. He more than likely saw it as a way to move everything out quicker.

There was going to be a clear need for me to be the proponent for our case again, and soon, when we refused to dump anything without full and complete inarguable documentation that we would not be held responsible for any loss. Considering that the bank hadn't released the state as a co-defendant when its position was no longer an issue, it didn't seem likely that we'd get the documentation from federal agencies, much less from the bank that seemed destined to lose big during a countersuit.

Sitting at home with a video camera and tape recorder, I sat ready to document the next step. The week was almost over, and surely nothing would take place yet here was another week gone.

The update the next week came from our attorney. The landlord had indeed demanded that his lawyer file a default judgment for past due rent. As our attorney said, there was simply no point in worrying about spilled milk. Instead, she was still trying to coordinate the removal of the wine.

My response was quite easy. The wine wasn't in our possession, or our responsibility to do anything with at this time but we should document the damaged product for our counterclaim. I suggested that we let the debtor in possession and the landlord solve the problem they had created. Let them get a buyer for the bottled wine, secure the proper documentation from federal and state agencies, pay the owed taxes and move it out.

We had neither a right nor a responsibility regarding anything that happened. And we certainly had no incentive. We had, at this point, lost everything.

Angee was to have a renal scan for more information about her lingering, persistent and painful left flank pain. On Monday I called, because no appointment had been set yet.

When I reached the assistant in the doctor's office, she told me that she didn't know what was to be scheduled and the doctor's files were elsewhere while he was in surgery. She promised to get back with me before the end of the day.

At 5:20 I called and left a message. The next morning she called. When I returned the call, she asked what the diagnosis was. I was tired and disgusted, but all I could do was laugh.

"Shouldn't that be the doctor's call?" I asked.

She laughed back, "Well, I need to have a reason for this procedure." How about the doctor's orders, which were already almost two weeks late?

"The doctor ordered it. Do you want the symptoms?"

"Yeah, that would be fine," she said.

I repeated what we had been saying for the last 18 months. "Persistent left flank pain that is exacerbated around the time of her period, a rise in temperature, difficulty peeing." She seemed satisfied.

"And when will her period start?" she said.

"Any day now…" I replied.

Angee received a call back for a two o'clock appointment. At 1:30 her period started, and although the pain would continue, she would begin feeling a little bit better, and for that I was happy.

Around the same time, I got an e-mail from our attorney inquiring as to my position on helping out. She insisted that we should be cooperative. And I was insistent on finding out her motivation to keep doing other highly paid lawyers' jobs.

The obvious answer was her obsessive desire to be in control of everything, but I believe she also had a strong need to show the court and the judge the extent of her capabilities.

She had tried in her e-mail to address the issues of legality of selling the wine, but the price per bottle had been reduced from $5 to $4.

I shot back a note questioning the change. What was even more important, I was adamant about her knowing the paperwork and releases we required to do anything. I was sure the documents would not come together. We wanted an unconditional release and to be held harmless for any action we took. Added to that, we wanted it from everyone involved: the landlord (who had just filed against us), the IRS, the ATF, the state of Indiana, revenue, excise and property tax divisions, and the bank. I wanted signatures, and cross signatures and threatened that I might take sperm samples as well.

Money would be needed for labels and labor, and no one was going to come up with that. Not only that, but I did not think the bank would not release us from action in helping it dispose of assets. It seemed a last-ditch effort to find something, or better, to cause something illegal or impeachable to happen. We wanted to remain steadfast and vigilant about not being caught in what I was convinced was their last attempt to trap us and reverse the outcome of the countersuit and the potential related damages that could be awarded.

As I showered to get ready to vote in the November election, I wondered about Angee's procedure, how she was feeling, and if this would finally provide us some long-term, effective solution. Surely going to vote wasn't going to change our legal problems. Yet I wasn't going to have anyone say that on all counts, I didn't try.

Before heading out, I tried one more time to connect with our attorney. I was surprised when she answered.

"You have time?" I said.

"Not really; go ahead…" she laughed.

"I'm afraid my e-mail was too harsh. What are you thoughts?" I left it open.

"We have a lot to gain by being cooperative. The landlord's lawyer is motivated to get the product out the door so he can rent," she said.

"But you don't have time for everyone else's work," I replied.

"It's cool-the landlord's attorney is doing it, and he has found a buyer and is making the calls to the attorney with the bank. What will happen from those proceeds is that taxes will get paid first, and then the lawyers, the landlord, and they will pay you to get things ready and labeled, out of the proceeds. The 25 cents that's left will go to escrow at the court."

Mentally, I quickly started going over the accounting. The buyer, someone from up north in the state, had offered five dollars, and the last e-mail quoted $4. Based on an unexplained reduction in sale price, perhaps lawyers don't make good sales people either. Who lets a bid go down for no reason?

Regardless, the end total wouldn't leave much of anything for anybody, and it was clear that no one else had done the math.

"We will also need labels, and from my conversation with Dave, we may not be able to put our labels on it," I said.

"We'll handle what we have to as it comes," she said calmly. "I want to be done with this, have us all get paid, so that we can start hanging out as friends."

I restated my absolute commitment to having every "I" dotted and every "T" crossed. "We're not going to touch anything without complete, full, undeniable release from everyone, including the bank."

"I know, let's see what the landlord's attorney gets accomplished, and let me give you the number for my new office," she said.

"Is your new boss okay with your time on this? "I asked pointedly. No sense in being surprised with a change from a new job.

"I'm doing both places still, he is just thrilled to have me at all, and I have already brought my minimum in for this month," she said. It was the fourth of the month and she had hit her goals-amazing time for lawyers in this economy. Even if it was business from drug felons, it was good times for crime.

"Okay, I'll be calm. I'm so sick of this dragging out and feeling like we have to clean up their crap and incompetence. But I won't bother you, just respond to e-mails, and you call if you need anything. I'm here for you!" I said.

"Cool, take care," she replied. I felt a little better, still frustrated but less so.

My conversation with Dave before my call to our attorney was more pointed but served to help align my attitude.

"I feel like we're being screwed and I have no motivation to help any more… this would be the seventh time we went in to save them," I said.

My calls to Farmer Dave always helped. He responded as passionately as I was feeling. "You need to be most cooperative. It's not you that doesn't want this resolved. You have consistently acted in good faith; continue to…these guys have taken everything, your business, your reputation, and now, during the holidays, they're going to put you out on the street. You'll have every juror in the box in tears" he prophesied. "This has been nothing but loaded with fraud and deceit, they have sold your assets for pennies on the dollar, and now they're going to take your house. And all you want to do is help, and be cooperative." Hearing him recount everything made it sound as bad as it was.

He continued to say what I already knew, but it was comforting to hear it repeated back to me. " List out everything you need to have from all the agencies, let them worry about getting it together, and then if—and I mean that's a big if—they can get every agency on board and you are completely released and protected, then go in and negotiate a rate to finish up the product and get it moved out. Let them know you can figure out an hourly rate later."

Immediately I figured that if, in fact, I was doing the job of the bank's lawyer, which I was, then the compensation must be in line. Three hundred and fifty dollars an hour sounded like a great figure to throw out and, as usual, it would be easy to support.

After a long spell of not feeling motivated to bring up the anger involved in dealing with all this, I received a push from the bank's attorney via the court.

The night before, I had found out I was not offered another job. This was despite having one of the best interviews of my life. There was convincing evidence that I had been on target with all four people within the organization. The day ended up being a waste of non-productive time.

Regardless of the fine weekend we had enjoyed, I was feeling very much a failure.

On Friday, Angee, Dawn and I had enjoyed a department party at the university. Our night of karaoke had rarely been so much fun, and for the night everything disappeared in to the background.

The next day we spent a relaxing Saturday preparing for what would be a fabulous multi-course non-commercial, but very much official, winemakers' dinner. Everyone had come together as friends and supporters, and although nothing about the winery was directly discussed, it was apparently on people's minds.

One guest had gone to a local retailer and bought a Gaia Wines blush and mead. Out of respect or nostalgia, it was appreciated.

Yet by Monday morning, after poor sleep and bad dreams, I found it impossible to even move my fingers in the general direction of the keyboard and commit anything to paper. I was also trying to ignore the fact that I had mentally set the end of November to complete the draft on this book and begin the editing process. I thought I had all the conviction in getting the book to press by the first of the year and meanwhile heading out on tour to support the book in the fall as I had been announcing.

Now I felt that a general manager position at a local retailer would be the best opportunity that the next stage of my life would have to offer. I was feeling so depressed that even the idea of that kind of monotony didn't add to the sucking feelings of failure. As I shuffled through the rain to the mailbox, I was hopeful for anything encouraging.

Instead, the envelope from the bank's firm seemed to pop out above the holiday rush of junk mail. I thought briefly of how an overall sense of failure was running throughout the entire country during the holiday time. The headline from the court was another disappointment.

ORDER PARTIALLY GRANTING PLAINTIFF'S COMBINED (A) NOTICE OF ABANDONMENT OF WINE INVENTORY FROM ORDER OF POSSESSION; (B) MOTION FOR APPROVAL OF SALE OF PROPERTY; (C) MOTION FOR AUTHORITY TO APPLY PROCEEDS FROM SALE OF PROPERTY; (D) MOTION FOR AUTHORITY TO RELEASE BOND.

Most unsettling was the assertion that there had been no objection submitted by counsel prior to the hearing. Yet all the objections had been very clear at the hearing. Again, I felt strongly that it made us look weak and unassertive of our position. My first response, feeling sucker-punched yet again, was to call our attorney. She was busy and distracted by her new job, which is where I found her.

"You sound upset, so let me take a minute I don't have to explain," she said condescendingly.

She went on to explain that she and the landlord's attorney were deeply involved in the process to get the product moved out of the space and to generate the funds needed to do so. What the court had allowed gave us the leeway to resolve this last issue, and it was a good decision, which she fully expected.

The details of the proceeds allocation were odd. From the $4 that had been promised—down from the original $5, which no one had yet explained—one dollar each would go to the court, the landlord, the bank and me. What still seemed unknown to the parties putting together this great deal was that it would be impossible to get the necessary releases from the federal and state agencies.

There would also have to be money up front for some kind of labels (although they would probably not be labeled as Gaia Wines) and the labor to make the wine sale-ready. Even after that, at that price, the money generated would go entirely to the outstanding liabilities. I had been directing every state and federal agency to those last remaining assets, knowing that was the only liability that could follow Angee personally.

It still seemed that no one was taking the time to listen to the real issues and leave this mess to the bank that had created it. I was angry that there was an attempt to save the bank again.

"It would just be nice to have the court acknowledge something in our favor," was my response as I fought back the tears I could feel coming on.

"Don't expect the court to be your advocate. The judge is making decisions based only on forcing the two parties to work together, to get this off his docket," our attorney explained emphatically. According to our attorney, I was supposed to accept that the courts, run on tax dollars, were not interested in anything that would require time or effort.

It was another clear indication that no one cared about the issues or about what was right, and like much of the medical care we were also receiving, if it took time or wasn't textbook easy, it was not going to get the consideration it required.

This was the reality of the results of our eight years of passion. How quickly could it be dismissed? At least, at this point, I felt that the big bank was getting away with everything it could, including all the bungling that had occurred. Were we right to think 12 jurors would feel any differently, any more outraged about the arrogance?

After reading it again, I felt somewhat encouraged by the second item in the judge's response. He deferred his response on the issue of selling the assets, applying the proceeds and releasing the surety bond.

I wasted no time sending an e-mail to our attorney to request our response to the second part the next morning. The judge was giving us an opportunity to make those issues part of the court records.

Subj: **Judge's response**
Date: **11/19/03 7:28:06 AM US Eastern Standard Time**
From: **GaiaWines**
To: **Our Attorney**

I, of course, had a few thoughts and requests of you, oh wise one.

I am concerned that the response states that no objections were filed prior to the hearing. I am sure it is just legalese, but it makes it look like nothing we said at the hearing was warranted. It looks like number 2 gives us that opportunity and I would like to have you file a response, with two strong assertions.

1. The bank never had the authority to sell that which was in their possession. We have to get this into court records, and my thought is that the judge is giving us an opportunity to do just that.

My conversation with the banker from down south stated clearly that unless they had written permission from the owner (Angee), they could not legally sell the assets.

Based on their request from the court, and the bank's attorney's statement in court that he met Angee when "she gave the assets to them" (pre-hearing banter), they are aware that they had no right to go to auction.

Rereading the transcripts from our last meeting with the TRO attorney (on tape), the agreement that they acted on was that they had the assets with the release of Angee's personal guarantee. When asked about documentation of that agreement in writing, the TRO attorney said they refused to give it. This needs to be made the issue of commercial unreasonableness that it is through the court.

2. When you do that, please include an objection to release of the surety bond, based on the damage done and perhaps the pending insolvency of the bank. At this time, will it make sense to object to the foreclosure based on their actions? It's an issue that has not been addressed in the judge's response, but, again, I don't want it to fall through any cracks, again saying that there was no response/objection.

Another thought was, is there some merit to getting a law student to do some research, project-based, to help us out from a time standpoint? I know you are running hard and fast, both with new responsibility and trying to work out the moving of the wine, but I don't want to miss other details that will strengthen our counter in March, [2003] as well as put us in the best position right now. I'll give you a few days to process and call on Tuesday at your new job!

M

Convinced that the releases that we required, especially from the bank, would never come, I resolved to try to relax. The focus would be to concentrate on issues that would do me the most good: finishing this book, preparing for publication, a fall book tour, and the upcoming Thanksgiving holiday.

Our attorney responded that day, and it was obvious that she had taken on a lot and I was an easy target to try to dismiss. Between the new job, still juggling the old employer, and taking on the bank's job with our case, she was frazzled.

Still, I was shocked and disappointed with her e-mail and her propensity to want, passively and aggressively, to bail out. After all, I thought we were the clients, and I hardly thought my once-a- month calls and e-mails were a major burden.

Subj:	judge's response
Date:	11/19/03 4:01:11 PM US Eastern Standard Time
From:	Our Attorney
To:	Gaia Wines

I got this. I understand your suggestions. I am going to re-read your e-mail again. What I am going to do is arrange to spend time explaining the Order to you; I owe you that.

I don't want you reading legal stuff and then believing that you understand it from one read and without at least $100K in student loan debt. There is a reason why it is stupid to represent yourself, and, further, to make assertions based upon that lack of knowledge, and believe you understand it. Yes, it is written in English, but the words have a different meaning from the common ones.

I appreciate your suggestions of about law student. We are struggling to pay an expert witness; we do not have more money to spend. I do my own research because I am a control freak. I will have more time to spend on you, and your issues, personal and professional, in about a week. You do not seem confident in my representation, and I appreciate your honesty. You may want to shop for somebody else, and you may find somebody who wants it, who really feels the cause and is not as worn out as I am over fighting this. Fresh meat. I would not be mad, and would fully support you and assist in the transition. I'm working my ass off, but you need more, your upkeep is a lot, but you deserve it, and any lawyer, I believe, does owe you that. I can't give you more than I have, I don't have It. You can find somebody better than me, who has more time and better diplomatic skills for fielding all of your suggestions. Let me know.

That night I gently explained to Angee that our attorney was again upset. That made Angee upset; as we rationalized, our trials had been significant enough to give us the upper hand on sympathy, or at the very least, empathy. After all, it was our house on the line, not the attorney's.

It was our passion of the dream we pursued that had been maligned by the bank's action. Without an aggressive legal offense, I felt that we had left action open to be reamed and dismissed by an disinterested legal system.

Perhaps we had put too much into the outcome in March, and as it grew closer, and without any movement from the bank, we wondered what we could do now to affect that event. I truly didn't believe that doing nothing was the best advice. Looking for another lawyer seemed a waste of time, but if our attorney was really going to crash, we had to have a backup.

It was impossible to tell how much of this was situational, or just how much she really wanted to bail out. Now in the comfort of a private practice, surely she could take or leave this struggle.

Two days before Thanksgiving, having calmed our attorney, I received a call from the landlord. Somewhat understandably, he was upset. Now, 60 days out, he still had wine that was drawing fruit flies and smell, and not the normal bouquet one wants from wine.

While he started out calmly, his temper, not normally bad, began to get worse. My remaining calm seemed to convey that I didn't care. There was simply no reason to play into his emotion. He expressed he had been accommodating during our lease. He was right.

No one was paying rent, and he felt strongly that no one would. He was missing an opportunity to lease the space, which was understandable. He also complained about the fact that his legal fees were continuing to mount—legal fees he had not been willing to pay to assist us in our organized process of closing eight months earlier. I recalled him saying it wasn't worth it.

He mentioned that we, as the winery, now back in possession, had dragged our feet and were not interested in helping, despite the court order.

At that, I got impassioned. "This has been 60 days that the bank has done nothing. And seven months before that. We have had that judgment for seven days. I want to help. I really do, I can't. I no longer hold a valid permit, nor does the winery. I understand from our lawyers that they are working on the required releases. I'd dump it tomorrow if we had the proper releases."

"All I know is my attorney has tried to secure a buyer for the good stuff. Is the remaining wine good stuff?" he questioned.

"I have no idea what condition the products are in. We haven't had access. I can't file federal and state tax returns because we don't have access," I replied.

"Why was no testing done? That's what we all came over to do after the hearing." he said.

I wondered if people didn't listen, think or both. "The bank had originally requested testing, and then changed its mind, because their people did not want proof as to their handling of the assets during the time of their possession," I said.

He was quiet, like it was something he had never expected to be so simple.

"I will not stand in your way of dumping what is in the big tank," I added.

"Is it bad? Can it be sold?" he asked.

"I truly don't know the technical state of anything in the space. I am sorry. I want an end to this as well, but we are not the party holding up the process."

"Well, I may draft a release saying I can dump it, and then just dump it," he said.

"You should probably talk with your attorney before you do anything," I cautioned sincerely. "I will e-mail our attorney to let her know we talked and what you want to do. Call me anytime."

He risked being pulled in further by dumping product, assets, without the bank's approval, but I don't think he understood or cared. He wanted his space back and to be out of the whole mess. My fear was that his action would cause more harm than good, and result in more legal fees then he ever expected.

Earlier that morning, Angee had called with the schedule for her laparoscopy. The pre-operative consultation would be December 23, and surgery would follow on January 5. When I asked about the pre-surgery consultation, I could sense a little of Angee's fear.

Because the procedure would be invasive, she would be required to have an electrocardiogram to make sure she was healthy enough to go through it. It was just part of the process, but it made the reality of all she had been through for so many years, on so many fronts, more clear. We both wanted only to see it end, but not just any ending. We were determined that the end to all our struggles would be positive. Angee would not just find out what was causing such consistent and unexplainable pain; she would also be able to determine a progressive, effective manner of care and recovery.

What was equally important, we didn't just want to end the almost year-long legal battle to close our business, but we wanted, even demanded, that justice be part of it, and that wrongdoing and all the mistakes of self-centeredness and insensitivity be uncovered and that someone learn from the process. The lesson, that the people in charge are not always right, should be learned.

We wanted to empower others. If we got some money to be able to have a secure future, which we had always planned that the winery would allow us to do, then that was a triple play that we would cele-brate. After all, the champagne was already chilled.

Later in the afternoon, I received a call from our attorney. Not recognizing the caller ID at first, I hesitated to answer. When I did, I wasn't prepared to properly document or respond to the information.

She had talked to the landlord's attorney, and the landlord was in fact going to dump the old 300 gallons of wine on the Wednesday before Thanksgiving. Could I be there? Did I want to be there?

Obviously, it should be videotaped.

Our concerns were similar. Knowing what I did as a previous permit holder, it felt like a setup regardless of what I did.

Angee's feelings were much more emphatic. She was sure we should not be there. I couldn't help think that, as the new custodians of the wine, thanks to the court's decision, we would end up at the countersuit being charged with improper and illegal disposal of assets. It struck me as just the thing to give our otherwise pristine countersuit a flaw. A major flaw.

I knew that Angee, as the actual winery permit holder, should have nothing to do with it. I was thinking strategically, and was strong about the belief that we should document the happenings via video to demonstrate what had exactly happened. As we still did not have keys, our presence could only be explained for that purpose.

When I called Farmer Dave, he was much more concerned, to the point where we came to a shouting match about opinions. All of his assertions were valid. While the landlord had said he would take responsibility, he had no authority to absolve us from ours. Even though the wine was undrinkable due to the bank's lack of care, it was still a legal asset of the corporation, under control of the bank.

There had not been any release from any of the federal or state authorities, and it was an illegal dumping of alcoholic product. Dave felt we might even have a fiduciary responsibility to notify the agencies. He suggested, with no mincing of words, that we should not be anywhere around the action. I could be an accessory to criminal actions.

As I read from the court's order, I stressed that I had been specifically ordered to be of assistance in the process. Still confused and feeling the pressure of the timeline, I called our attorney back to discuss the concerns. After leaving a voice message, I reiterated my concern by e-mail.

Still uncomfortable over what action to take and what involvement to document, I called David. He quickly understood and asked the right questions, surmising that I was seriously between a rock and a very hard place.

Could the dumping be put off? Could we ensure that everyone was present? Up to this point, eight months out, not only we were failing to elicit action from the bank and its attorney, but even federal and state agencies were not even returning calls. According to our attorney, she had been calling for three weeks but had not had the courtesy of a call back from regulatory groups.

David felt that getting everyone involved made the most sense, sending e-mails and following up with faxes and registered letters of the e-mails. Then, make calls and record the participation, or lack thereof. He even made the suggestion of the hold-hostage trick: get a daily paper with the date and record it as part of the timing of every-thing.

Even though I trusted everyone I had called on, I was as unclear on what to do here as with any issue we had faced. When our attorney called back, I tried to be succinct and cover my own confusion. We discussed all the concerns I had heard, in the few short minutes of impassioned calls, and she seemed to share and confirm my concerns. It was a double-edged sword.

She was able to tell me that the landlord's attorney had been in contact with the agencies, and was still trying to secure approval. But this was a holiday week, and the likelihood of finding anybody to show up, much less make a decision, was slim. I understood the delay. No agents wanted to make calls on an issue they had never had to deal with.

Our attorney wisely pointed out that all the agencies had been notified with regard to the hearing and no one had bothered to show up. That would serve as their response.

The bank had been called by our attorney, and both the bank and its attorney were not interested in coming. Further, they expressed that they did not care what happened to the wine in the stainless steel tank. Again, nothing was in writing but the court order. I hated the fact that the sides of the issues were not being evenly documented.

No culpability. It sounded like a good idea. I was more than happy at our attorney's suggestion that I simply give her the video camera and not enter the building. That simple act apparently would keep me from direct responsibility for any actions that occurred. I would have no first-hand knowledge.

Even though we had never received from the bank a copy of their tape from the taping of our assets conducted in March, I found it curious that the bank people requested a tape of the dumping occasion. I made a mental note to remind our attorney to wait for the official invitation— a subpoena.

Another surprise comment from the bank: Our attorney said that the bank, through its legal counsel, wondered if we would entertain a settlement. The surprise came from the fact that nothing had been done or said for eight months! The bank had stopped paying rent and was surely liable for some action from the landlord if he got angry enough. She told the bank's attorney to put something in writing. I wanted to tell her to make sure that in the process they did not insult us.

We were at attempt number seven to assist in resolving their mess, and I was not inclined to trust that the bank was behind any offer. The bank's attorney was merely trying to back out, like he had requested the day of the hearing. We were 90 days out, and the bank had proven they were unable to make a decision, good or bad.

Secretly, I hoped for their understanding of their liability as we went to countersuit, and as a result, an offer that would put a respectable end to this resource wasting and an emotionally draining nightmare.

Realistically, I prepared for a significant action in the case. It was poorly timed—before the first holiday that I did not have to work in eight years. Thinking that it was never too early for resolutions, I committed to let our attorney do the lawyering; I would not allow the recent events to ruin a peaceful, long weekend.

As I had promised, it would be a weekend to focus on Angee's health and a plan of action that would give us direction as we both thought about the upcoming surgery and a first-quarter visit to the Mayo Clinic in Jacksonville, Florida.

The night passed without a lot of the usual anxiety I would feel about an event or the related decisions. In the morning, I headed over to Angee's workplace to borrow the video camera from her co-worker. I stopped by Dawn's office to bring her updated news.

As I left, I thought about the fact that it was best that I didn't even pull up in front of the winery, so I called our attorney's office to ask her to meet me at the coffee shop down the street.

As I pulled up to the coffee house, I began to leave a message. The receptionist put me through to our attorney as I heard her calling across the office in the background.

"Great news: I got a fax from the feds, we're cool," she said. My sales training taught to me clarify what "cool" was. "What does that means?" I inquired.

"I talked to them, they don't care, and there may be some excise tax due; just tape it so we're good to go," she said.

I got specific. "You have the faxed copy?"

"Yes."

"Okay, well then, I will be there and you can do your magic; I'll tape," I said.

"Love you, mean it so much. See you soon," she replied.

I followed up with a call to Angee, just so she wouldn't worry. A quick muffin and a hot chocolate later, I was pulling up to the storefront where I had spent eight years of my life.

Before I got out of the car, I saw the landlord's wife. She unlocked the door while I got quarters to feed the parking meter. I stepped inside and we exchanged light pleasantries.

"So, I hear the bank's going out of business," she mentioned casually. I replied just as casually, "You got that from their attorney?" It was both a question and a statement, and she nodded her head yes.

"Well, they have had some trouble. It seems there are more loans than just yours handled improperly," she replied. I was at once happy and concerned. There was a small amount of satisfaction that the very entity that had called our efforts a failure was unable to pull out of its own self-created hellhole.

She went downstairs to open the door, and I stepped out to meet our attorney. I smiled as she pulled up. She looked rested and well. I could barely say hello before telling her what had been said.

A big smile came over her has she exclaimed, "Excellent. Then there might be some credence to the bank's counsel's offer. His tenor was a little different, like this time he would follow up on it. I said, 'I can make the ladies go away, show me something.' "

"Make sure that you get it in writing, and warn him in advance not to insult us," I said.

Even though I had never shared our goal for results with our attorney, I was aware that in Indiana we could get triple damages, and I knew what hard assets losses were and what we could prove. That would put a jury award, without punitive dollars, into seven figures.

I felt that the bank's offer would not be in that range. But I left what was possible up in the air for everyone to figure out in his or her own time.

We all waited around, only to find out 20 minutes into it that the landlord either was not coming or would be running late. His meeting to dump the wine, which he claimed he had to have, proved to be not so essential. I stood there not moving and not mentioning the federal release.

Finally, the landlord's wife began to dispose of the ruins that had been the best chardonnay Angee had ever produced. As she opened the tank, a sudden and pungent smell hit our noses like a hammer. Before long you could feel it burn your eyes. The wine had not been maintained at all. Brown ponds of scum and mold floated on top and swirled with the sucking that the pool pump was causing. I started videotaping, as we made insignificant talk.

Not feeling sad about what was happening made me even sadder. We talked about what was going to happen next, and I promised to call next week and remove the personal items that remained. That would allow us not only to pack up the last of the personal belongings but also to complete the already overdue personal and corporate taxes.

Before our attorney left, I could hear her confirming the bank information with the landlord's wife. She continued to share with her that the bank's accounts had been frozen and that the landlord had not been paid rent in four months.

Our attorney and the friend she had come with left shortly before lunch, and she asked me to stay and videotape the empty tank. As it was finishing up, the landlord arrived and helped his wife with what was left to do. We moved leftover holiday decorations remaining from the auction into another bay so the new tenant could continue his build-out.

The staircase we had once thought about putting in as a second entrance looked perfect and didn't take up as much space as we had originally thought it would. The space was becoming someone else's dream. It looked right.

The last few minutes of the tape showed an empty tank, and with that, $25,000 worth of what had been award-winning, excellent wine was gone.

The landlord asked if we were going to go after the bank. My guess was that people had other things going on in their lives and were not as attached to this process as I was. That was okay, so I downplayed our pending countersuit by asking if there was anything to go after. Would the landlord do the same?

He responded as if he had already made his decision, "Well, at some point the legal fees outweigh what you can get. I got to spend a couple of thousand to make a couple of thousand, so I don't know." I thought about how lucky we were to have our attorney joining our passion to have this all made right.

I recounted the landlord's suit against us. Yet he had displayed an obvious reluctance to go after the bank. It proved that it was another sign of choosing to go after whoever was easiest. It was a sad commentary on business and what was considered right in the world.

We talked about how things had gone, and his wife confirmed again that she had heard the bank had sold the assets prior to the auction. No fewer than three people had shared with me that this action was trickery. It was good information if we ever needed to pull out the big guns.

I still believed that the bank couldn't actually close, but could only quietly and secretly sell without any customer knowledge. It was a common practice within the financial world. Sticking by the thought that no one would buy an institution with outstanding litigation put a small, happy spring in my step as I walked out of the building for what would be one of the last times.

Retuning the camera to Angee's co-worker, I recounted the short version of the details to Dawn and Angee. Later that afternoon, Angee would jump on the FDIC Website and uncover the fact that the FDIC had indeed closed another bank two weeks ago. So perhaps it was possible. She also found on the website that 5,500 bank checks had been reported missing from our ex-bank. A prime example of their ability to manage business appropriately!

There was also an FDIC report of two loans made to bank officers. How nice it must be to have your own personal source of funds, even when your business is in trouble, even when you are not paying your attorney or the landlord holding your precious, expensively seized assets, and even as you are destroying those assets.

After the Thanksgiving weekend, I went in to evaluate the damage and ascertain what had to be done to remove what was left of our corporate records. I can't say that it was a sad moment, seeing everything in shambles, versus the beauty that had been our winery. But it did feel different. Almost empty and void of emotion as I was and try as I did, it didn't feel sad. All I felt was emptiness for the destruction that had occurred.

How long this had gone on, when the bank's action was started by its desire to speed up the process. Now here I was standing among the trash of what was left, eight months later, still with no one caring. All the precious assets that were supposedly at risk if we remained in control were now full of dirt and dust, unorganized and undocumented. Here I was, now in charge of doing something with what remained. It felt victorious and ridiculous at the same time.

Doors that had been locked to avoid our actions were now open to the general public, with a new tenant redecorating the private-function space, and contractors coming and going through an open back door.

Cases with full bottles of wine were full of dirt and dust. Adding labor to the cleanup and making the remaining wine salable would cost the bank twice what it would have paid just months ago. Despite our attorney's assertion from their counsel that the bank wanted to make an offer, she was surprised when three weeks later there had not been any communication.

Only when I demanded an e-mail from the bank's attorney, allowing us to remove what was ours, personally and professionally, did we hear anything. While he agreed, his arrogance reared its head again when he included his client's desire to accept our assistance in the "profitable and reasonable" sale of the wine.

Convinced that he didn't care about how he was making his ultimate job more difficult, I remained calm and resolved to add one more event of their arrogant disrespect towards us to the cost of the settlement.

As the holidays approached, Angee's body experienced a flare up and it stayed that way. Left flank pain coupled with joint pain brought back the need to walk with a cane. Slumped over to one side, she limped on her knee and hip while trying to balance the sore elbow on the other side. She looked 81, not 41.

Every step broke my heart. As always, when we were able to go out to do something I offered my arm for support. Only one event—shopping, lunch, a movie, or a book fair—was all she could do in any one day. After her monthly period ended, usually a good time, she could work only two days before needing to take three days off.

That Monday was focused on setting doctor appointments that we had aggressively, and after much discussion, we agreed needed to be more proactive. This was no way for her to live.

That afternoon we got in to see the family-practice doctor, a caring man who seemed to take Angee and her pain very seriously. He expressed as much frustration as we had. He could see the pain in her face even before she started to cry.

We had surmised over the previous weekend that there were two issues. One was solving the pain problem and getting the lupus under control, and the other was making the current situation as comfortable and functional as possible.

It was easy for me to go off, angry and resentful, back to the time when this had all started. As we had sat in the loan officer's office 18 months earlier, he allowed his boss to pontificate on the process of foreclosure on our house in the event we could not pay off the line of credit.

The loan officer's boss struck me as an ugly man, not physically but emotionally. As it was explained to me later by another banker, hatchet men at banks tend to be loners and significant losers as people. They have no friends inside or outside the organization. How could they? They are angry at the loan officers and underwriters for making the loans in the first place. Who is going to sympathize with someone who takes homes from people who are trying their best to make it in today's business world?

How would any day ever be full of anything other than misery? Yet, when they had a choice, the idea that they might be logical escaped them! How could they possibly expect to function in the outside world? They become like any other too-powerful entity, stopping at nothing regardless of the sense or legality of it.

In the early 1990s, I remembered with horror, there was a tragic IRS story that had been well covered in the media. A couple had been running a business and began receiving notices of late or missing IRS payments. The couple tried in vain to resolve the issue, providing documentation, being proactive.

When they were at their wits' end and about to lose their home, the husband committed suicide and left a note to his wife to use the insurance money to pay the debt that had continued to mount. She instead hired a lawyer and fought the battle.

In the end, the issue was resolved and proved in favor of the couple. As a newscaster sat with the IRS agent, he asked if the agent or his organization had ever apologized to the wife and the family. For $300,000 in insurance money, a man was dead because of the arrogance and stupidity of one agent and one organization. A man was dead and his family forever affected.

The IRS never admitted wrongdoing. It never apologized.

We wonder how atrocities occur in other, underdeveloped countries. When did we in the United States fail to be human and possess understanding in our own country?

Had the bank gone through with any of the process or actually made their threats a reality, it might have been different. Other than that, I felt it was just intimidation. The same technique employed by a stupid grade-school bully on the playground or a hit man for the mob. It was all designed to browbeat us into a position were no compromise or resolution was possible.

Instead, our attorney had been able to lay out a payment plan, something the bank had suggested earlier, before its troubles. It was something we had requested, as an obligation we could logically meet without fail. However the bank refused.

I was resolved to make this right for Angee. We would never give up the fight to make it right, and to hold the bank responsible for the part it had played in causing stress to an already potentially deadly disease.

When Angee headed home to rest, I headed to the drugstore again for new pain medications, hoping to restore some normalcy. I remembered the last e-mail I had received from our attorney that day about the offer. She said to expect that the bank would offer only to walk away from the damage it had caused. It was so incredibly late for that that it wasn't even on the clock of lateness.

Angee and I chose instead to look at the damage that had taken place. Of course the bank would be happy to walk away: it had received five times the original debt in assets. I don't know of a bank that would-n't be happy with that scenario. I asked our attorney to do some serious mind-fucking with the bank's attorney the next time they talked.

We would not agree to walk away with nothing at all. Not with the knowledge that the state allowed a jury to give three times easily proven damages. Surely we could count on punitive damages, as well as damages for the effects on Angee's health and for our mental and emotional pain and suffering.

I fought the desire to make it be about money. But then the bank already had made that the issue nine months earlier. What else could it be about? How could anything feel rectified without our day in court?

Despite the fact that everyone was sure this mess was going to be resolved by year's end, we would carry on the struggle into the next year, awaiting the jury date and a jury decision to make it right.

As Dawn would say, "I will tell my story, and they will cry for me." I had only to add that the bank would then compensate us for all this gross abuse and injustice. Lack of common sense, and arrogance would have a price, and it would not be cheap.

At a standstill, I was blindly unaware of just how much would change in our constant battle.

CHAPTER FOURTEEN

SURVIVAL OF THE TENACIOUS

*"I spent so many nights, thinking how you did me wrong,
and I grew strong. I learned how to carry on."*
Gloria Gaynor, *I will survive*

"There is no failure except in no longer trying."
Elbert Hubbard

"We have not yet begun to fight."
John Paul Jones

"Never, Never, Never, Never give up."
W. Churchill

I have no idea what will happen. Even so, our options seemed as clear as ever. We could still save our house by dropping the counter-claim. We had come to realize that this was what the bank really wanted, even more than the bankruptcy it had tried to threaten us into filing.

That option would leave a mess to clean up, and no method or resources to do so. Complete responsibility would be wiped clean from the bank's actions, the very actions that had breached their own agreement allowing us 90 days for an organized sale. Actions which, by unanimous opinion of those I spoke with, directly conflicted with wanting to get paid promptly and without damage.

We set out a best estimate of their cost to pursue this amount equal to the debt. The Small Business Administration guarantee has not been activated, and I wondered how carte blanche the government would be with the charges in our counterclaim pending.

There had to have been $30,000 to $50,000 in legal fees, which might or might not have been paid. According to the bank's own attorney, the bank had stopped paying rent and legal fees months ago. Rent for seven months was over $28,000. While in possession, the bank became responsible for tax liabilities past and present, because it seized and continued to hold the assets required to pay them.

As was uncovered on the day of the abandonment hearing, almost $120,000 of product had been ruined by the gross lack of knowledge and arrogance. No one had been in there since the auction, which was obvious. The bank's thought of being able to walk in and cash checks during all the bullying and damaging of assets was a strong error in judgment. These people had seriously misjudged what we would consider reasonable.

Soon they would add the sale of the house to the list of assets seized and disposed of at a loss. Every action continued and remained unchallenged through the courts. No one took the time to analyze the damage and effect of such brazen tactics.

Why? You should be asking. As we have heard often, because it was a bank. An institution which, as a collective society, we believe is rarely ever wrong. And the mistakes, thus far, were a cost multiple of the gains that could have existed.

"Let it go." I heard that sentiment from the landlord and the state, who were creditors in line to benefit from any reasonableness. "It's the bank, and you will not win." It wasn't even a consideration. And it seemed clear to them there was no sense in the legal fees, the time and frustration. That is how it happens, every time, without fail. If you don't give up right away, you enter into a heavily leveraged waiting game. This is really the basis of law. It's sad and misleading to think it's about right and wrong, and justice.

Other options to settling were talked about before trial. But every offer had been about 60 days behind what was acceptable. Until June, it was about being able to open and maximize the return, which we were able to do so convincingly that weekend in May.

After June, it became more about walking away clean, getting mounting taxes, penalties and fees taken care of, and, of course, keeping the house.

Giving the bank enough room to "trip over their own dicks," as our lawyer put it at the hearing, added significantly to the weight of our position. At this point, offers to walk away were showing ignorance added on top of their arrogance. Or was it vise versa?

The once-balked-at costs to save the wine and sell it before the auction indeed had the possibility of looking like the best deal since the Louisiana Purchase. However, now, with nothing to lose, the playing had become a battle of the heart, mind and spirit. We felt positioned to win on all counts.

Over lunch, I discussed the scenarios with Dawn. Were there twelve jurors, all of whom were either unemployed, underemployed, or had at one point cradled both the American Dream and the difficulty of understanding a bank?

Would a jury understand the impact these actions had on our future? How the bank had stopped our ability to walk away from our dream as we had planned, as whole as possible? Would they appreciate our desire and commitment, even in this economy, to honor the responsibility of taking care of those partners we enjoyed through the journey?

Would they understand and reward our resolve, a willingness to make a stand? At the same time, would they be willing to send the message to big business, big banking, and big government? Could they look at the whole picture not the one-sided view? Would they be able to keep their own egos and fears in check?

Could we find 12 people with the same passion as an entrepreneur? Would they find the strength to send a message that could begin repair and heal and begin to make each of us feel some control and be proud of the responsibilities and risks we had taken? Could it become the success story of the city, our own little Enron experience of wrongdoings made right? Would the jury be able to say that at some point this has to stop? How long does did it take for questionable legal actions to be made right?

How dare the bank create its own reality of right and wrong and then pass judgment on the passionate pursuits of others. It was not a mind set that would take us as a whole into the next stage of our journey as a torn, disheartened society. I had so many questions. I longed for the answer—from anybody.

In an effort to understand what position the bank might be trying to assert, my morning call was with to a gentleman, a referral from my friend David. He was a consultant to banks and, ultimately its clients, small businesses. His group of experts moved in, saving companies at the last moment or offering assistance in taking things to the next level. That always made more money for everybody! He was responsive, nice, and asked decent questions.

This expert found it unusual the bank had taken the stance it had. I should have invited him to join the club. There were a number of problems that the bank could be facing, he offered.

The ratio of loan rate to deposit growth could be off. What the bank's people faced, in reality, was the possibility that account holders could put a run on the bank. If it was suddenly exposed that the FDIC might no longer insure deposits, everybody rushes to the bank and, in a panic, removes his or her money, and presumably stuffs it under the mattress.

Regardless, all banks had three options in the scenario as it unfolded. "Take a haircut" was the process of writing down the loan value, trimming it so that it was payable. Banks could encourage clients to shop the loan around, and, at times, even help in the process of moving the loan so that it would disappear favorably from their books.

We had been asked to do this during the line of credit negotiations. However, our bank lacked the industry knowledge and relationships to be of any assistance in moving the loan to another bank. Let's face it, if it a perceive problem for the bank, how many other institutions are rushing to sign you up? The bank never had an answer for my requests.

If the bank was sure a company was going out of business, they wanted it in bankruptcy. Since all three scenarios had been part of our experience, it was hard to determine what the bank's next move would be. When did it trim the loan and what was the status?

As I talked with this banking expert he was almost positive there were, or could be, criminal issues involved, and the bank's strong opposition was a reaction to keeping everything under wraps. Together we both wondered if the solvency of the bank was an issue.

For our side, he felt the counterclaim was valid and a "stroke of genius" as a strategy. But we were serious; we wanted to be made whole from what had happened. The lack of definitive response from the courts during the last hearing he saw as a positive sign from a sympathetic court unimpressed by the bank's heavy-handed scare tactics.

Finally, there was a strong argument to make in court regarding the market value in our house and that the bank should not be allowed to continue to be commercially unreasonable with assets. Our efforts to deal in good faith were apparent to this gentleman during our less than one-hour conversation.

I ended the conversation feeling good about the vote of confidence from someone so close to the industry, with an understanding of what should and shouldn't have happened. Except that the future and the actions that would come along were as uncertain as ever.

We waited, now way past the hearing. No direction, no resolution. No action that was moving us even closer to our court date. With nothing to react to, Angee and I tried to balance the calm of the coming fall with a real need to find another place to call home through the holidays.

I feared a worst-case scenario recalling the evil banker Mr. Potter from the movie *It's a Wonderful Life* —a scenario of moving in the cold of winter and surrounded by the holidays. The first set of major holidays when we did not find ourselves tied to the environment of entertainment and retail sales. We would hang in the balance.

For the first time in nine years we could have tended to each other. Instead, we would find ourselves struggling for shelter, while the last of what we had created together, a welcoming home, was to apparently fall to the auction block in a city already reeling in unemployment, consumed by failures of business, real estate, and the human spirit.

You're not going to be happy with this…

Has the idea come across that I like to do things differently? Usually I think it's better, as well as different. But mostly it's just a different way of doing things, a different mind set of how to react and respond to what we face.

The idea of writing a book with no real conclusion to the conflict was odd. I worked my time schedule backwards and was insistent on getting out to tour. Lack of a conventional conclusion would not stand in my way. It would have been one more impedance we allowed the bank to make.

That meant there would be no real resolution before our court date. We had always expected that a settlement would be forthcoming at each disastrous uncovering of our charges of deception, wrongdoing, commercial unreasonableness, and incompetent arrogance.

We always believed that the courts and related proceedings would justify our position and resolve matters in our favor. Ultimately, we believed that the court would tell the bank exactly what it had to do. That somehow it would right all the wrongs and make us believe in the American justice system. That no matter how small the challenger, individuals and small businesses could receive justice without buying it.

I think we may have been strong and passionate, but slightly naive.

Should the lessons be so easy that they can be recounted here? My guess is that rather than dollars, we have gained sense. What can we take from the experience that will provide enduring lessons and wisdom?

If you truly trust in what you are doing, and a dozen or so experts agree, then it is a good bet that the you should resolve to believe in it as well. Remember, when someone you are dealing with protests too much, or regularly acts counter intuitively to what a normal, intelligent person would do, it's safe to assume you are not dealing with normal, intelligent people.

There is probably a reason why. Is the whole organization incompetent and arrogant? It's possible that it is a trait that people huddle to rather than challenge. Think about the dozen other people within the banking organization that could have, at many points through the battle, interceded and brought a logical end to the issues. Instead, each one chose to be removed from the challenges of trying to figure a better way out. Why?

It was easy. It was the fact that they lacked a passion for what they were doing.

So, conversely, what have we brought away from the experience?

We challenged ourselves and those who love us. We were challenged to understand, stay with the our conviction and believe in the power of that passion. At each critical moment, we had a chance to back down, fold and walk away. Yet we developed the fortitude to go forward, even though it wasn't easy.

I feel like we each got better at distinguishing between trust and falsity. Whether it was in friends, customers, people who knew a lot or knew very little, the responses we garnered from each uncovering were paramount to understanding the breaking point within each of us.

Our attorney learned that the law isn't about a 30-day resolution. It is many times about willful persistence. Just like love and business.

People will continue to lie, to paraphrase the BB King Song "everybody lie a little." If they are able to make their perception the reality, then they have won.

When someone shows he is incapable of an action, believe him. If he is unable to be professional and proactive, understand and accept that it is not within his current ability to offer these traits. Then act accordingly.

People act on their time frames and not yours, for whatever reason. The most you can hope for is to find their motivation to impact that time frame.

The best deal is not the first one, nor is it the fifth. As long as they keep coming, keep entertaining the options, because each new one offers much more than was originally is presented. It allows insight into what priorities are or are not.

You can't help people who don't want to be helped. Sometimes the situation is so far gone that they don't even realize what is happening. At the same time, it is never too late. Leave yourself open to help if it remains in your best interest.

At the right time, it does help to be brutally honest. Even if it doesn't get you anywhere, you have planted a root for your own passion to grow. You may find that it motivates others to question theirs.

Angee and I learned what will keep us together. Also that ultimately, nothing pulls you apart. It lies within the relationship you have built, and the trials and tribulations you have shared together. Talk about it, regularly and ad nauseum. The creative ramblings of late-night bitch sessions often spark the re-formation of your passion, your path and your tactics. It is wonderfully refreshing. It is the spontaneous brilliance that is born from exhaustion and mass confusion.

Taking control was important. But sometimes staying out of the control process is the asset that others have relinquished. But know when to take that control by letting go. Allow the other side to make all the mistakes they will. If you are not moving forward together, they will never catch up.

You may not be happy about this, but the last chapters are still to come. Regardless of how you continue our journey of Passion versus Arrogance, I hope you have found it fascinating and enlightening.

SOME THOUGHTS

There are only two issues hurting America. There are only two reasons we find ourselves where we are, personally, professionally and as a society. The forces that hate America have some of it right. Still they have no chance to be righteous. They are guilty of the same age-old, class-defining struggle.

Our issues struggle among themselves. Quite simply, we are run by fear and greed. It's what you have just read about, it's what you experience every day in your families, your homes and your workplaces. The simplest driving force behind everything that happens in America is greed and fear.

Greed to acquire more education is generally accepted as positive. It's about self-betterment and what that can bring to an individual, a family, and a society.

In the same vein, fear of snakes is a good thing. You never know what those pesky, quick little slithery creatures are going to do. On a less personal note, fear can be a motivator or it can remind us of an earlier lesson learned.

That's not what functions we have allowed those emotions to serve. They have become emotions run amuck. We are afraid of everything. No matter how big and powerful we become, we are afraid: of the unknown, of the barely known, and mostly of the known.

Everyone might agree that losing your house can be a frightening experience. But let's sketch it out for a moment. There are always options. Always. I mean all the time. We have choices. Now, I am not saying that you have to like all the options, or that staying in your home isn't your first choice. It may very well be. It shouldn't be considered to have the same importance as a world crisis or death, although each of those can be dealt with equally as effectively.

What should remain foremost in your mind is that you have the power to placate that fear. Fear about anything, really. Call it rationalizing, denial, or blind optimism. But what can't you really overcome? Or deal with? Or not be afraid of?

I have friends and enemies (a few) and have interviewed hundreds of people, from someone thinking it would be cool to work in a winery (it is!), to new and old millionaires, presumably secure in their happy ways.

But I find that it takes less and less time to find out the underlying fear. Loss of job, loss of riches-they are afraid of the next thing. I will never understand why someone who has truly earned his or her first million think it's not possible to do it again. If you don't have the job you have today, will you never work again? Are the forces of labor excluding you permanently from the ranks? (Actually, that sounds like a good idea, never work again)!

Why have we chosen fear? I have a thought about that. We have lost our passion. This brings us back to the book you have just read. (You did read it, right?) If we hold to that passion we have for what we do, we have a hard time remaining fearful for very long.

In our own case, we quite literally lost everything, one moment after another, while facing the fear and apprehension of failing health. But I can say that very little time was spent being fearful.

We had a passion for what we did. What we had created came from nothing but our minds and hearts, and developed into worldwide acceptance and praise. That feeling is unwavering and empowering.

It was the one shield we possessed against the forces of greed, fear, incompetence and the arrogance that we faced. It was the most powerful. It rendered us invincible.

At any time the bank could have used a very simple Number 2 pencil and removed whatever loss it felt it was going to face and moved onto bigger and better things: more profitable, better financed entities and real estate. Secured endeavors that would have most likely taken it to greater heights than any of its people could have imagined.

But, as I guess must be the case with most bankers, they either lost, or, even more sadly, never had a passion for what they were doing. They could have overcome any of the obstacles they faced externally, or any challenges, even when they started creating them for themselves.

The antidote for fear is passion. My hope is that you find your passion—in a person, a hobby, a sky, a sunset, an endeavor. Then, I recommend that you immerse yourself and those you love in it. It will, in fact, keep you warm at night. It will keep you young, and laughing through the hard times.

Be not frightened, but be forward-thinking about every day of your future. It may even become the answer for peace and harmony. Failure becomes opportunity. Fear becomes the challenge to learn something new and valuable. Each event becomes a bigger part of the "you" that was and the "you" that might be.

That is what once made America great. Remember, it was called the "American Dream." It was because people took risks, and gained support and praise for trying, even if it didn't always end up the way it was supposed to.

I hear all the time how banks and venture capital are looking for the next Microsoft. Instead, I challenge you to see the qualities that are good and honest about each venture, without comparing it to an unreasonable, on one occasion icon.

There may never be another big easy! It might be big, but it won't be easy. Conversely, what may be easier may not be as big. I believe there is plenty of room for each opportunity to turn into a successful venture, if we can, for some brief time, look beyond what was, and fearlessly, with hope and passion, look to what can be. My wish is that you all have the chance to feel that passion. Remember to forget the arrogance!

Secure the courage to forever and constantly ask questions, and question answers. It will uncover brilliance and passion, ignorance and arrogance. In all cases, you will be infinitely better off. My wish for you is the right kind of success; however you and yours may define it.

Cheers! Margaret

Glossary

Banking & Financial Terms

Acceleration Making demand for payment in full for a debt that has not yet matured. Usually a remedy provided in a loan document for the lender to use in the event of default by the borrower.

Amendment A revision to a document. A UCC financing statement can be amended by filing a designated amendment form, usually UCC-3.

Capital (1) Usually refers to the total of the equity accounts in a firm. For a bank, the equity accounts are common and preferred stock, surplus, and undivided profits. For other corporations, equity accounts are common and preferred stock, surplus, and retained earnings. For bank capital, see tier 1 and tier 2 capital. (2) Sometimes used as a synonym for common stock, as in capital stock.

Cash flow A finance and accounting term used to describe the net amount of cash generated by a firm's operations. In traditional and over-simplified usage, cash flow is defined as the sum of net income after tax plus all noncash expenses such as depreciation. More modern and sophisticated usage defines cash flow to include the net difference between all cash outflows and cash inflows.

Commitment letter A legally binding letter in which a lender documents the terms, prerequisites and conditions under which it agrees to provide financing to an applicant. Commitment letters may be used in almost any lending transaction but are most common in commercial real estate transactions.

Current assets The group of assets considered the most liquid. Usually comprised of cash, accounts receivable, inventory, and a few minor items. The sub grouping of assets into current and long-term categories is common for all financial statements except for firms in the financial industry.

Current liabilities The group of liabilities considered to be the shortest term. Usually comprises accounts payable, short-term bank debt, bank overdrafts, other short-term accounts or notes payable, current portion of long-term debt, and a few minor items. The sub grouping of liabilities into current and long-term categories is common for all financial statements except for firms in the financial industry.

Debt Funds owed by a debtor to a creditor. Outstanding debt obligations are assets for creditors and liabilities for ebtors. May or may not be covered by written agreements

Debt-to-worth ratio The simplest way to measure leverage. Calculated by dividing total liabilities by total equity.

Debtor (1) A party who owes money or other performance to another party. Under the UCC, debtor includes the seller of accounts or chattel paper. (2) For the purposes of UCC provisions dealing with collateral, debtor also applies to the owner of collateral given as security for the debt of another.

Debtor in possession In some bankruptcy proceedings, the debtor, rather than a trustee, may continue to operate the business. The debtor in possession is the same person or company that controlled the business prior to the bankruptcy, however, the debtor in possession is a different legal entity.

Default (1) noun — A condition in which a loan or investment is not performing as expected because of the debtor's failure to act or refrain from acting in ways contractually agreed upon. As in "the loan is in default" or "an event of default."

(2) verb — A debtor's failure to act or refrain from acting in ways contractually agreed upon in the loan documents. Most often, default is the debtor's failure to pay.

Expenses Outflows or other reductions of assets or increases in liabilities (or a combination of both) from delivering or producing goods, rendering services, or carrying out other activities that constitute the entity's ongoing major or central operations.

Federal Deposit Insurance Corporation Improvement Act (FDICIA) 305 A section in the FDICIA that requires the FDIC, the Office of the Comptroller of Currency (OCC), Office of Thrift Supervision (OTS), and the Federal Reserve to add an interest rate risk component to bank and thrift capital requirements

Firm commitment An agreement with an unrelated party that is binding on both parties and that is usually legally enforceable. In FAS 133, FASB specifies that the following are both satisfied for a firm commitment: a) the agreement specifies all significant terms, including the quantity to be exchanged, the price at which the quantity will be exchanged, and the timing of the transaction. b) The agreement includes a disincentive for nonperformance that is sufficiently large to make performance probable.

Forbearance agreement An agreement between a creditor and a debtor. A forbearance agreement is utilized when a debtor has defaulted or is likely to default. Under the terms of the forbearance agreement, the debtor is given more time to make loan payments, a reduction in the amount of loan payments due each month or both. Typically, the lender agrees not to exercise rights to foreclose or accelerate during the forbearance period. In return, the debtor agrees not to contest any actions taken by the creditor to collect the debt in the event that the debtor fails to comply with the payment schedule or other terms specified in the forbearance agreement. In some forbearance agreements, the debtor may grant the creditor a deed in lieu of foreclosure if the terms of the forbearance agreement are not met. Sometimes called a drop dead agreement

Foreclosure A remedy provided by state law for creditors secured by an interest in real property to obtain title to the property under certain conditions.

Fraudulent conveyance A transfer of an interest of the debtor made within one year prior to the filing of bankruptcy that is either made by the debtor with the intent to defraud its creditors or for which the debtor receives less than reasonable consideration. A fraudulent transfer may be set aside (reversed) by a bankruptcy judge.

Haircut A lender's informal expression for a collateral margin. Commonly used with repurchase and reverse repurchase agreements informally called repos and reverses.

Inventory A category of goods defined by Article 9 of the Uniform Commercial Code. Inventory is goods held for sale or lease. It includes raw materials, work-in-progress, finished goods, and materials used or consumed in a business

Judgment A sum due for payment or collection as a result of a court order.

Judgment clause A provision in bank promissory notes or guaranties. In this clause, the borrowers or guarantors authorize the bank to create a judgment lien at any time after the documents have been executed. The bank only has to take the documents to a court. Many states prohibit judgment clauses.

Lender liability An informal term referring to various manifestations of actual or potential legal liability arising from the conduct of a financial institution lender. Generally, lender liability arises from allegations that a lender has violated a duty (whether implied or contractual) of good faith and fair dealing owed to the borrower or has assumed a degree of control over the borrower resulting in the creation of a fiduciary duty owed to the borrower or its other creditors or shareholders.

Line of credit A type of credit facility. The specific meaning of the term varies from bank to bank. Since the various uses often cause confusion, two definitions are presented here. In this book, the second definition is used. 1) A type of loan that permits a borrower to draw funds, up to a specified maximum, for a defined period of time. Sometimes called a nonrevolving line of credit. 2) Any loan that permits the borrower to borrow funds up to a specified maximum, make repayments in any amount at any time, and obtain any number of readvances so long as the maximum is not exceeded. Sometimes called a revolving line of credit. The distinguishing feature of a line of credit is that it rebounds, which means that the amount borrowed can be paid down and reborrowed, or readvanced, as the borrower's needs change.

Operating income An income statement subtotal that is variously called operating income or operating profit. Gross profit minus operating expenses. A credit balance here, shown as a positive number, indicates that the firm makes money on its principal operations. . A debit balance, shown as a negative number, indicates that the firm loses money on its principal operations

P & I Principal and interest as in the principal and interest required for periodic loan repayments.

Perfection The name for a procedure established by Article 9 of the Uniform Commercial Code. Creditors must comply with this procedure in order to establish the priority of their security interest in personal property relative to the priority of security interests in the same property that may be held by other creditors. (It may be used when an interest in collateral is provided by the debtor or by a guarantor or other third party.) Perfection does not normally constitute the actual agreement between the secured party and the debtor. By itself, perfection does not create a security interest and must therefore be supported by a separate security agreement or pledge agreement. There are several different procedures that can be used to achieve perfection of a security interest in a debtor's personal property. The most common method is perfection by filing a financing statement. See financing statements and security agreement.

Projections Projected financial statements showing predicted income, cash flow, and/or balance sheets. Unlike pro forma statements, projections typically cover multiple time periods — sometimes as many as five future years.

Promissory note A written contract between a borrower/debtor and a lender/creditor in which the borrower agrees to repay a loan granted by the lender. The contract specifies the amount of the loan and the terms of repayment.

Quit claim deed A document by which title to real estate is conveyed from one party, the grantor, to another party, the grantee. The distinguishing characteristic of a quit claim deed is that it transfers only such interest, title, or right that the grantor has at the time of conveyance to the grantee. A quit claim deed is common in divorce or other situations such as equitable interests, in which the grantor's interest is not clearly defined.

S corporation Legal entity that is a special kind of Corporation. An S corporation offers shareholders the same limitations on personal liability that are available to corporate stockholders. At the same time, S corporations are taxed similarly to partnerships, that is, the income or loss incurred by the S corporation is allocated to the stockholders for tax purposes. S corporations are subject to limits on stockholders and may not be part of affiliated corporate groups.

Security agreement An agreement between one or more debtors and one or more creditors in which the debtor grants the creditor an interest in the debtor's personal property as collateral for the debt. (Alternatively or in addition, the collateral may be property owned by a guarantor or by another third party.) As used in Article 9 of the Uniform Commercial Code, it is an agreement that: is in writing; gives the names of the parties; is signed or authenticated by the debtor; describes the collateral; and includes language stating that the debtor is granting or giving the security interest in the collateral to the creditor. While the security agreement establishes the creditor's interest in the collateral, it does not establish the priority of the creditor's interest relative to the interests of other creditors. See financing statements and perfection.

Underwriter The investment bank, commercial bank, or brokerage firm that works with an issuer to sell a new issue. Issuers may select underwriters by obtaining bids or on a negotiated basis. Potential underwriters may form groups called underwriting syndicates to bid collectively.

Underwriting The name used to describe the process of analyzing and structuring a proposed loan. Good underwriting is the most important aspect of secured lending. Outside of banking, the term primarily refers to the purchase of risk.

Uniform Commercial Code (UCC) A compilation of laws relating to commercial contracts involving personal property. The code does not address real property. In addition, a few types of personal property are also excluded. While the UCC has been adopted by all 50 states, there are differences among the versions adopted in each state. Secured lenders tend to focus on UCC Article 2A covering leases, Article 8 covering securities, and Article 9 covering all other personal property collateral.

Working capital In accounting and finance, used to describe the amount, if any, by which a business's current assets exceed its current liabilities. Also used more loosely to describe the funds a firm has available to run its day-to-day business affairs.

Legal Terms

Affidavit A written, sworn statement of facts made voluntarily, usually in support of a motion or in response to a request of the court.

Allegation The assertion, declaration or statement of a party to a lawsuit often made in a pleading or legal document, setting out what the party expects to prove at the trial.

Answer A pleading by which defendant endeavors to resist the plaintiff's allegation of facts.

Appeal A request to take a case to a higher court for review.

Appearance The formal proceeding by which a defendant submits himself or herself to the jurisdiction of the court.

Arbitration The hearing and settlement of a dispute between opposing parties by a third party whose decision the parties have agreed to accept.

Attorney of record The attorney whose name appears as counsel to a party in the permanent records or files in a case.

Breach of contract - A legally inexcusable failure to perform a contractual obligation.

Burden of proof In the law of evidence, the necessity or duty of affirmatively proving a fact or facts in dispute.

Case Any proceeding, action, cause, lawsuit or controversy initiated through the court system by filing a complaint, petition, indictment or information.

Cause A suit, litigation or action, civil or criminal.

Cause of action The rights which a party has to institute a judicial proceeding.

Claim The assertion of a right to money or property.

Consideration - Something of value given in return for another's performance or promise of performance; generally required to make a promise binding and to make agreement of parties enforceable as a contract. Consideration may be either executed or executory, express or implied.

Contract - A legally enforceable agreement between two or more competent parties made either orally or in writing.

Costs An allowance for expenses in prosecuting or defending a suit; ordinarily does not include attorney's fees.

Counterclaim A claim presented by a defendant against the plaintiff in a civil action, that the plaintiff has injured him or her.

Court reporter Person who records and transcribes the verbatim testimony and all other oral statements made during court sessions.

Damages - Monetary compensation that may be recovered in the courts by any person who has suffered loss, detriment, or injury to his or her person, property or rights, through the unlawful act or negligence of another.

Default The failure of a party to respond in a timely manner to a pleading; a failure to appear for trial.

Defendant A person sued or accused.

Defamation - That which tends to injure a person's reputation. Libel is published defamation, whereas slander is spoken.

Deposition The testimony of a witness not taken in open court, but in pursuance of authority given by statute or rule of court to take testimony elsewhere.

Discovery A proceeding whereby one party to an action may learn of facts known by other parties or witnesses.

Due process Law in its regular course of administration through the courts of justice. The constitutional guarantee of due process requires that every individual have the protection of a fair trial. Due process requires that everyone receive such constitutional protections as a fair trial, assistance of counsel, and the rights to remain silent, to a speedy and public trial, to an impartial jury, and to confront and secure witnesses.

Escrow A writing or deed delivered by the grantor into the hands of a third person, to be held by the latter until the happening of a contingency or performance of a condition.

Evidence A fact presented before a court such as a statement of a witness, an object, etc., that bears on or establishes a point in question.

Exhibit A paper, document or other article produced and exhibited to a court during a trial or hearing.

Expert evidence Testimony given in relation to some scientific, technical or professional matter by experts; i.e., persons qualified to speak authoritatively by reason of their special training, skill or familiarity with the subject.

Fiduciary A term derived from the Roman law meaning a person holding the character of a trustee, in respect to the trust and confidence involved in it and the scrupulous good faith and candor which it requires. A person having a legal relationship of trust and confidence to another and having a duty to act primarily for the other's benefit, for example, a guardian, trustee, or executor.

Fraud An intentional perversion of truth; deceitful practice or device resorted to with intent to deprive another of property or other right or in some manner to do him or her injury.

Hearing An in-court proceeding before a judge generally open to the public.

Hearsay Testimony given by a witness who relates what he or she has heard said by others, not what he or she knows personally.

Injunction A mandatory or prohibitive order issued by a court.

Interrogatories Written questions propounded by one party and served on an adversary, who must provide written answers under oath; discovery procedure in preparation for a trial.

Judge An elected or appointed official with authority to hear and decide cases in a court of law; Nebraska judges are selected and retained according to the merit plan.

Judgment The official decision or decree of the court upon the rights and claims of the parties.

Jury (or petit jury) A jury of 12 (or fewer) persons, selected according to law, who are sworn to inquiry of certain matters of fact, and to declare the truth upon evidence laid before them.

Liable - Legally responsible.

Litigation - A case, controversy, or lawsuit.

Lien An encumbrance upon property, usually as security for a debt or obligation.

Limitation A certain time allowed by statute in which litigation must be brought.

Litigant Person or group engaged in a lawsuit.

Litigation A judicial controversy.

Malfeasance Evil doing; ill conduct; the commission of some act, especially by a public official, which is positively prohibited by law.

Mandate A command from a court directing the enforcement of a judgment, sentence or decree.

Material evidence Such as is relevant and goes to the substantial issues in dispute.

Motion Oral or written request before, during or after a trial on which a court issues a ruling or order.

Negligence The failure to do something which a reasonable person, guided by ordinary considerations, would do; the doing of something which a reasonable and prudent person would not do Failure to exercise ordinary care.

Objection The act of taking exception to some statement or procedure in trial; used to call the court's attention to improper evidence or procedure.

Perjury The willful assertion as to a matter of fact, opinion, belief or knowledge, made by a witness in a judicial proceeding as part of his or her evidence, whether upon oath or in any form allowed by law to be substituted for an oath, and known to such witness to be false.

Plaintiff The person who brings an action; the party who complains or sues in a personal action and is so named on the record.

Pleading The process by which the parties in a suit or action alternately present written statements of their contentions, each responsive to that which precedes, and each serving to narrow the field of controversy, until there evolves a specific point or points, affirmed on one side and denied on the other, called the "issue" upon which they then go to trial.

Power of attorney Document authorizing another to act as one's agent or attorney in fact (not an attorney at law).

Precedent Previously-decided case which is recognized as an authority for determining future cases.

Preliminary hearing The hearing given a person charged with a crime to determine whether he or she should be held for trial.

Probable cause A constitutionally prescribed standard of proof; a reasonable ground for belief in the existence of certain facts.

Prosecution Act of pursing a lawsuit or criminal trial.

Pro tem "Temporary."

Reasonable doubt An accused person is entitled to acquittal if, in the minds of the jury, his or her guilt has not been proved beyond a "reasonable doubt"; that state of minds of jurors in which they cannot say they feel an abiding conviction as to the truth of the charge.

Retainer Act of the client in employing an attorney or counsel; denotes the fee which the client pays when retaining an attorney to act for him or her.

Settlement - Agreement resolving a dispute between parties in a lawsuit without trial. Settlements often involve the payment of compensation by one party in satisfaction of the other party's claims.

Slander Base and defamatory spoken works tending to harm another's reputation, business or means of livelihood. Both "libel" and "slander" are methods of defamation, libel being expressed by print, broadcast, writings, pictures, signs or other forms of side publication, while slander is expressed orally.

Special performance A mandatory order in equity; where damages would be inadequate compensation for the breach of a contract, the contractor will be compelled to perform specifically what he or she has agreed to do.

Subpoena A process to cause a witness to appear and give testimony before a court.

Summary judgment The termination of a lawsuit, usually before trial, upon the judgment showing that there is no issue of fact in the case, and that one party or another is entitled to prevail as a matter of law.

Summons A writ or order directing the sheriff or other officer to notify the named person that an action has been commenced against him or her in court, and that he or she is required to appear, on the day named, and answer the petition or complaint in such action.

Temporary restraining order (TRO) - Prohibits a person from an action that is likely to cause irreparable harm. This differs from an injunction in that it may be granted immediately, without notice to the opposing party, and without a hearing. It is intended to last only until a hearing can be held.

Testimony - Evidence given by a competent witness, under oath, as distinguished from evidence derived from writings and other sources.

Third-party claims An action by the defendant that brings a third party into a lawsuit.

Tort A civil wrong or breach of a duty to another person, as outlined by law. A very common tort is negligent operation of a motor vehicle that results in property damage and personal injury in an automobile accident.

Transcript The official record of proceedings in a trial or hearing.

Undue influence Whatever destroys free will and causes a person to do something he or she would not do if left to himself or herself and creates a ground for nullifying a will or invalidating a future gift. The exercise of undue influence is suggested by excessive insistence, superiority of will or mind, the relationship of the parties or pressure on the donor or testator by any other means to do what he is unable, practically, to refuse.

Verdict In practice, the formal and unanimous decision or finding made by a jury, reported to the court and accepted by it

Witness One who testifies to what he or she has seen, heard or otherwise observed or concluded from observations.

INDEX

The story's not over for Passion v. Arrogance

Keep updated on the on-going story!
Order a Book Autographed by the Author!
Request the Author come speak at your function!
Additional Book Order Form

Quantity	Cost		Total
	$29.95 each	$	
	Add 6% Indiana Sales Tax	$	
	$4.95 first book plus $1.95		
	each add'l book to same address		
	Grand Total	$	

(6 or more call for discount volume pricing)

Payment Options: mailed check   debit card   credit card
Card # _____ expires___/____/____

Purchaser: _____ Ship To: _____

Name_____
Organization / Dept. _____
Address 1 _____
Address 2 _____
City/ State/ Zip _____
Phone _____
Fax _____
Email _____
Please e-mail me updates on the story!

Mail Complete Form to: Passion Power Press
Post Office Box 127 INDIANAPOLIS, IN 46204-0127

To have Margaret Broderick speak at your function, please contact
Passion Power Press at **PASSIONBOOKS@AOL.COM** or *317-356-6885*